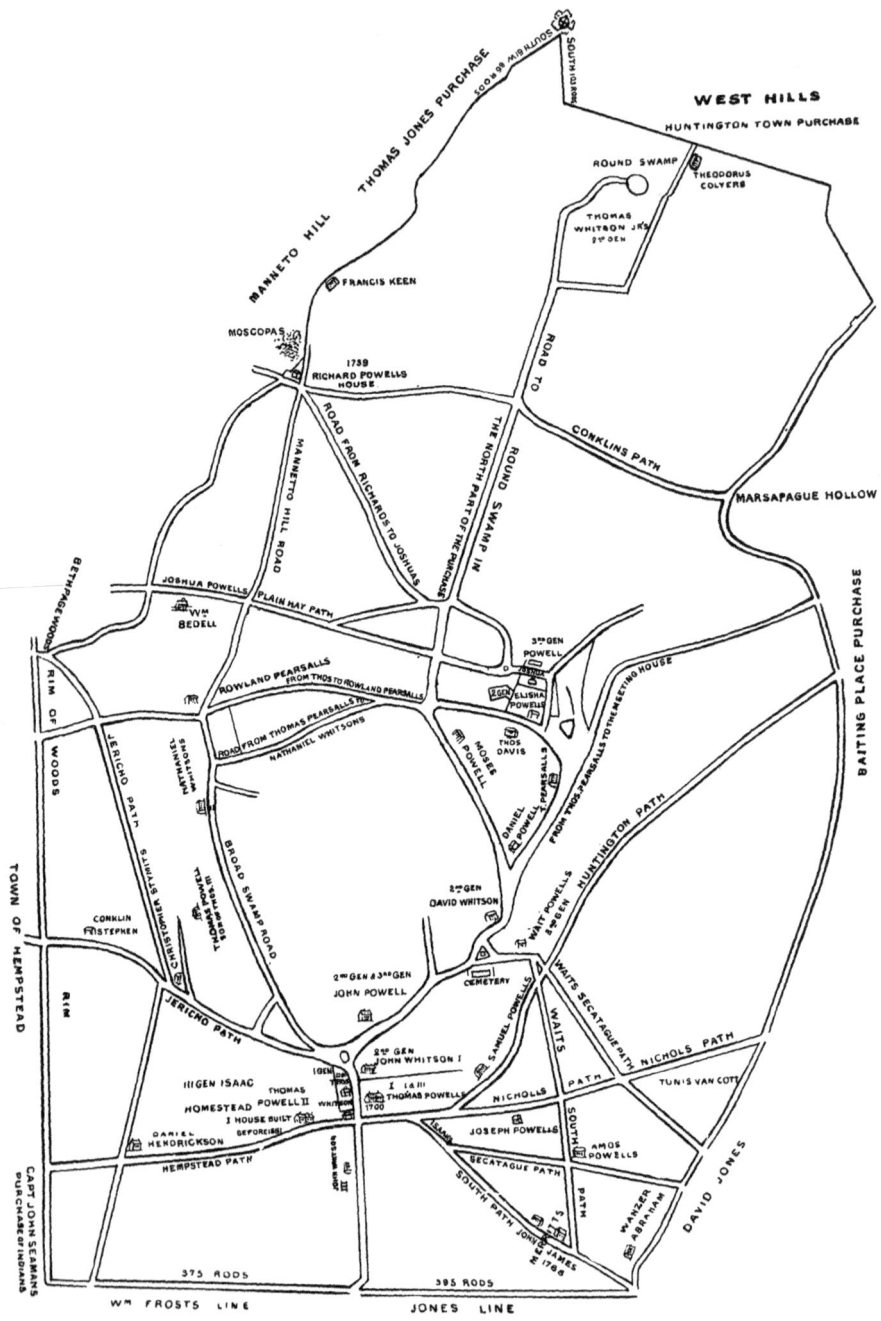

LONG ISLAND GENEALOGIES.

Families of Albertson, Andrews, Bedell, Birdsall, Bowne, Carman, Carr, Clowes, Cock, Cornelius, Covert, Dean, Doughty, Duryea, Feke, Frost, Haff, Hallock, Haydock, Hicks, Hopkins, Jackson, Jones, Keese, Ketcham, Kirby, Loines, Marvin, Merritt, Moore, Mott, Oakley, Onderdonck, Pearsall, Post, Powell, Prior, Robbins, Rodman, Rowland, Rushmore, Sands, Scudder, Seaman, Searing, Smith, Strickland, Titus, Townsend, Underhill, Valentine, Vanderdonk, Weeks, Whitman, Whitson, Willets, Williams, Willis, Wright, and other families.

BEING KINDRED DESCENDANTS OF

THOMAS POWELL,

OF BETHPAGE, L. I., 1688.

COMPILED BY

MARY POWELL BUNKER.

CLEARFIELD

Originally Published
Albany, New York
1895

Reprinted
Genealogical Publishing Co., Inc.
Baltimore, Maryland
1976

Reprinted for
Clearfield Company, Inc. by
Genealogical Publishing Co., Inc.
Baltimore, Maryland
1990, 2003

International Standard Book Number: 0-8063-5055-5

Library of Congress Cataloging in Publication Data

Bunker, Mary Powell Seaman, 1820-
   Long Island genealogies.

   Reprint of the 1895 ed. published by J. Munsell's Sons, Albany, N. Y., which was issued as no. 24 of Munsell's historical series.
   1. Long Island—Genealogy. 2. Powell family. I. Title.
F127.L8B9 1976   929'.1'0974721   76-11845

PREFACE.

Thirty years of interesting study examining many and various town, county, State, church, family Bible, and other records (at all times taking notes), have enabled me to compile therefrom the within matter, which I hope will give as much pleasure to some of the other descendants of the early settlers of Long Island as the gathering of it has given me.

As "to err is human," I must ask indulgence for errors, and offer to endeavor to correct them if brought to my notice.

Several pages in the fore part of the book are devoted to deeds, wills and records of the early Powells, with some accounts of the coming of the first Thomas, progenitor of all the rest.

The Powell genealogies follow in the order of the *first Thomas*. Then, *Powell* descendants of his oldest son; then, Powell descendants of his second oldest son; then, Powell descendants of his third oldest son, and so on through the Powells.

Three of the children of Thomas Powell having married into the Willets family, I have deemed it proper that the genealogy of the Willets family should come next. Edmund Titus' genealogy follows; then, Henry Willis' genealogy; then, Capt. John Seaman's genealogy; then, William Hallock's genealogy; then, John Carman's genealogy. All these were original settlers, and the first Thomas Powell's children married into their families.

The other genealogies of old Long Island families follow in alphabetical order.

Lastly, the will of John James, the first town clerk of Hempstead, and some other interesting matter.

I am, with great respect for my ancestors and their descendants,
MARY P. BUNKER,

A descendant of three successive Thomas Powells and many other early settlers of Long Island.

RECORDS.

A Copy of the Will of Thomas Powell.

Last will and testament of Thomas Powell Sen late of Bethpage now of Westbury in the limits of Hempstead in Queens County on Nassau Island in the Colony of New York

Whereas the certainty of mortality is before me and the uncertainty when the time of my dissolution shall come, and now being indifferent in health and of perfect memory do hereby make and ordain and appoint this my last will and testament for the disposing of what is disposable by me, and in order thereunto I do in the first place give and bequeath my soul to God my Maker from whom I have received mercy and hope and believe I ever shall as I keep in his fear and stand in his counsel through Jesus Christ my Lord and Savior who suffered the shameful death of the Cross without the Gates of Jerusalem and ascended on high and led captivity captive and hath given gifts unto men for the edifying of the Body his church for the perfecting the Saints among whom my lot is fallen as well to believe the Gift as to Receive it, so that by the prevailing of the Gift — the giver working with it — I come to know his Righteousness, imparted as well as imputed to me and in a sense thereof my Soul doth praise the Lord Jehovah who with his Glory

Enlighteneth His Holy City the Lamb is the Light thereof and the Nations of them that are saved shall walk in the Light thereof so that by the Revelation of the Son of God in my inward parts which is manifested by the Light, (for whatsover makes manifest is light) I come to witness the light of the knowledge of the Glory of God in the face of Jesus Christ, but we have this Treasure in our earthen vessels that the Excellency of the Power may be of God and not of us, and with the holy Apostle Paul to witness that God who commanded the light to shine out of Darkness to shine in our hearts.

Secondly I give my Body to the Earth from whence it was taken to be buried in a decent manner at the discretion of my executors herein after named.

And as to my outward Estate, after all my just debts are paid I do dispose of it as followeth,

Imprimis I will and Bequeath unto my son Thomas Powell and to his heirs and assigns forever, Twenty acres of Plain Land that I bought of John Westcoat, and all other Land and Right of Land that I have given him Deeds of Gift for.

I will and bequeath unto my daughter Abigail Willets one wainscot chest, and a Box of Small Drawers that was her mothers, together with what other things she has already had,

I give and Bequeath unto my Sons John Powell and Jonas Powell and Caleb Powell and Wait Powell and Elisha Powell, to them and their Heirs and Assigns forever all the land and Rights of land and Meadows as is particularly mentioned in their Several Deeds of Gifts for the same.

I will and Bequeath unto my Son Caleb Powell and unto my son Elisha Powell and to their Heirs and assigns forever the Equal two thirds of said lot of Meadows lying on the Great Neck at Huntington South lying on the west side of the third part of said lot of meadow that I sold to my son Thomas Powell to be equally divided between them or their Heirs and assigns forever, and I bequeath unto my youngest son Solomon Powell the sum of Two Hundred Pounds of Current lawful money of New York to be paid unto him when he shall arrive to the age of one and twenty years or shall have some lawful issue begotten by his own body or which of them shall first happen, — but if my Son Solomon Powell happen to die before he arrive at one and twenty years of age and have no Lawful issue begotten of his own Body Then the above said Two hundred Pounds shall be, the equal two thirds parts thereof Divided between all my Daughters that I have now living, and the children of my Daughter Elizabeth Titus to have one equal share divided amongst them, and all my daughters to have an equal share and share alike. and if my daughter Abigail Willets shall die before my son Solomon Powell, and my son Solomon Powell before he arrive at the age of one and twenty years, or have any lawful issue her part and share of said money shall be equally divided amongst all her children.

And whereas the said Two Hundred pounds Bequeathed unto my son Solomon, and in case of his decease before he ariveth at the age of one and twenty years or have any lawful Issue the equal two thirds parts thereof Bequeathed to all my daughters and is now due in the hands of my son Thomas Powell, my will is that all the mean profits and rents thereof shall also be equally divided as the said two thirds part of the said two hundred pounds. Allowing to my Executors all their just charges about the executing this my will, and in case my son live to the age to receive his portion above said he shall also have all the mean profits and Rents thereof, allowing the charges of the executors above said. I will and Bequeath if my son Solomon die without lawful issue or before he be one and twenty years old the equal one third part of the Two hundred pounds Bequeathed to him be equally divided between all my sons viz My son Thomas Powell and my son John Powell and my son Jonas Powell and my son Caleb Powell and my son Wait Powell and my son Elisha Powell and in case of any of their decease to their Heirs and also the mean profits and Rents thereof as above said I will unto them. And I will unto Samuel Titus the sum of one pound and ten shillings current money of New York in full of the remaining part of his wife's portion.

I will and Bequeath unto my two youngest daughters Sarah Powell and Amey Powell my Bed and Bedding and furniture belonging unto it. I will and bequeath unto my son Elisha Powell all my apparel and wearing clothes, and all the remaining part of my estate in money goods and chattels after my just debts are paid shall be equally divided amongst my six youngest daughters viz my daughter Mercy Powell and my daughter Sarah Powell and my daughter Amey Powell and my daughter Hannah Willis and my daughter Phebe Willis and my daughter Rachel Willets.

I do hereby constitute, authorize, and appoint and ordain my Loving Brother Thomas Townsend and my trusty and loving Friend Benjamin Seaman and my two sons in law William and Henry Willis to be my Executors of This my last Will and Testament and I do hereby Disallow Revoke and Disannul all and every other former Testaments, Wills, Legacies, Bequests, and Executors by me in any wise named and bequeathed or Willed and Bequeathed. Ratifying and confirming this and no other, to be my last will and Testament.

In witness whereof I have hereunto set my hand and seal this third day of the first month one Thousand seven hundred and nineteen, twenty.

The words to whom, and the words the equal two thirds part thereof Bequeathed, interlined before signing and sealing thereof.

      THOMAS POWELL. [L. S.]

Signed sealed published, pronounced and delivered by the said Thomas Powell as his last Will and Testament in the presence of us the Subscribers
    NATHANIEL SEAMAN,
    SILAS TITUS,
    JOHN WILLIS,
    JACOB WILLIS,
    WILLIAM WILLIS.

WILL OF THOMAS POWELL THE SECOND.

The last will and testament of Thomas Powell of Bethpage in the Township of Oyster Bay in Queens Co. on Nassau Island made the sixteenth of ninth month in the year of our Lord Christ one thousand seven hundred and thirty one, revoking whatsoever by me formerly made, and this being my last will and testament I being weak of body but perfect in mind and memory, I being willing to dispose of my outward estate as followeth and my will is that all my just debts shall be well and duly paid as I shall hereafter duly appoint by my Executors hereafter named.

Item. In the first place I give and bequeath to my well beloved wife, Mary Powell my dwelling house and the use and profit of one third part of all my lands and meadows everywhere, and my will is that my wife shall have half of my moveable Estate in the house: one third of my movables without doors excepting my Carts, Ploughs and Tackling, belonging to them and my Smiths Tools. My will is that my wife shall keep *them* till such time as our youngest son Isaac Powell shall come to the age of twenty years. Then to return back to my sons equally amongst them. And my will is that my son Tho's Powell shall have four acres of Land and house that stands upon it, — my fathers homestead, more than any other of my sons: meaning the four acres of Land with the house and orchard to him his heirs and assigns forever. And I give all the rest of my Land and meadows both Salt & fresh to my Seven Sons, viz. Thomas Powell, Wait Powell, Amos Powell, Moses Powell, Richard Powell, Joshua Powell and Isaac Powell to be equally divided amongst them their heirs and assigns forever. And if either of my Sons die without children or before they take their part in possession it shall be that their part shall be equally divided amongst the surviving Sons. In the next place I give unto my six daughters by name Abigail Hallock, Mary Pryor the wife of Samuel Pryor, Elisabeth Powell, Hannah Powell, Martha Powell and Deborah Powell the one half of all my movable Estate that is not already disposed of and two thirds of my movables without doors which are not already disposed of, to them, their heirs and assigns forever, and in case any of my daughters shall die without issue or before they are in possession of their portion, it shall be equally divided among my

Surviving daughters. My will is what I have given to my wife is during her widowhood. My will is if she marry again she shall have half the indoor movables, and one third of the out door movables, to her for her own disposal.

I do constitute and appoint my son Thomas Powell and my son Wait Powell and my brother Wait Powell and my wife Mary Powell all to be my Executors hoping they will this my last Will Execute according as it is the intent of it. And lastly, I desire my Brothers in law Richard Willets and Samuel Underhill to oversee and assist my Executors. In witness whereof I have hereunto set my hand and Seal the day and year above written. Before Signing and Sealing my will is that my Executors shall have full Power to sell land when they think best for to pay the debts and their Deed or Deeds shall be good.

THOMAS POWELL. [L. S.]

Signed Sealed published and declared this my last Will and Testament in the presence of the Subscribers.

JOHN WHITSAN,
DAVID WHITSAN,
HENRY WHITSAN.

Will of Thomas Powell the Third.

I Thomas Powell of Bethpage in the Township of Oyster Bay in Queens County on Nassau Island, yeoman being this the second day of second month called February in the year of our Lord one thousand seven hundred and fifty five much indisposed of body but of perfect mind and memory do make and ordain this writing to be my last will and Testament in manner following. I first order that my debts and other incidental charges about my estate shall be fully paid out of my movable Estate in some reasonable time after my decease. Item. I will and bequeath unto my well beloved wife, Abigail Powell, the issues and profits of the one third part of all my Lands and Meadows wheresoever, for her support and the east dwelling house that I dwell in all for her to use during the time she remains my widow. Item. I will unto my son Samuel Powell his heirs and assigns forever the lot of land I bought of Caleb Powell which was John Powells. Item. I will and bequeath unto my son Thomas Powell, his heirs and assigns twenty acres of my land before a division be made in general amongst my sons. Item. I will and bequeath unto my son Joshua Powell his heirs and assigns forever Ten acres out of my Lands before division be made. Item. I will that my son Samuel Powell has five acres of land. Item. I will that after my son Samuel has five acres, of land, my son Thomas twenty acres, my son Joshua Ten acres of Land, that then all the remainder part of my houses, lands, Rights of land and meadows whatsoever and wheresoever shall be equally divided amongst my eight sons viz, Samuel, Thomas, Joshua, Joseph, Elisha, Amos, Israel and Jesse, and to remain unto them in severalty their heirs and assigns forever, so to be understood as not to infringe or debar my wife from her privilege of my house lands & meadows above mentioned to her during her widowhood and I do hereby fully and absolutely empower my Executors or such of them as shall Execute this my will, to make a full and clear division of my Lands amongst all my sons in quality according to the above devise as they shall judge equal and just, and the division so made by my Executors or such of them as shall qualify as aforesaid shall be good stable and authentic to my sons, and to each of them in fee simple in as full a manner as if I had done it myself in my lifetime to all intents & purposes whatsoever; And my will is after my debts are fully paid and other charges accruing about my estate, that the remainder part of my movable Estate be divided thus : my wife to have the Indian girl named Boda during her widowhood, and then my daughter Mary Powell to have the said Indian girl to her disposal. I also will unto my daughter Mary Powell so much out of my movable estate as will make her portion equal with one of my two daughters or what each of my two daughters have had that are married. Then my will is that my wife shall have the one equal third part of the remainder of my movable Estate and the other two thirds to be equally divided amongst my three daughters viz Elizabeth Post, Ruth Mott & Mary Powell to their free disposal. And my will is what I have above given to my wife shall be taken and esteemed in lieu of her right of dower and not otherwise.

And my will is further that my Executors shall be tutors and guardians for all my children under age, and shall have full power to put and bind my three youngest sons out to trades according to their inclinations, and further to explain my will in respect to what I have given my son Samuel, which is thus. The lot before mentioned which I bought of Caleb Powell is to be reckoned as part of his portion to be equal with the common division amongst my sons, only the five acres to be taken out first before the common division is made aforesaid. Lastly. I do constitute, ordain and appoint my brother Isaac Powell, my brother in law John Whitson and my cousin Richard Willets of Islip to be my Executors of this my last Will and Testament and every article, clause and condition above expressed and further to make division with the rest of the *Proprietors* of *Bethpage*, and to take what Land falls to my right and to give releases when the division is finished, to the other Proprietors as fully as I could myself in my life time if I were personally present.

In witness hereunto I have set my hand and fixed my seal the day and date above expressed.

THOMAS POWELL. [L. S.]

Signed, Sealed, Published, Pronounced and declared by said Thomas Powell as and for his last Will and Testament in the presence of the subscribers who subscribed as witnesses in the presence of the testator.

MARY POWELL,
HENRY WHITSON,
SAMUEL WILLIS.

Marriages.

15-3-1690. Richard Willets and Abigail Powell took each other to be wife and husband at a meeting appointed at the house of Thomas Powell Huntington.

Witnesses who signed the certificate

Thomas Powell	John Cock	Tamison Fry
Joseph Wood	Thomas Whitson	Sarah Cock
John Seaman	Nathaniel Pear-	Thomas Willets
John Townsend	sall	Dinah Willets

Hugh Cowperthwait	John Dole	Martha Seaman
John Adams	Daniel Kirkpatrick	Hope Willetts
Benjamin Seaman	Samuel Titus	William Willis
William Fry	Elizabeth Adams	John Feake
	Martha Seaman	Elizabeth Feake
		Elizabeth Phillips

2^{day} of 9th mo. 1690. At a meeting at Edmond Titus Westbury, Thomas Powell, late of Huntington and Elizabeth Phillips of Jericho were married by Friends ceremony.

Witnesses

John Townsend	Edmond Titus	John Willis
Thomas Powell jr	Martha Titus	Benjamin Seaman
Thomas Whitson	Hannah Titus	William Eastland
Richard Willets	Henry Willis	
Joseph Wood	Mary Willis	Mary Smith.
	William Willis	
	John Dole	

6 of 9th mo 1691. Married at the house of Thomas Powell jr Bethpage by Friends ceremony, Samuel Titus of Westbury and Elizabeth Powell daughter of 1st Thomas Powell.

Witnesses who signed the certificate

Thomas Powell	Robert Field	William Willis
Edmond Titus	Phebe Field	Mary Willis
Hannah Titus	Benjamin Field	John Fry
Samuel Titus	John Rodman	John Dole
Joseph Wood	Hugh Cowperthwait	John Underhill
Benjamin Seaman	Isaac Smith	Sarah Cock.

At the same time and place Thomas Powell jr. of Bethpage and Mary Willets daughter of Thomas & Dinah, became husband and wife by Friends ceremony.

Witnesses

Thomas Powell	William Fry	Mary Willets
Thomas Willets	John Fry	Hope Willets
Edmond Titus	John Dole	Richard Willets
Joseph Wood	Robert Field	Phebe Field
Hugh Cowperthwait	Benjamin Seaman	Martha Seaman
		John Rodman
John Underhill	Isaac Smith	

Ancestry.

"We represent the hereditary influences of our race, and our ancestors virtually live in us.

"The sentiment of ancestry seems to be inherent in human nature, especially in the more civilized races.

"At all events we cannot help having a due regard for our forefathers. Our curiosity is stimulated by their immediate or indirect influence upon ourselves. It may be a generous enthusiasm or, as some might say, a harmless vanity, to take pride in the honor of their name.

"The gifts of nature, however, are more valuable than those of fortune, and no line of ancestry however honorable, can absolve us from the duty of diligent application and perseverance or from the practice of the virtues of self control and self help."

"They haunt your breezy hillsides, and thundering floods;
They linger by your gliding streams, and mid your moss draped woods;
They sit beside the green old graves; in shadow and in sheen,
And move among your household gods, though voiceless and unseen.

Records.

"Then ye, who make your happy homes, where once *their* homes
   have been,
Deem also *this* your heritage, to keep their memories green;
To shield within your heart of hearts, the glorious trust you hold,
And bear unstained the names they bore, those brave, proud men
   of old."

Thomas Powell (progenitor of all the Long Island Powells — most if not all of these in the State of New York — many in New Jersey, Pennsylvania and Maryland — and some in the other States) was born in 8th month, 1641. The names of his parents and place of his birth do not appear to be on record in this country.

The various branches of his descendants claim that he came from Wales, and we have reason to believe that tradition is, in this case, correct.

In 1619 First Journal of House of Delegates for Virginia says Burgesses were chosen. William Powell for James City, George Yeardly Knight and Govenor of Virginia, and others.

A great-grand-daughter of Thomas Powell Ist of Bethpage, told her children that the Virginia Powells were relatives of the family.

The Court Records of Huntington Dated — 1662 first introduce him to our notice as giving written testimony in the suit of law, brought at that time against Joanna Wood, widow of Jonas Wood Hal. Jonas Wood Hal was drowned when attempting to ford Peconic River near Riverhead, in 1660, consequently T. Powell was not more than 19 years old at the time of the transaction.

At a Court held in Huntington July 29, 1662.

Thomas Matthus plaintiff against Joanna Wood widow and Administratrix to Jonas Wood. An action of debt for fifty-four pounds 2 shillings and two pence.

Mr. John Simmons of Hempstead appeared in the case as attorney for Joanna Wood.

After relating the circumstances of the case Thomas Powell gave testimony in writing that, "What was in my Master's book—that particular about Master's Good Wood and Good Higbie touching the six pipes of wine and three hhds of rum,—when it was writ my Master read it to him or them and asked if it was well, and one of them answered it was. This was at Oysterbay in Daniel Whitehead's store.   living with my Master almost nine years I never knew my master's books questioned in the least."

J. Matthews produced his books in Court and the case was decided in his favor.

    JAMES CHICHESTER,
    RICHARD WILLIAMS,
    THOMAS JONES,
    SAMUEL TITUS,
         Jurymen.

Thomas Matthews sometimes called *Captain* Matthews was at Flushing, L. I., in 1649, trading with John Bowne delivering goods, &c. In 1659 he was bringing goods in partnership with Jonas Wood and Edward Higbie.

In 1669. Thomas Powell, Attorney for Mr. Thomas Matthews, sold land in Oysterbay to Joseph Ludlam.

In 1667. John Matthews, son of Thomas, sold land in Huntington to Thomas Wicks.

He died Dec. 7, 1686—his son John was of age in 1679.

1663. A copy of a deed from John Westcoat to Thomas Powell:

Know all men by these Presents that I John Westcott late of Fair— have bargained, sold and doe by these presents make over from me my Executors, Administrators and assigns forever, all my accommodations where Moses Hayte and myself bought of Rich'd Ogden in Huntington, that is to say my home lot, meadow and hollows commonage, and all privileges belonging to the accommodations, as also land upon the plains which belonged to Rich'd Ogden when I bought the accommodations of him.

I the aforesaid John doe bind myself, my heirs and assigns, to clear all Rates and Taxations that shall be demanded and found from the beginning of the World to this day, as witness my hand this 8th of December 1663.

JOHN WESTCOTT.

WITNESSES { THOMAS SKIDMORE, CALEB WOOD.

This is a true copy of the Original Deed extracted by me

THOMAS POWELL *Recorder.*

This appears to have been the first land purchased by T. P. although the Records show that he had a home and corn in 1662.

In 1667 Thomas Powell was Constable, John Todd, John Rogers Overseers, for Huntington, L. I.

Under the Duke's Laws, promulgated when the English took possession in 1865, 8 Overseers were to be chosen the first year, to hold office 2 years, & 4 to be elected every two years afterwards, and a

Constable was to be elected every year out of the Overseers of the previous year.

The Constable and Overseers managed the Town affairs, and had power to make orders & rules concerning fences, highways and similar matters. Constables were to attend Courts, and they had power to arrest, those who were overtaken with strong drink, or found swearing, or Sabbath breaking, Vagrants night walkers, provided taken in sight of Constable, or proven information from others or if in beer or disorderly places

" Every Constable shall have a Staff six feet long with the Kings arms on it, as a badge of his authority"

The Town Court had Jurisdiction of assault, Slander, and disorderly conduct generally, One offense was defined " as giving false news and lying about another." The penalty was a fine of 40 shilling if Paid" if not paid to sit in the stock or be whipped 40 strokes and give satisfaction.

T. P. was then 26 years old.

Huntington Records show that Thomas Powell was frequently elected to fill important positions in the Township — the first of which appears to have been in 1663, when at the age of 22 he was made Recorder. this office he held most of the time for about 20 years.

In 1666 Thomas Powell, John James, James Chichester, Ebenezer Platt, Isaac Platt, Thomas Platt John Bailey & Jonas Wood; were Trustees of the Freeholders of the Town of Huntington, and their successors. and the Patent was issued in their names, on behalf of the Company.

1684 T. Powell and one of the others were sent to Gov Nichols. to obtain a pattent from him. These patents were both at Huntington a few years since, probably are there still.

The court consisted of a Justice of the Peace (or in his absence) Constable and two Overseers.

T. P. was Constable in 1667. 1668, 1669, had to carry a club four feet long. appointed Surveyor 1670, to lay out land in the East Riding. Overseer 1672. 1680 &c &c

1682 Chosen Constable but refused to serve being "scrupulous of swearing as the law directs"

The constable had to swear to levy and collect the Church Rates.

1686 Chosen Committee Man to go to Southampton to act with others on behalf of the Town.

1666 Attorney for Thomas Matthews in the sale of land in Oysterbay, Joseph Ludlam, Purchaser.

The following is on record at Huntington 1670. Whereas, Henry Whitson of Huntington, deceased in the year 1669, and after the will was proved according to law, the estate being divided by order and consent of the widow of Henry, and Thomas Whitson son of deceased, and 2^d Thomas Whitson being under age,—he with the consent of his Grandfather Foster and the rest of his friends have thought good to make choice of Thomas Powell of Huntington to be his Trustee and Guardian of him the said Thomas Whitson, for the care and supervision of the Estate of him the said Thomas Whitson until he accomplish the age of one and twenty years, during which time the aforesaid, Thomas Whitson doth promise not to bargain sell or alienate any of his Estate without the leave and consent of his said Guardian, but in all things expedient be subject to his advice and counsel,

as witness my hand
THOMAS WHITSON.

In 1679. It was agreed that Thomas Powell and Thomas Whitson take in an addition to their land at Cow Harbor,

In 1689. Thomas Powell gave a deed jointly with Thomas and Martha Whitson for a piece of land in Huntington.

In 1700. Thomas Powell gave Thomas Whitson a Deed for one third of all his Bethpage purchase of land,—and they together built the two houses which were afterwards their homes, and the homes of their respective descendants, for many, many years. The places are both owned by descendants of T. Powell to this day—have never been out of the families.

In 1678 the Council ordered the Constable and Overseers of Huntington to distrain for Church and Ministers Rates, but the order does not appear to have been attended to for several years. T. P. was Overseer in 1681. Same year we find charged against him for Ministers Rates the follows sums, viz.:

1676.	1.	15.	00.	1679.	1.	10.	09.
1677.	1.	13.	03.	1680.	1.	02.	05.
1678.	1.	09.	06.	1681.	1.	04.	11.

Altogether £8. 15. 10.

In 1692 he was ordered by a Writ from the King to appear at Court at Riverhead to show cause why this should not be taken from him per force. There does not appear to be any Rec. of a settlement of the claim in any manner, and it is thought that the Authorities let the case drop out of sight.

Meantime T. P. sold his property in Huntington and bought a large tract of wilderness, of the Marsapaque Indians, called it Bethpage, took possession in 1688, built a house for his eldest son Thomas, (said house is now standing on the Bethpage turnpike, and has always been in possession of his descendants. Got his deed from the Indians in 1695, and as has been said sold one third to T. Whitson in 1700. T. P. purchased a second plot of the Indians in 1699. The Deeds are both Recorded at Jamaica.

The following is a copy of the boundaries of the two purchases, with the names and marks of Indians who made the sale.

1695.

We Marinus, Sowamicus, Wm. Choppy, and others for £140, sold to Thomas Powell Sen., land Beginning at the west Corner, at a dirty hole upon the brushy plains near Mannetto kill, from thence up a hollow the south side of Mannetto hill and out of that hill across the hills eastward pretty near Huntington South line to the bushy plains on the east side of the hills, and so along the east side of the hollow that goes to the east branch of Marsepequa the head of the swamp being the South east Corner, and from thence along Wm. Frosts line until we come to West Neck northeast bounder belonging to Oysterbay, and from the s^d north east bounder of West Neck, so to run on the west side of the hollow that comes from the west branch of Marsepequa swamp so far as there is any trees;—from thence to the aforesaid hole of dirt and water near Mannetto hill called by the Indians Moscopas. Part of the above land having been in the possession of Thomas Powell 7 years, Indians reserving unto themselves liberty of hunting, and gathering huckleberries.

    + SOWWAMACUS (his mark).
    × W_M CHOPPY (his mark).
    T SOUREEKENNY (his mark).
    Z WAMASSUM (his mark).
    6 SASCOMOMA (his mark).
    O RUAMPASS (his mark).

Deed No 2. 12 March 1699.

Land, bounded southwesterly by Oysterbay Neck line, west by the line or bounds of the Town of Hempstead, so running northerly to a certain marked tree of Rob't Williams his bounds, thence along by a Ridge of Trees between the bushy plains and the great plains until it comes to a swamp or hole of water called by the Indian name of Mosscopas near the Mannetto hill; east by Thomas Powells (former purchase of) land.

 1684 THOMAS POWELL for Huntington,
   THOMAS TOWNSEND for Oysterbay,
Chosen to settle the boundary between the Towns.

 1688. T. P. Our Surveyor was still busy laying out lands for the Town. After this period he appears to have been more engaged with appointments in Friends meetings than in public business. He was evidently very useful as a member of the monthly meeting, held part of time at Jericho and part of the time at Westbury. The last mention of his name on the records were on this wise.— 28, 12mo 1721 Died Thomas Powell Sen'r being well respected as a worthy Friend, —and died in unity with Friends.

Thomas[1] Powell divided two thirds of the land which he purchased of the Indians and named Bethpage between three of his sons, namely Thomas Powell the second, whose house is still standing on the Bethpage Turnpike. John Powell whose house was north of the pond.

The site is now known as the Mott Place and Elisha Powell, his place was north east of the Meeting house & Friends burial ground. The whole purchase covered an area of five miles from north to south and about three and a half miles from east to west, of this Thomas Whitson had one third, not all lying together in one piece, but divided out in various different parcels & pieces.

In this way the homes of the different families as they became more numerous were scattered over the premises in all directions.

Of the other sons of T.[1] P. it appears that Caleb, Jonas & Wait were settled in Huntington first, and that probably Jonas & Wait lived after a while in the neighborhood of Oysterbay & Jericho.

Solomon lived at Westbury.

In 1727. Friends Meetings were held once a month on first days at [2]Thomas Powell's house.

In 1744. A meeting house was built, near where the present one stands.

The first purchase in the Town of Huntington was made by Theophilas Eaton Gov of New Haven in 1646,—a peninsula on the north side, known as Eaton's Neck.

The first purchase made by actual settlers (of which we have any record) was made by Richard Holbrook, Robert Williams and Daniel Whitehead in 1653.

It lay from Cold Spring Harbor on the west to Northport Harbor on the east, and extended South to the middle of the Old Country road, it was called the old purchase. In 1657-8 several necks of meadow on the South Side of the Island, were purchased of the Indians by Jonas Wood and others.

In 1673. T. Powell was Rated £104. 1683 £233.

1673. There was a division of lands by lot among the proprietors and that called the fifth farm lying at Fresh Pond Neck fell to Thomas Skidmore, Jonas Wood, James Chichester and Thomas Powell, which they bound themselves and one another to occupy or cause to be occupied built upon and improved within 3 years.

 1668. At Town meeting T. P. was voted 6 acres of land.

 1668. The Division of Santipagne gave T. P. considerable land.

 1699. T. P. bought of Nathaniel Williams.
  " " " John Rogers.

 1689. T. P. sold to John Adams, 1895 to Joseph Wood.

 1699. " " " John Sawneys, 1,700 to Thos. Smith.

 1701. " " " Jonas Wood, 1,717 to Isaac Sammis.

POWELL FAMILY.

THOMAS[1] POWELL, born 8th mo 1641, died at Westbury, L. I. 28, 12, 1721, 1st wife unknown, children:
    Thomas[2] m. Mary Willets 6, 9, 1691 at Bethpage, he d. 27, 9, 1731.
    Abigail[2] b. 18, 4, 1668 m. Richard Willets 15, 3, 1690 at Huntington L. I., she d. 2, 9, 1757.
    Elizabeth[2] m. Samuel Titus 6, 9, 1691 at Bethpage, she d. 9, 2, 1704.
    John[2] m. Margaret Hallock 10 mo 1704, he d. 1738.
    Jonas[2] m. Anna.
    Caleb[2] m. Sarah, he d. 1741.
    Wait[2] d. 1750   m.   no ch.
    Elisha[2] m. Rebecca, he d. 1739.

THOMAS[1] POWELL, m. 2d Elisabeth Phillips of Jericho, L. I. 2, 9, 1690, (at Edmund Titus' in Westbury), children.
    Hannah[2] b. 28, 5, 1691, m. Wm. Willis 1712 at Bethpage.
    Phebe[2] b. 10, 6, 1693 m. Henry Willis 1712 at Bethpage she d. 1751.
    Rachel[2] m. Thomas Willets 1719.
    Mercy[2] b. 1702, m. Jacob Seaman 1726 she d. 13, 3, 1759.
    Solomon[2] m. Ruth Carman 1730, he d. 23, 2, 1736.
    Sarah m. Nathaniel Seaman 1722.
    Amy.

Elizabeth Phillips was prob. dau. of John[2] Townsend and widow of Theophilus Phillips of Flushing m. Theophilus 1685, he d. 1686, she was his 3d wife.

THOMAS[2] POWELL (Thomas[1]) m. Mary dau. of Thomas Willets of Jericho and Dinah Townsend and had children :

Thomas[3] b. 30, 5, 1663 m. 12, 1724 Abigail Hallock he d. 1, 3, 1757.
Mary[3] b. 4, 11, 1694, died 2 mo. 1695.
Abigail[3] b. 13, 12, 1695 m. 1733 Peter Hallock.
Mary[3] b, 16, 3, 1697 m. 16, 8, 1728 Samuel Prior b. 1692 she d, 21, 5, 1776.
Wait[3] b. 29, 9, 1698 m. 15, 1, 1723 Mary Mudge, he d. 1782.
Amos[3] of Islip b. 9, 5, 1700 d. single 14, 1, 1749.
Moses[3] b. 4, 5, 1702 m. 1732 Catharine Hallock, he d. 1774,
Richard[3] b. 17, 4, 1704 m. 1737 Freelove Weeks m. 2d 28, 7, 1748 Jerusha Week, he d. 7, 3, 1774.
Elizabeth[3] b. 11, 10, 1705.
Hannan[3] b, 18, 7, 1707 m. Henry Whitson, b. 1705 she d. 1790,
Joshua[3] b. 18, 5, 1709 m. 1744 Phebe Post dau. Richard.
Isaac[3] b, 4, 1711, m. 2, 1, 1733 Martha Whitman he d. 1794.
Martha[3] b. 29, 6, 1713 m. Francis Keen she d. 24, 3, 1773.
Deborah[3] b, 28, 10, 1715, m. 1744 John Whitson.

Thomas[2] lived and died at Bethpage. Their home was the first house built in that vicinity. There were Indian Wigwams in the neighborhood.

In the year 1747, Amos Powell accompanied John Woolman through Connecticut, when he Woolman was on a Religious visit to New England.

Powell Family.

THOMAS[3] POWELL (Thomas[2] Thomas[1]) m. 24, 12, 1724 Abigail dau. of John Hallock (and Hannah) of Brookhaven, L. I., children:
Samuel[4] b. 10, 11, 1725, m. 23, 3, 1748 Mary Wood, he d. 1797.
Elizabeth[4] b. 2, 7, 1727, m. 1761 Micah Post.
Thomas[4] b. 3, 2, 1729, m. 1757 a collier.
Ruth[4] b. 31, 3, 1731, m. 1748 Jehu Mott.
Joshua[4] b. 9, 12, 1732, m. Margaret (called Gretie) Ellis.
Joseph[4] b. 25, 12, 1735, m. 1757 Deborah Scott he d. 12, 2, 1789.
Elisha[4] b. 20, 12, 1737, m. 1766 Rachel Ham, she b. 9, 8, 1749, d. 27, 8, 1825, he d. 22, 2, 1824.
Mary[4] b. 30, 10, 1739 m. 3, 8, 1765 John Cornelius, she d. 21, 3, 1826.
Amos[4] b. 20, 10, 1741, m. 1st 1767 Jerusha Allen, 2d Annie nee Willets, wid. Powell.
Israel[4] b. 17, 2, 1744, m. dau. Amos Seaman.
Jesse[4] b. 7, 8, 1746, m. Margaret called Peggy.
Thomas and Abigail lived, died and buried at Bethpage.

SAMUEL[4] POWELL (Thomas[3] Thomas[2] Thomas[1]) m. 23, 3, 1748 Mary Wood, children:
Samuel m. 1787.
Martha m. 1784 Jesse Brundige.
Jacob, a weaver, m. 1793 Hannah Pearsall, dau. of John, moved to New York in 1804.
Mary b. 1754, m. William Stillwell, he b. 1757, d. 1799, she d. 1844.
Abigail m. Caleb Wood, he d. 4, 9, 1828.
Kesia m. 1794 John Darby.
Hannah m. 1793 John Pearsall, dau. of John.
Stillwell children of Wm. and Mary:
Abigail b. 1781, m. Jonah Powell, she d. 1825.

Samuel b. 1787, d. 1790.

Wood children of Caleb and Abigail:

Elkanah m. 1st Annie Rushmore, dau. of James Rushmore and Deborah Whitson, dau. of John and had : Dr. James R. Wood of New York, b. 9 mo, 1816. He was a noted surgeon.

Samuel Darby, mariner, and Hannah, his wife, came to L. I. from Salem, Mass. in 16—.

SAMUEL[5] POWELL (Samuel[4] Thos.[3] Thos.[2] Thos.[1]) m 1787 Kesia and went to Coeymans, N. Y., children :

James[6] m. and had eel potpie for his wedding dinner.

Mary[6] m. a Halstead.

Phebe[6].

Rachel[6].

Elisabeth[6].

THOMAS[4] POWELL (Thos.[3] Thos.[2] Thos.[1]) m. 1757 a Collier. In 1762 moved with his family from Bethpage, L. I., into the limits of Purchase. Monthly meeting. Was at Stephentown now Somers 24, 9, 1792. Children :

Thomas[5] b. 4, 4, 1758, m. Catharine Ham, she b. 13, 3, 1753, he d. 1840.

John[5] m. and lived in Westchester county, N. Y.

Unknown,[5] killed by a shark.

Hannah.[5]

Katie.[5]

THOMAS[5] POWELL (Thos.[4] Thos.[3] Thos.[2] Thos.[1]) m. Catharine Ham, b. 13, 3, 1753. Children :

Elisha[6] H. b. 15, 12, 1793, m. Hannah Powell b. 2, 7, 1795, dau. of John and Phebe (Halstead) Powell.

Frederick.[6]

John H.[6] had son Edward.

Sarah[6].
Some of their descendants still live at Coxsackie.
Children of ELISHA[6] H. and Hannah (Powell) Powell were:
Phebe[7] b. Aug. 24, 1814.
Katharine[7] b. Feb. 28, 1816,
Coenrad,[7] b. Jan. 27, 1817, m. Martha G. Bedell, dau. of Daniel and Miriam and had Alice and Ella.
Luman[7] b. Jan. 27, 1819, m. Abigail Bedell, dau. of Daniel and Miriam.
Prudence[7].
John Wm.[7]
Rebecca[7].
Hannah Jane[7].
Elisha B.[7]
Thomas Collier,[7] m. had ch. Omar Powell and others.
Children of LUMAN[7] and Abigail (Bedell) Powell:
Alonzo G.[8] m. and had Maud, Clarence, Mabel, Satie and Stanley.
Daniel E.[8] m. and had Edith and Arthur.
Benjamin B.[8] m. and had Lela.
Jennie H.[8] m. a Slingerland and had Luman and Claude.

JOSHUA[4] POWELL (Thos.[3] Thos.[2] Thos.[1]) m. 1757 Margaret Ellis. He was disunited with Friends 1757 for bearing arms to save paying his *fine*, children:
Sally[5] m. Richard Totton.
Abigail[5] m. Cornelius Van Cott, son of Gabriel.

JOSEPH POWELL (Thos.[3] Thos.[2] Thos.[1]) m. 1757 or 1760 Deborah Scott, b. 1739, children:
Catherine[5] b. 1760, m. Jacob Covert.
Martha[5] b. 1761.
Abigail[5] b. 1764, m. Richard Whitson.

Rachel[5] b. 1766, m. Isaac Whitson.
Wm.[5]
Rowland.[5]
Jerusha[5] b. 1776, m. Jas. Seaman.

Joseph[4] Powell was a carpenter, lived at Bethpage.

Huntington Rec. give account of a verbal Will made in 1789 after a severe injury caused by the giving way of a ladder upon which Joseph[4] Powell was standing while engaged in building a house; his death followed soon and the will was allowed.

ISRAEL[4] POWELL (Thos.[3] Thos.[2] Thos.[1]) resided in Dutchess county, N. Y., m. a dau. of Amos Seaman, children:

Annie b. 5, 3, 1760.
Stephen b. 10, 2, 1768.
Charles b. 2, 8, 1772, and perhaps Phebe and Abigail.

ELISHA[4] POWELL born at Bethpage, settled in Dutchess county, about 100 years ago. He took his family to Medway in Greene county. There he made a home, reared his family and when he died in 1824, Feb. 22, he was buried in a beautiful little cemetery of his own selection on his farm. His wife and many of his descendants lie around him A granddaughter and her husband and family were living on the farm in 1890.

ELISHA[4] POWELL (Thos.[3] Thos.[2] Thos.[1]) m. 1766 Rachel Ham, b. Aug. 9, 1749, she d. Aug. 27, 1825, children:

Mary[6] b. Feb. 17, 1767, m. Thomas Hallock.
Thomas E.[6] b. July 22, 1768, m. Catharine O'Blenis.
Frederic[6] b. Feb. 5, 1771, m. Deborah O'Blenis.
Abigail[6] b. Jan. 17, 1773, m. Wm. Bedell.
Elisha E.[6] b. July 12, 1777, m. Rachel Carmen.

Elisabeth[6] b. Nov. 8, 1778, m. Henry O'Blenis.
John E[6] b. Sep. 22, 1782, m. Sarah Smith.
Margaret[6] b. Oct. 21, 1783, m. Jonathan Miller.
Israel[6] b. Aug. 15, 1785.
Samuel H.[6] b. Oct. 12, 1787, m. Jane Smith.
Henry[6] b. Dec. 16, 1789, prob. d. young.
Oliver[6] b. Dec. 4, 1794, m. Deborah Rundle b. 1795, d. Aug. 5, 1886, he d. Dec. 6, 1866.
OLIVER[5] POWELL (Elisha[4] Thos.[3] Thos.[2] Thos.[1]) m. Deborah Rundle, children:
Samantha m. Reuben Washburn.
Perline m. Oliver Marcus Daboll.
Ann P. m. Isaac Smith.
Susan H.
Israel B. m. Amanda Shepherd.
Jane m. Benj, Hilton.
Araminta m. Stephen Washburn.
Mary Elisabeth.
Warren B. m. Lydia Newman.
AMOS[4] POWELL (Thos.[3] Thos.[2] Thos.[1]) m. 1767 Jerusha Allen, 2d Annie nee Willets, widow of Z. Powell, children:
Thomas[5] m. Stacy Conklin.
Allen m. a Birch.
James m. Elisabeth Van Cott.
Anne m. a Den Eyke.
Martha m. R. Whitson.
Willet d. single and wealthy in the West Indies.
THOMAS[5] POWELL (Amos[4] Thos.[3] Thos.[2] Thos.[1]) m. Stacy Conklin, children:
Jerusha m. Joshua Carman.
Jesse.
Conklin m. Esther Wanzer.
Ann m. Wm. Wanzer.
Phebe m. a Noel.

Sylvanus m. Martha Haff and had a son.
Isaac.
James.
JAMES[5] POWELL (Amos[4] Thos.[3] Thos.[2] Thos.[1]) m. Elisabeth Van Cott, children :
Mary Weeks.
Martha m. R. Tooker.
Allen.
Amos.
James m. Amelia Ketcham.
John.
Jervis.
Willet.
Zebulun.
Andrew.
Elizabeth m. Dennis Middleton.

JESSE[4] POWELL (Thos.[3] Thos.[2] Thos.[1]) m. Margaret, and went to Nova Scotia after the War of Independence, children :
Thos.
Samuel T.
John.
Jesse.
Israel.
Joseph.

WAIT[3] POWELL (Thos.[2] Thos.[1]) b. 1698, m. 1723 by a justice of the peace Mary Mudge b. 1701, dau. of Moses and Mary, children :

    Jane[4] b. 2, 22, 1725, m. 1742 Samuel Willets of Islip.

    Mary[4] b. 11, 31, 1727, m. 1749 Nathaniel Whitson, son of John.

    Anna[4] b. 7, 22, 1730, m. 1748 Rowland Pearsall, son of Henry.

    Wait[4] b. 4, 30, 1733, m. Hannah Willets b. 1734, dau. of Amos.

Powell Family. 37

Jemima⁴ b. 1, 31, 1736, m. 1762 Samuel Cocks, son of Henry.

Esther⁴ b, 2, 23, 1738, unm.

Sarah⁴ b. 8, 23, 1745, m. Silas Whitson Aug. 10, 1772.

Esther Powell's will, 1781, gives her property to niece Mary wife of John Seaman, sister Mary Whitson, niece Jemima Willets wife of Amos Powell, Amos Powell, Jemima Cock.

WAIT⁴ POWELL (Wait³ Thos.² Thos.¹) m. 1756 Hannah Willets, children:

    Willets b. 1757, m. 1781 Ruth Whitson b. 1761, and had Charles b. 1783, Sarah b. 1788, Hannah b. 1792, Wait b. 1795.

    Rachel b. 1759.

MOSES³ POWELL (Thos.² Thos.¹) m. 1732 Catharine, dau. John and Hannah Hallock of Brookhaven, will dated 1774 at North Castle, Westchester county, N. Y., children:

    Moses⁴ b. 26, 1, 1733, d. 1737.

    John⁴ b. 11, 10, 1734-5, m. 1745-6, 11, 11, Elisabeth Kipp b. 1738, 4, 9, dau. of Benj. Kipp.

    Anna⁴ b. 26, 10, 1737, m. 1757, 3, 17, Samuel Quimby and had Catharine and Jane.

    Nathaniel⁴ b. 1739, m. 1767 Anna Sutton b. 1751, 11, 1, dau. of Joseph and Deborah, he d. 12, 2, 1807.

    Moses⁴ b. 5, 11, 1741, m. Hannah Wheeler.

    Hannah⁴ b. 5, 11, 1742-3, m. 1761, 12, 17, Benedict Carpenter.

    Obadiah⁴ b. 16, 5, 1744.

    Catharine⁴ b. 30, 3, 1746, m. a Hunt and had Mary Ann and Rebecca.

    Edward⁴ b. 5, 3, 1748, m. had children.

    James⁴ b. 25, 12, 1750, m. 1st unknown, 2d Martha Townsend, April 1, 1804.

Samuel b. 30, 9, 1752.

Elisabeth b. 25, 1, 1755, m. 7, 20, 1775, Zebediah Dickinson and had Daniel, Isaac and Jacob.

Mary b. 23, 5, 1757, m. a Gleason.

Isaac b. 8, 8, 1759, m. 1788 Phebe Fowler.

In 1754 Moses Powell sold his home and lands at Bethpage to Joseph Prior, and removed to Westchester county, N. Y.

JOHN[4] POWELL (Moses[3] Thos.[2] Thos.[1]) m. 11, 11, 1754–6 Elizabeth, dau. Benj. Kipp, she b. 1738, 4, 9, children:

Jacob.
Daniel.
Ann.
Sarah.
Abigail.
Nathaniel.
Benjamin.

JACOB[5] POWELL (John[4] Moses[3] Thos.[2] Thos.[1]) m. ———, children:

James[6] died.
Henry J.[6] m. Judith Rider.
James[6] m. had five children.
Ammon[6] m. had five children.
Ruth[6] m. 1st ——— Booth, m. 2d Benjamin Shelden.

HENRY J.[6] POWELL (Jacob[5] John[4] Moses[3] Thos.[2] Thos.[1]) m. Judith Rider and had children:

Jonathan K.[7] m. 1st Elizabeth Stark, 2d Anne Morrell.
Wilson M.[7] m. Sarah, dau. of Samuel Browne.
Albert G.[7] m. Eva.
Maria[7] m. Edwin Blackburn.
Mary.[7]
Louisa[7] she died Nov. 27, 1884.

JONATHAN K.⁷ POWELL (Henry I.⁶ Jacob⁵ John⁴ Moses³ Thos.² Thos.¹) m. 1st Elizabeth Stark, 2d Anne Morrell and had children:
Henry A.⁸ m. Julia.
Lefferts M.⁸
Jonathan.⁸
Anna L.⁸

WILSON M.⁷ POWELL (Henry I.⁶ Jacob⁵ John⁴ Moses³ Thos.² Thos.¹), a noted lawyer of New York city, m. Sarah, dau. of Samuel Browne and Rachel (nee Hopper), dau. of Isaac T., had children:
Samuel B.⁸
Rachel H.⁸
Henry I.⁸
Wilson M.⁸
Elsie.⁸
Melville.⁸

ALBERT G.⁷ POWELL (Henry I.⁶ Jacob⁵ John⁴ Moses³ Thos.² Thos.¹) m. Eva, had children:
Arthur Albert.
Eva m. Christopher Howard.
Henry Yarwood d. early.
Yarwood Henry, d. early.

NATHANIEL⁴ POWELL (Moses³ Thomas² Thomas¹) m. Anna Sutton, dau. of Joseph and Deborah. Removed from North Castle, Westchester county, to Salt Point, Dutchess county, 12 miles north-east of Poughkeepsie in 1772, 7, 14. Children all born at Salt Point.
Stephen⁵ m. had three children.
Joseph⁵ m. had seven children.
Nathaniel⁵ m. Martha Haight.
Henry⁵ not married.
Anna⁵ m. a Hoag, several children.
Phebe⁵ m. a Hoag, several children.

Elisabeth⁵ m. a Halstead, five children.
Catherine⁵ m. a Duel, two children.
Emma⁵ m. a De Garmo, seven children.
Mary⁵ not m.
Hannah⁵ m a Bowman, four children.
Esther⁵ m. a Ryder, four children.
Lydia⁵ m. a Culver, three children.
Deborah⁵ m. a Quimby, three children.
STEPHEN⁵ POWELL (Nathaniel⁴ Moses³ Thos.² Thos.¹) m.   Children :
Mark⁶.
Anna.⁶
JOSEPH⁵ POWELL (Nathaniel⁴ Moses³ Thos.² Thos.¹) m. had children :
Jacob.⁶
Clark.⁶
Henry.⁶
Nelson.⁶
Lydia.⁶
Elisabeth.⁶
NATHANIEL⁵ POWELL (Nathaniel⁴ Moses³ Thos.² Thos.¹) m. Martha Haight, had children :
Ruth Ann⁶ m. Henry Dickinson.
Esther Maria.⁶
Caleb H.⁶ m. Mary Jane Haight.
Probably there were others.
MOSES⁴ POWELL (Moses³ Thos.² Thos.¹) m. Hannah Wheeler, children :
John⁵ b. 16, 4, 1771, m.¹ Phebe Halstead, m.² Rebecca Hallock, he died 19, 11, 1859.
Isaac.⁵
Nicholas.⁵
Daniel.⁵
Edward.⁵

Peter.[5]
Pherris.[5]
JOHN[5] POWELL (Moses[4] Moses[3] Thos.[2] Thos.[1]) born at North Castle, Westchester Co., lived at Coeymans, m' Phebe Halstead (dau. of Joshua and Mary), she b. 15, 1, 1767, children :
    Hannah[6] b. 2, 7, 1795, m. Elisha[6] H. Powell, son of Thos.[5] & Catherine.
    Joshua[6] b. 13, 11, 1796.
    Moses[6] b. 13, 1, 1798, m. Jerusha Hicks of —— & Margaret.
    David[6] b. 19, 1, 1800.
    Mary[6] b. 21, 8, 1801.
    Isaac[6] b. 11, 4, 1803.
    Phebe[6] b. 12, 10, 1804.
    Prudence[6] b. 16, 4, 1806.
JOHN[5] POWELL m.[2] 1829, 3, 29, Rebecca Hallack, dau. of Edward and Susanna, she b. 13, 11, 1780, one child :
    Phebe[6] b. 5, 7, 1823.
OBADIAH[4] POWELL (Moses[3] Thos.[2] Thos.[1]) m. had children :
    Obediah.[5]
JAMES[4] POWELL (Moses[3] Thos[2] Thos.[1]) m. 1st unknown, 2d Martha, children :
    George[5] m., had several children.
    Moses[5] m.
    James[5] unm.
    Amy[5] m. Shepherd, three children.
    Phebe[5] m. Montross, six children.
    Catharine[5] m. Combs, four children.
    Elizabeth[5] m. Fedenburgh, four children.
    Sarah[5] m. Dean, five children.
    Dorcas[5] m. John Bedell, seven children.
    Deborah[5] unm.

JAMES[4] POWELL m. 2, 1804, 4, 5, Martha, dau. of John Townsend and Susanna (Shotwell), children:

Jane[5] m. Macy, two children.
Townsend[5] m. Catharine Macy.
Susan[5] m. Mulineaux, nine children.
Grace F.[5] m. 1st Ricketson, one son, 2d Robinson.
Shotwell[5] m. Clapp, dau. of Thomas, three children.

TOWNSEND[5] POWELL (James[4] Moses[3] Thos.[2] Thos.[1]) m. Catharine Macy of Hudson, dau. of Abraham Macy and his wife Elizabeth, dau. of Elihu Coleman, children:

Aaron M.[6] m. Anna Rice, had one dau. d. an infant.
Elisabeth[6] m. Bond, one son Edwin Bond. She is a widow and is now Dean of Swarthmore College, Penn.
George[6] m. Marcia, has several children, and is a noted agriculturist living in Ghent, N. Y,

SAMUEL[4] POWELL (Moses[3] Thos.[2] Thos.[1]) m. Phebe Fowler, had children:

ISAAC[4] POWELL (Moses[3] Thos.[2] Thos.[1]) m. Phebe Fowler, had children:

Henry[5] m. Phebe Haight.
Caleb[5] m. 1st Elisabeth Barnard, 2d Crosby.
Caleb[5] and Elisabeth had dau. Phebe, m. Oliver Macy, and had two sons.

HENRY[5] POWELL (Isaac[4] Moses[3] Thos.[2] Thos.[1]) m. Phebe Haight, dau. of Reuben and Sarah (Wright) Haight, b. 1794, she died 1883, 12, 16, aged nearly 90 years, children:

Sarah C.[6] m. Isaac D. Brown of David S., and has two children, son Franklin[7] Brown, m. Jennie Crosier, and dau. Louisa,[7] m. Edward Cornell, their son Franklin Edward[8] Cornell.
Henry H.[6] m. Emma Blanchard, has two children: Edna and Irene.

Henry[5] Powell and Phebe lived at Poughkeepsie, son Henry H.[6] still lives there.

The Brown family live in Brooklyn, N. Y.

One of the descendants of De Garmo and Emma,[5] dau. of Nathaniel Powell, is at present President of Swartmore College, Penn.

3, 30, 1739. *To the Monthly Meeting of Friends at Westbury:*

DEAR FRIENDS — These lines may acquaint you that I am under concern of mind for my misstep in ye way that I was married.

Which was on this wise. I having made my application to her that is now my wife, not doubting but that we might come before the meeting and be allowed to pass the same, and having gone so far that we could not reverse our desires and being discouraged from making application to the preparative Meeting by some of the members thereof, did unadvisedly and without ye counsel and advice of Friends procure a license from the Governor and was married by a Justice of the Peace.

Which hasty and unadvised marriage, contrary to the practice and good order used and established amongst Friends I do condemn, and do desire that for the future I may walk more circumspectly.

From your friend,
RICHARD POWELL.

Richard Powell's acknowledgment was acccepted by the Meeting, as satisfactory, and he remained a useful member of the Society the rest of his life.

Powell Family.

EXTRACT FROM THE MINUTES OF WESTBURY MONTHLY MEETING OF FRIENDS HELD IN 1762–3.

"In the matter of Henry Powell marrying out of the unity of his Friends, to his first cousin, which was again resumed and considered of, it appears to be the sense and judgment of the meeting that inasmuch as he was sufficiently treated with, in a dissuasive manner to desist from proceeding in marriage with his near kinswoman before marriage, and he hath not received the counsel and advice of Friends, but gone contrary to the rules of our Discipline, and left Friends. Therefore, he is disowned as a member in unity with us, until he is sensible that he has gone contrary to the order of Truth and condemns the same with sincerity of mind to the satisfaction of Friends.

Signed by order of the Meeting by
SAMUEL WILLIS,
Clerk.

RICHARD[3] POWELL (Thos.[2] Thos.[1]) m. 1737 Freelove Weeks, dau. of Henry Weeks & Susanna Alling. They lived and died at Bethpage, L. I., near Mannatts Hill, children :

Henry[4] b. 1741, m. his cousin Mary Keen, dau. of Francis.

Richard[4] m. 1762 Phebe Whitson.

RICHARD[3] POWELL m.[2] 1748, 7, 28, Jerusha (nee Lewis), widow of Robert Weeks, brother of his first wife, child:

Silas[4] m. 1780, April 30, Ann Allen. They had son Daniel[5] who m. 1808 Julianna Carle and had son Timothy,[6] who m. and had son Allen[7] Powell.

Powell Family. 45

HENRY[4] POWELL (Richard[3] Thos.[2] Thos.[1]) m. Mary dau. Francis Keen and his wife Martha[3] Powell, dau. Thos.[2] The marriage was at St. George's church, Hempstead, L. I., 19 Dec. 1762, by Samuel Seabury, Rector, children:

Freelove[5] m. Jacob Parrish.
Jacob[5] not m.
Thomas[5] m. Mary Ludlow.
James[5] was drowned 1782.
Martha[5] m. Benjamin Townsend.
Elisa[5] m. William Seymore.

THOMAS[5] POWELL (Henry[4] Richard[3] Thos.[2] Thos.[1]) m. 1802 Mary Ludlow, dau. of Robert, children:

Henry[6] not m.
Robert Ludlow[6] m. Louisa Orso.
James Augustus[6] drowned 1828.
Jacob[6] died 1816.
Francis Elisabeth Ludlow[6] m. Homer Ramsdell, he died 1894, their children were: Leila Rains Ramsdell, Homer Stockbridge Ramsdell, m. Maud Clarkson; James Augustus Powell Ramsdell m. —— Van Nostrant; Thomas Powell Ramsdell, died 1893 or 4; Francis Josephine, m. G. W. Rains, U. S. A.

ROBERT[6] LUDLOW POWELL (Thomas[5] Henry[4] Richard[3] Thos.[2] Thos.[1]) m. Louisa A. Orso, dau. of Jean Baptiste Orso. She was a Creole. Children:

Francis E[7] died young.
Mary Ludlow[7] m. Isaac Sebring Fowler.
Henrietta[7] m. W. A. M. Culbert.
Children of Isaac Sebring Fowler & Mary[6] Ludlow were: Robert Ludlow Fowler, Julia Fowler, Thomas Powell Fowler and Isabella Fowler.

RICHARD⁴ POWELL (Richard³ Thos.² Thos.¹) m. 1762 Phebe Whitson, dau. of John and Martha (Whitman) Whitson, children :
  Richard⁵ b. 14, 7, 1769, m. 1790 Amy Saxton.
  John⁵ b. 9, 7, 1773, m. Sarah Latting.
  Henry⁵ b. 1782, m. Sarah Wood, of West Hills.
  Esther⁵ b. 10, 1, 1768, m. 1789 Charles Willets, no children.
  James⁵ b. 1, 7, 1784, m. 1808 Prudence Peters.

RICHARD⁵ POWELL (Richard⁴ Richard³ Thos.² Thos.¹) m. Amy Saxton, dau. of   , children:
  Ephraim⁶ m. widow of French, ex. of Mannetto Hill.
  Henry.⁶
  John⁶ not m.
  Ann⁶ m. Capt. Kendal Towne, and had :
    Rebecca m¹ Aaron Oakley, m² Samuel Post.
    Ruth m. Ira Ketcham.
    Sarah m. Abner Chichester, of West Hills.
    Hattie not m.
    Kendall m., he had two children.
    Anne m. Frederick Bunce of Babylon.
    Lana m. Willett Powell of Hempstead.
    Phebe m. John Wood of Amityville.
  Abner and Sarah Chichester had Josephine & Irving; Frederick and Anne had Virginia Bunce; John Wood and Phebe had Hannah; Wait Powell and Lana had Annie and Harriet.

JOHN⁵ POWELL (Richard⁴ Richard³ Thos.² Thos.¹) m. Sarah Latting, children :
  Oliver⁶ m. Charlotte Wood, no children.
  Henry⁶ m. Rachel Colyer.
  Elwood⁶ m. Susan Kortwright.

Powell Family. 47

HENRY[6] POWELL (John[5] Richard[4] Richard[3] Thos.[2] Thos.[1]) m. Rachel Colyer, children :
  Charles[7] died.
  Edward.[7]

ELWOOD[6] POWELL (John[5] Richard[4] Richard[3] Thos.[2] Thos.[1]) m. Susan Kortwright, children :
  John K.[7] m. Ida Cornelius, dau. of John & Ida.
  Sarah Emma[7] m. Epenetus Ketcham and had Susan and Alexander.

HENRY[5] POWELL (Richard[4] Richard[3] Thos.[2] Thos.[1]) m. Sarah Wood, children :
  Andrew[6] m. Jane Duryea of Norwich, and had Esther m. Benjamin Willis.
  Esther m. Jesse Bryant of Comac, had Esther m. Ira Hubbs.
  Elisa[6] m. Wait Powell of John and Ruth.

JAMES[5] POWELL (Richard[4] Richard[3] Thos.[2] Thos.[1]) m. Prudence Peters, children :
  Richard[6] unm.
  Phebe[6] m. James Powell of John and Ruth.
  Ansalem[6] m. Hannah Ketcham of Amityville.
  Charles[6] m. Eliza Ann Weeks of Mannetto Hill.
  Janett[6] unm.

ANSALEM[6] POWELL (James[5] Rich'd[4] Rich'd[3] Thos.[2] Thos.[1]) m. Harriet Ketcham Powell, had :
  Antoinette[7] m. Carle Baylis of Melville, and had Alice, Alexander, Gertrude and George.
  Alexander[7] m. Nellie Thomas.
  Mary Alice[7] m, James Davy of Flatlands, children : Bessie and Hattie.
  George W.[7] m. Hattie Boroughs of Brooklyn, child : Herbert.
  Ansalem[7] m. Anna Powell of Brooklyn, children : Mabel and Wesley.
  Josephine[7] unm.

Thomas[7] unm.
Willie[7] died.
Children of Charles[6] and Eliza Ann (Weeks) Powell:
Mary Celia.[7]
Mary Lavina.[7]
Charles Augustus[7]
Phebe Emma.[7]
Sarah Elisabeth.[7]
Richard.[7]
Hattie[7] died.
The children of Francis and Martha Keene were:
Mary m. Henry[4] Powell, son of Richard.[3]
Martha m. Jacob Titus.
Thomas m.
Isaac m.
Francis Keen was noted for being very active and quick motioned. They lived at Herricks, North Hempstead, L. I., after selling their place at Bethpage.
Martha Keen was dau. of Thomas[2] and Mary (Willets) Powell.

WILL OF RICHARD POWELL 1774.

I Richard Powell of Bethpage in the Township of Oysterbay in Queens County on Nassau Island in the Province of New York — being this seventh day of third month called March in the year of our Lord Christ one thousand seven hundred and seventy-four in perfect health of body though pretty far advanced in years yet judgment and memory quick and good not knowing how soon my final change may come being therefore willing to set my house in order do make and ordain the present writing to contain my last Will and Testament in manner following

First I do order and direct that all my just and lawful debts and funeral charges be fully paid and satisfied by my executors herein after named before any division be made in my estate in general.

Item, I give and bequeath unto my Daughter-in-law Jemima Weeks one Bed and full furniture and so much money as to make the whole amount to thirty pound as it may be appraised.

Item I give and devise to my eldest son Henry Powell all the Land that lyeth at Cold Spring that I have any right to under what circumstances soever it may be to him and his heirs and assigns forever, also the one equal half of a piece of Plains Land containing twenty one acres, and two thirds part of an acre cituate in the Township of Oyster Bay and in the Williams Purchase it being a piece of land given me by my brother Amos Powell. Item I give and bequeath to my son Henry above named the full sum of one hundred pound currant lawful money to be paid unto him in some Reasonable time after my decease. Item I devise to my son Richard Powell, the dwelling house that he now lives in together with barn and improvements thereto belonging, also the land whereon it now stands, and the lot of land lying before the south of the house as the fence now standeth, also all the land northwardly up the Hollow on the west side of the road, I also devise to my son Richard a certain lot or parcel of land lying the east side of said hollow to extend northwardly to a certain line fixed as a bounds between my son Richard and my son Silas Powells land, and to extend eastwardly to the road that leadeth from Bethpage to John Whitson's, comprehending all the land lying the south side of the division line, to the land belonging to Francis Keen and Tice Lane extending eastwardly to the road that leadeth from Bethpage before mentioned together with one other piece of land lying westward from my dwelling house and near the great plains — it being the lot lying before or south of Silas Smith's house, beginning the northeast corner of said lot and running southwardly as the fence now standeth to Silas Smith's land thence westwardly to the next fence, all which several pieces of land above mentioned I give and devise unto my son Richard Powell to remain unto him and to his heirs and assigns forever.

Item, I give and devise unto my youngest son Silas Powell all my buildings as house and barn and also all the land of my homestead extending westwardly to Silas Smith's land and the land given to my son Richard — and northerly to a piece of land belonging to Silas Smith, thence extending eastwardly straight with Silas Smiths line until it comes to the road that leads from Joshua Powell's to Mannetto Hill, also a piece of plain land lying westward and near Silas Smiths as the enclosure now stands. Also a piece of wood land lying the south side and eastwardly and joining Tice Lane's land, southwardly to the Country road and also all the land lying northwardly of a certain line above mentioned as a bounds between my two sons, Richard and Silas Powell, also one other piece of land lying the east side of the road that leads from Bethpage northwardly to John Whitsons—containing about twelve acres more or less all which pieces of land above given to my son Silas Powell I do ratify and confirm unto him to his heirs and assigns forever.

Item, I also give and bequeath unto my son Silas Powell above mentioned the full sum of one hundred and fifty Pound currant lawful money to be paid to him at some Reasonable time after my decease. Item, I give and devise all my other lands and rights of lands, meadows and plains land that I have in the Township of Oysterbay or the Township of Huntington to be equally divided between my two sons Richard and Silas Powell — to be equally divided between them and to remain unto them in severalty to them and to their heirs and assigns forever, Item — my will farther is that my son Silas Powell should have one bed and full furniture, and that all my other moveable estate after legacies are paid, should be equally divided between my three sons namely Henry, Richard and Silas Powell, and my will farther is that if my son Silas should die before he doth arrive at lawful age or without lawful issue — that in such case the portion above given him should be equally divided between his surviving brothers or their heirs.

Lastly I do constitute ordain and appoint my son Richard Powell and Nathaniel Whitson and Thomas Pearsall, all of Bethpage in the Township of Oysterbay my executors of this my last Will and Testament, giving and hereby granting unto them or either of them full Power and Authority to execute this my Last Will and Testament in every part thereof.

RICHARD POWELL.

WITNESSES { JOSHUA POWELL, AMOS POWELL, PHEBE POWELL.

JOSHUA^3 POWELL (Thos.^{2} Thos.^{1}) m. 1744 Phebe Post, dau. of Richard and (?) Phebe, children:
  Hannah^4 b. 15, 10, 1745, m. 1765 Jacob Willets, son of Daniel, of Islip.
  Willets^4 b. 11, 6, 1747, m. 1779 Catharine Seaman, dau. of Obadiah, children: Deborah and Udall,

Phebe[4] b. 17, 9, 1749, m. 1774 Amos Willets, of Jericho.

Amos[4] b. 27, 4, 1752, m. 1773 Jemima Willets, dau. of Samuel & Jane, he d. 1828.

Joshua[4] b. 15, 10, 1754, m. 1891 Phebe Willis, dau. of John, he d. 1817.

Richard[4] b. 2, 11, 1757, m. 1781, Jemima Pratt, no children, he died 1836.

Benjamin[4] b. 13, 2, 1760, m. 1792 Elsie Smith.

AMOS[4] POWELL (Joshua[3] Thos.[2] Thos.[1]) and Jemima, had children:

Jervis[5] b. 1774.

Joshua[5] b. 1775-6, m. had Joshua[6] 1807, Rachel[6] 1809.

James[5] b. 1779.

George[5] b. 1783, m. Sarah Powell, dau. of Thomas & Martha.

Phebe[5] b. 1787.

GEORGE[5] POWELL (Amos[4] Joshua[3] Thos.[2] Thos.[1]) and Sarah, had:

Willets[6] b. 1820, m. Mary Jane.

Ruth W.[6] b. 1824.

WILLETS[6] & Mary Jane Powell, had:

Antoinette[7] b. 1843.

Wait[7] b. 1849.

Mary Seaman[7] b. 1852.

Charles[7] b. 1862.

Jennie[7] and Willet[7] died.

JOSHUA[4] POWELL (Joshua[3] Thos.[2] Thos.[1]) and Phebe (Willis) had:

Edmond[5] b. 17, 2, 1785, not m., he d. 1844.

Elisabeth[5] b. 18, 8, 1786, not m.

Mary[5] b. 2, 7, 1788, m. 1810 Samuel Titus, son of Stephen & Phebe.

John W.[5] b. 29, 5, 1790, m. 1813, Sarah M. Johnson, dau. of Wm. & Anna, of New York.

Powell Family. 53

Phebe[5] b. 12, 12, 1796, not m.
JOHN[5] W. POWELL (Joshua[4] Joshua[3] Thos.[2] Thos.[1]) and Sarah had:
Mary[6] m. Adam Mott, son of Henry.
Mathilda[6] m. Stephen Rushmore, son of Isaac.
Sarah[6] m. Jacobs Willets son of Samuel.
Phebe[6] m. Jehiel K. Hoyt.
BENJAMIN[4] POWELL (Joshua[3] Thos.[2] Thos.[1]) m. 1792 Elsie Smith, children:
Richard[5] S. m. Sarah Underhill, dau. of Richard.
Walter[5] m. Maria Seaman, dau. of John.
Damaris[5] m. James Whitson, son of Eliphalet.
Phebe[5] single.
Hannah[5] m. Samuel Robbins, son of Scudder and Elisabeth (Cornelius).
RICHARD[5] S. POWELL (Benjamin[4] Joshua[3] Thos.[2] Thos.[1]) and Sarah had:
Phebe[6] b. 1829, m. Harrison Young.
Alice.[6]
Thomas[6] m. Hannah Ann Ketcham.
Hannah[6] m. Robert Carpenter.
Walter[6] m. Lucy Harned, dau. of Andrew, have Sarah[7] T. and Ruth.[7]
Caroline[6] m. James Reed.
Pamela[6] unm.
Children of Phebe[6] (Powell) and Harrison Young:
Frank m. Phebe C. Smith, dau. of Ephraim and Sarah Jane (Powell) Smith.
Sarah P. m. Hewlett Nostrant.
Harrison, Jr. m. Martha Smith of Elbert.
Children of Hannah & Robert Carpenter:
Richard.
A. Lincoln.
Edward.

WALTER[5] POWELL (Benjamin[4] Joshua[3] Thos.[2] Thos.[1]) m. Maria Seaman, children:

Mary Alice[6] unm., died.

Benjamin[6] unm.

Edward Harnett (*ord*, sometimes spelled one way, and sometimes the other) and family, were at Salem, Massachusetts, in 1640, and later suffered for harboring Quakers. Their son Edward, Jr. m. Elisabeth Porter, dau. of Jonathan and Eunice, and came to Huntington, L. I. about 1653 with the Porter family. Jonathan Porter died 1660, left wife and children, viz.:

Eunice Porter m. James Chichester.

Mary Porter m. Stephen Jervis.

Elisabeth Porter m. Edward Harned, Jr.

In 1672 Jonathan Harned was on the Huntington Records, in 1714 he was at Huntington, West Neck, a brother-in-law of Elias Cornelius. In 1790 Jacob Harned joined Friends Meeting at Bethpage, and in 1816 Mary Harned also became a member amongst Friends.

ISAAC[3] POWELL (Thos.[2] Thos.[1]) m. 1733-4 in the Church at Huntington Martha Whitman, dau. of Zebulum and Sibbel (Lewis). The youngest son of Thomas[2] Powell. Isaac and his descendants have always occupied his father's homestead, it being the original first house built in the Bethpage purchase, children:

Martha[4] m 1756 Thomas Titus, son of William.

Zebulun[4] m. Nov. 11, 1773 Anna Willets, dau. of Samuel and Jane.

Sibbel[4] b. 31, 7, 1747, m. 1778 Jonas, son of Daniel Powell, she d. 9, 4, 1785.

Thomas[4] b. 1752, m. 1774 Martha, dau. of James and Annie Cox Titus.

Powell Family. 55

Jonah[4] m. July 28, 1779 Jane Ryder.
Phebe.[4]
ZEBULUN[4] POWELL (Isaac[3] Thos.[2] Thos.[1]) and Annie (Willets), children :
  Sarah[5] m. 1797 Libni Pinkham, had Zebulun and Ann.
  Jonah[5] b. 22, 12, 1776, m. 1798 Abigail Stillwell, dau. of William.
  Amy[5] unm.
  Zebulun[5] died a young man.
JONAH[5] POWELL (Zebulun[4] Isaac[3] Thos.[2] Thos.[1]) and Abigail, had :
  Wm. Stillwell[6] d. 1798.
  Samuel[6] d. 1801.
  Mary Ann[6] d. 1803.
  Eliza[6] b. 1805, m. 1st Col. Stone, 2d —— Allen.
  William Stillwell[6] 1806, m., had several daughters.
  James Edwin[6] b. 1813, unm.
SAMUEL[6] STRINGHAM POWELL b. I715, m. Huldah A. Frazier, had sons who died early, one son
  Thomas[7] b. 1837, m., lived in Brooklyn.
  Samuel[6] S. Powell was mayor of Brooklyn in 1857–58–59–60, again in 1872–3, was city controller in 1875–76, was treasurer of Brooklyn at his death in Feb., 1879.
  Libni Pinkham was son of Ebenezer and Elisabeth of Nantucket, who removed to Nine Partners, N. Y. after the Revolutionary War. Libni had certificate from Nine Partners to Jericho Monthly Meeting in 1793.
THOMAS[4] POWELL (Isaac[3] Thos.[2] Thos.[1]) m. Martha Titus, children :
  Isaac[5] b. 1774, m. 1797 Ruth Post.
  James[5] b. 1777, m. Susanna.

John[5] b. 1780, m. Ruth Whitson, dau. of John.
Annie[5] b. 1782, m. Eliphalet Whitson, son of John.
Sarah[5] b. 1787, m. George Powell, son of Amos.
Willet[5] b, 1792, m.
Phineas[5] b. 1795.
Jarvis[5] b. 1797, m. Sarah Bedell.
Jonah[5] b. 1801, m.[1] Rachel Mott, m.[2] Mary Hubbs, dau. of Selah.
Whitman[5] b. 1805.

JOHN[5] POWELL (Thos.[4] Isaac[3] Thos.[2] Thos.[1]) and Ruth Whitson, children:
James[6] b. 1, 7, 1784, m. Phebe Powell, dau. of James & Prudence (Peters).
Zebulun.[6]
Wait[6] m. Eliza Powell, dau. of Henry & Sarah (Wood).
Sarah Ann[6] not m.
Mary[6] not m.
Phebe.[6]
Ruth Ann.[6]
Hannah[6] m. Charles Wood.

JAMES[6] POWELL (John[5] Thos.[4] Isaac[3] Thos.[2] Thos.[1]) and Phebe, had:
Emiline[7] not m.
Charles Sylvester[7] m. Antoinette Powell.
John J.[7] m. Louisa Powell.
James W.[7] m.[1] Emma Travis Sanders, m.[2] Mary Shaw.

CHARLES[7] SYLVESTER POWELL & Antoinette had Wellington[8] & Charles Sylvester.[8]

JOHN J.[7] & Louisa Powell had Antoinette[8] & Phebe Mary.[8]

JAMES[7] W. and Emma[1] Powell had Emma,[2] and by second wife May had Charles,[8] Catherine Emmeline.[8]

WAIT[6] POWELL (John[5] Thos.[4] Isaac[3] Thos.[2] Thos.[1]) and Elisa, had :
Ruth[7] m. William Remsen of Jamaica.
Zebulun[7] not m.
Mary Emma[7] m. Richard Van Wyck Powell.
Elisabeth[7] died.
Celestine[7] not m.

JONAH[4] POWELL (Isaac[3] Thos.[2] Thos.[1]) m. Jane Ryder, July 25, 1779, had children :
Whitman.[5]
Nicholas.[5]
Phebe[5] m. a Hageman.
Martha[5] m. John Dorland.

JOHN[2] POWELL (Thomas[1]) m. 10th mo. 1704 Margaret, dau. of John Hallock and Abigail (nee Swazye) had children :
John[3] b. 24, 10, 1705, m. Jan 11, 1739, Martha Oakley.
Philena[3] b. 12, 10, 1707, not m.
Clement[3] b. 27, 12, 1709, m. 1731 David Whitson.
Mary[3] b. 22, 8, 1713, m. 1736 Daniel Powell.
Phebe[3] b. 13, 6, 1716, m. 1765 John, father of Elias Hicks, the celebrated Quaker Preacher. She was his 2nd wife, she had been clerk of Westbury Monthly Meeting of Friends several years previous to her marriage.
Amy[3] b. 6, 1, 1718, m. 1745 or 6 Daniel Willets.
Rachel[3] b. 1, 4, 1720, m. 1754 Thomas Pearsall, she d. 1759. They had one daughter.
Sarah[3] b. 10, 2, 1723, m. 1755 Thomas Underhill.
Hannah[3] b. 17, 6, 1725, m. 1744 Jacob Willets, son of Amos.

John[2] Powell lived and died at Bethpage, widow Margaret m. 1640 Richard Willets of Secatague, see Willets, Gen.

From David Whitson descended Edward H. Magill, A. M., Ex-President of Swarthmore College, Pa.

JOHN[3] POWELL (John[2] Thos.[1]) m. Dec. 24, 1739, Martha Oakley, had children:

John[4] b. 1740, m[1] Elisabeth Underhill, dau. of Thomas, m[2] Phebe Post, children.

Isaac[4] b. 1744, m. 1769 Margaret Powell, dau. of Daniel & Mary.

Martha[4] b. 1747, died 1748.

William[4] in 1775 had certificate from Bethpage to Purchase.

Sarah, dau. of *John*, Powell, perhaps John,[3] m. 1767 Joseph Walters of Cortland Manor.

JOHN[4] POWELL (John[3] John[2] Thos.[1]) m. Elisabeth Underhill, dau. of Thomas and Sarah, children:

Martha[5] b. 3, 3, 1767, m. Willet Leaycraft.

Sarah[5] b. 27, 6, 1769, m. a Hawhurst.

Ann[5] b. 5, 5, 1771.

Jeffrey[5] b. 16, 3, 1773.

Ezra[5] b. 25, 9, 1775.

Thomas[5] b. 1, 8, 1777, m. 23, 5, 1803, Esther Lax.

John[4] P. m. 2, Phebe Post, children:

William[5] b. 17, 8, 1783, m. Harriet Valentine.

Eliza[5] b. 10, 9, 1785, m. Samuel Leggett.

John[5] b. 18, 10, 1787, m. Elisabeth Cox, dau. of George, she b. 1796, he d. 1873,

THOMAS[5] POWELL (John[4] John[3] John[2] Thos.[1]) and Esther (d. of Thomas and Isabella Lax) b. in Eng. 15, 10, 1783, had children:

Ann Isabella[6] b. 1804, m. William R. Whiting.

Elisabeth[6] b. 1805, m. John M. Ferris and had 3 children who died.

Thomas L.[6] b. 1811, m. Sarah Ann Snedeker.

John Ferdinand[6] b. 1814, m. Eliza Farrington.

George Edgar[6] b. 1817, m. Harriet Farrington.

Esther L.⁶ b. 25, 9, 1818, m. Samuel Poole.

Mary L.⁶ b. 1823, m. Daniel Duryea Cox, son of Peter, of Richard, of Samuel and Jemina (Powell).

THOMAS⁶ L. POWELL (Thos.⁵ John⁴ John³ John² Thos.¹) and Sarah Ann, children :

George S.⁷ m. Hannah Jackson, dau. of George and Elisabeth.

Charles C.⁷ m. Gertrude Burt.

Whitney⁷ m. Jane Lent.

Mary Esther⁷ m. George Paine.

JOHN⁵ POWELL (John⁴ John³ John² Thos.¹) and Elisabeth Cox Clinton, children.

William⁶ b. 1827, d. 1828.

Martha⁶ b. 1829, m. Jacob Valentine.

Sarah⁶ b. 1830, d. 1848.

Harriet⁶ b. 1831, m. Van Rensalaer Abbott.

Adaline⁶ b. 1835, unm.

ISAAC⁴ POWELL (John³ John² Thos.¹) m. 1769 Margaret, dau. of Daniel Powell and Mary, children :

Amy⁵.

Phebe.⁵

Mary.⁵

Rachel⁵ lived and died at Samuel I. Underhill's, Jericho.

Jacob⁵ m. Elisabeth Sands, went to New York where his descendants still live.

JACOB⁵ POWELL (Isaac⁴ John³ John² Thos.¹) and wife Elisabeth Sands had children :

Platt⁶ one son, m. —— Joralemon, dau. of Joralemon, formerly owner of the Brooklyn Joralamon street property a part of which is still in the possession of his grandson Tunis Powell, son of Platt.⁶

Isaac.⁶

Jeffrey.⁶

Stoddard.[6]
Uriah.[6]
Mary Ann[6] m.
Eliza[6] m.

JONAS[2] POWELL (Thomas[1]) m. Anna ———, believed to have had a family of whom one named

Daniel[3] m. 1st a dau. of Caleb Powell of Huntington, 2d Mary, dau. of John[1] and Margaret Powell of Bethpage.

1699, Jonas Powell bought land at Jericho of John and Mary Dole.

1761, Daniel Powell requested to be received a member amongst Friends of Westbury Monthly Meeting, lived at Bethpage.

In 1719 Jonas Powell and Anna his wife sold land to Wait Powell, described as all Lusum joining Jacob Willets, that Richard Willets bought of Hope Williams and Garret Albertson.

It seems probable that Jonas Powell married into either the Champion or the Eastlake family, and went to New Jersey with them, taking most of his family with him.

Anna wrote her name to the deeds of land when they sold the different pieces. Most of the women of that day made only a mark.

DANIEL[3] POWELL (Jonas[2] Thos.[1]) m[1] dau. of Caleb Powell, no children, m.[2] Mary Powell, dau. of John and Margaret, and had children:

Jacob[4] b. 2, 6, 1737, drowned in the South Bay.

Deborah[4] b. 10, 10, 1739, not m.

Margaret[4] b. 11, 12, 1743, m. 1769 Isaac Powell, son of John[4].

Jonas[4] b. 24, 4, 1745, m. 1778, Sibbel[4] Powell, dau. of Isaac,[3] he d. 24, 2, 1815.

Daniel[4] b. 22, 1, 1749, m.

Rachel[4] b. 17, 2, 1753, d. 1759.
Mary[4] b. 29, 1, 1755, m. John Whitson, son of John & Martha (Whitman).
JONAS[4] POWELL (Daniel[3] Jonas[2] Thos.[1]) and Sibbel[4] had children :
 Martha[5] b. 1779, m. John Plummer, son of Enoch & Abigail, she d. 1843.
 Mary[5] b. 1782, not m., she d. 1854.
 Sibbel[5] b. 29, 12, 1784, m. 1810 Stephen Loines, son of John, she d. 1864.
Children of Sibbel[5] & Stephen Loines :
Mary b. 1811, d. 1814.
Jonas b. 1814, d. 18—.
John b. 21, 2, 1818, m. 1843 Mary Bunker, he d. 5, 3, 1854.
Jonas P. b. 27, 4, 1821, m. Martha Macy, he d. 15, 12, 1873.
Robert b. 17, 5, 1824, m. Caroline.
Children of Martha[5] & John Plummer :
Mary m. 1839 Richard Titus had one son died early.
Abigail m.[1] Jarvis Whitson and had Mary Malvina[6] and Sidney, he d. 1891 or 2, she m[2] Isaac Coles, she d. 1891 or 2.
John J.[6] m., has a family.
Enoch Plummer, an Englishman in King George's Army. married at Hempstead, L. I., Abigail Batty, dau. of David Batty & his wife Abigail (nee Seaman), widow of Samuel Jackson.
 CALEB[2] POWELL (Thomas[1]) m. Sarah, children:
 Sarah[3] m. John Albertson, of Derrick.
 Caleb[3] m. 1742 Clement Hallock, dau. of John and Hannah of Brookhaven. They removed from Oyster bay to Westchester county, N. Y., in 1742.

Will of Caleb Powell, proved in 1741.

Know all men by these presents that I, Caleb Powell of Oyster Bay in Queens county on Nassau Island on the tenth day of ye fourth month Called June, in the year of our Lord Christ one thousand seven hundred and forty one, being but weakly in body and subject to infirmity, but my understanding sound and memory quick and good — for which I return thanks to God for the same — do make and ordain this and no other to be my last Will and Testament in manner following

Payment of just debts etc. etc.

I do will and bequeath to my Son in law Daniel Powell the sum of six shillings — and upon receipt of the same ye s^d Daniel Powell shall give a full acquitance and discharge to Executors — I do will and bequeath to my daughter Sarah the wife of John Albertson 1 pound, and the household goods already delivered to her and she to give a full discharge to my executors.

I will and bequeath to my only son Caleb Powell all and every part of the remainder of my whole estate of what nature or kinds whatsoever.

CALEB POWELL.

Witnesses { Thomas Powell. Henry Whitson. Jesse Willets.

Executors { Richard Powell. Wait Powell of Oyster bay.

ELISHA[2] POWELL (Thos.[1]) m. Rebecca. His will proved 3 mo. 1739, says: Sell my negro boy Ben and Oxen and give my wife Rebecca the proceeds thereof, etc. Children:

Isabel[3] m. Thomas Davis, had son Elisha mentioned in his grandfather's will.
Abigail[3] m. May 30, 1738, Samuel Pearce.
Elisabeth.[3]
Rebecca.[3]
Johanna.[3]
Charity.[3]

Thomas Davis and his family had a home willed to them by her father. It was located in the eastern part of the Bethpage purchase.

Portions of land were also given to the single daughters for their homes, and the rest of his large land estate was ordered to be sold and the money divided amongst them all.

WAIT[2] POWELL (Thomas[1]) m., had no children: His will proved 1750, made in 1746.

Witnesses { Joseph Clement. Sarah Seaman. Samuel Willis.

Gave £50 to Wait[4] the minor son of his (cousin) Nephew. The Estate to Wait[3] Powell jr., father of said minor.

1710, Nathaniel Seaman and Thomas Powell were appointed by Westbury Monthly Meeting of Friends to speak to Wait[2] Powell and John Fry about their attending the marriages of two of their neices, Hannah and Mary Willets, daughters of Richard Willets, dec., said marriages were accomplished by the assistance of a Priest.

1724, Another Committee reported to the Monthly Meeting that they had spoken with Wait[3] Powell about his marriage out of the order of Friends — also with his uncle Wait[2] about assisting him in said marriage.

Thus with no children of his own he, Wait[2] Powell, seems to have been a convenient uncle to help other people's children to have their own way.

SOLOMON[2] POWELL, son of Thomas[1] and his second wife Elisabeth, was the only one that was born at Bethpage. He was young when his mother died and his father soon took him and some of his sisters to Westbury to reside. He never had a home in Bethgate afterwards, his share in his father estate being money, £200. His will dated 23, 2, 1735 or 6, executors, Henry Willis, Jacob Seaman & Baront Van Wyke. He m. 1730 Ruth Carman, dau. of Thomas, had children:

Stephen[3] b. 1731, m. Jan. 5, 1754, Elisabeth Petitt.
Thomas[3] b. 1733, m. 1755 Sarah Sands, he d. 1781.
Solomon[3] b. 1735, m. 1758 Jerusha Hinton.

(Baront Van Wyke m. Hannah Carman, sister of Ruth.)

STEPHEN[3] POWELL (Solomon[2] Thos.[1]) m. Elisabeth Petitt and had children:

Stephen[4] m. Abigail Smith.
Ruth[4] m. a Mott.
Betsy[4] m. a Carman.
Mary[4] m. a Mott.

STEPHEN[4] POWELL (Stephen[3] Solomon[2] Thos.[1]) and Abigail (Smith) had children:

Thomas[5] m. Sarah Cornwell dau. of William and Sarah (Culver) Cornwell.
Benjamin[5] m.[1] Fannie Southard, m.[2] Mary Ann Waters.
Harry[5] m. Bertha Mills.
Joel[5] m. Jemima Ingard.
Robert Townsend[5] m. Wealthy ———.
Charles[5] m. Fanny Bedell.
Sarah[5] m. a Bailey.

Phebe[5] m. a Brower.

Maria[5] m. a Carman.

THOMAS[5] POWELL (Stephen[4] Stephen[3] Solomon[2] Thos.[1]) and Sarah (Cornwell) had children:

William,[6] Henry[6] S, Stephen,[6] Gideon,[6] Thomas,[6] David[6] B. reside in Hempstead.

CHARLES[5] POWELL (Stephen[4] Stephen[3] Solomon[2] Thos.[1]) and Fannie (nee Bedell) had children:

Charles[6] m. dau. of Raynor Rock Smith.

And others.

CHARLES[6] and wife (Rock Smith) had children:

Charles[7] postmaster at Freeport, L. I., in 1894, m., has daughter.[8]

Daughter[7] m. Harvey Rock Smith, has children:

THOMAS[3] POWELL (Solomon[2] Thos.[1]) m. Sarah Sands, dau. of Samuel Sands and Mary (nee Pell.), children:

Solomon[4] b 1756, m. —— Smith.

Samuel[4] b. 1759, no children.

Thomas[4] b. 1762, m. 1781 Martha Smith.

Mary[4] b. 1765, m. 1783 James Peters.

Richard[4] b. 1768, m. Elisabeth Jackson.

James[4] b. 1774, m. Sarah Smith.

David[4] b. 1777, no children.

Mary Pell was daughter of Thomas Pell, whose wife was said to be the daughter of an Indian chief, so say the records. Town records say that, " in 1684 Indians granted to Henry Pell 50 acres at Matinecock, L. I., as he has married an Indian woman named Jane, one of our own nation, the Narragansetts." The Youngs and Coverts now have the place.

The above Thomas[3] Powell d. 1681 ; gave silver tankard to his wife, Sarah Powell.

SOLOMON[4] POWELL (Thos.[3] Solomon[2] Thos.[1]) and wife had children :

Solomon[5] m. and had George[6] Joshua[6] Catherine.[6]

Thomas[5] m. Ann Strattan, had Thomas,[6] William,[6] Susan,[6] Catherine.[6]

Mary[5] m. John McFall.

Sarah,[5] no children.

Oliver,[5] no children.

THOMAS[4] POWELL (Thos.[3] Solomon[2] Thos.[1]) and Martha (Smith). Children :

Thomas[5] m. Elizabeth Stymits; had but one child, Martha, b. April 13, 1811, m. Alfred Seaman, b. 1809. She d. Oct. 6. 1861.

Joshua[5] m. Elizabeth Covert.

James[5] m. Jane Covert.

John[5] m. Catherine Smith.

Jarvis[5] m. Deborah Saxton.

Samuel[5] m. Deborah Ketcham.

George[5] m. Maria Mitchell.

Charles[5] m. Mary Wood, and had Charles[6] and Henry.[6]

Epenetus[5] m. Martha Van Wyke, and had Benj.,[6] Annie,[6] John[6] and Mary.[6]

Nancy[5] m. Gershom Saxton.

Sarah[5] m. Eliphalet Hendrickson.

Ruth[5] died.

JOSHUA[5] POWELL (Thos.[4] Thos.[3] Solomon[2] Thos.[1]) m. Elisabeth Covert, and had :

Jane[6] m. John Jarvis.

Letty[6] m. William Jervis.

Naomi[6] m. —— Garret.

Nelson[6] m. Hannah Nichols.

Elisabeth[6] m. Henry Bedell.

Ruth[6] m. James Van Size.

Maria[6] m. Jervis Whitson.

Powell Family.

JAMES[5] POWELL (Thos.[4] Thos.[3] Solomon[2] Thos.[1]) and Jane Covert had:
William[6] m. Leonora Nostrant.
Martha[6] m. George Smith.
Sarah Jane[6] m. Ephraim Smith.
Samuel[6] m. Harriet Perry.

JOHN[5] POWELL (Thos.[4] Thos.[3] Solomon[2] Thos.[1]) and Catharine (Smith) had:
Smith[6] m. Sarah Ann Nichols.
George[6] m. 1st —— Gildersleeve, 2d Sarah Bumford.
Charles[6] m. Delia Ketcham.
Elbert.[6]

JARVIS[5] POWELL (Thos.[4] Thos.[3] Solomon[2] Thos.[1]) and Deborah (Saxton), had:
Phebe[6] m. Thomas Sulivan.
Ruth[6] m. Jesse Conklin.
Charry Ann[6] m. James Barrett.
Susan[6] m. Edwin Smith.

SAMUEL[5] POWELL (Thos.[4] Thos.[3] Solomon[2] Thos.[1]) and Deborah (Ketcham) had:
Margaret[6] m. John Robbins.
Elisabeth.[6]

GEORGE[5] POWELL (Thos.[4] Thos.[3] Solomon,[2] Thos.[1]) and Deborah (Mitchell) had:
Thomas[6] m. Martha Ann Post.
George[6] m. Ann, school teacher.
Martha[6] m. Gowdy.

JAMES[4] POWELL (Thos.[5] Solomon[2] Thomas[1]) and Sarah Smith had children:
Sands[5] m. Rachel Boylson, she d. 1886.
David[5] m. Mary Johnson.
James.[5]
Phoeby.[5]
Samuel[5] m. Ellen Marsden, had Mary and Margaret.

William[5] m. Maria Baldwin, had Samuel and Willets.
Elisabeth[5] m. Pettit.
Ann Amelia.[5]
SANDS[5] POWELL (James[4] Thomas[3] Solomon[2] Thos.[1]) and Rachel Boylson had:
Theodore.[6]
Amanda.[6]
Sands.[6].
Franklyn.[6]
James[6] m. Cornelia Wood and had Percy[7] and May.[7]
Adaline[6] m. Robert Hendrickson and had Bertha[7] C.
Annie S.[6] m. Eugene Bedell and had Viola[7] Sands Bedell.
DAVID[5] POWELL (James[4] Thos.[3] Solomon[2] Thos.[1]) and Mary Johnson had:
Calvin,[6] who m. and has three children, Helen[7] Clifford[7] Calvin.[7]
RICHARDSON[4] POWELL (Thos.[3] Solomon[2] Thos.[1]) m. Elisabeth Jackson and had:
David[5] died without children.
Richard[5] m. Mary Baldwin and had John[6] and Frank.[6]
Jackson[5] m. Letitia Powell of Stephen Ch. Elisebeth[6] m. —— Hicks and Stephen.[6]
STEPHEN[5] POWELL (Mary[4] Thomas[3] Solomon[2] Thos.[1]) m. Phebe Stymits and had:
Allie[6] died.
John[6] m. Margaret M.
Letitia[6] m. Jackson Powell.
Stimusson[6] m. Mary Bergen, 2d m. Mary Wiggins.
Joseph[6] m. Jane Lott.
STIMUSSON[6] and Mary (Bergen) Powell, children of:
Jacob[7] m. Sarah A. Oakley and had Stimusson[8] M. and Lucretia O.[8]

Stephen B.⁷ m. Jane Cox and had Cora.⁸

Phebe Ann⁷ m. Henry A Manolt and had Edmond Willets⁸ Mary Emma⁸ and Harry.⁸

SOLOMON³ POWELL (Solomon² Thos.¹) m. 1758 Jerusha Hinton, children :

Abraham⁴ m. 1784 Mary Dickerson.
Robert⁴ b. 1767, m. Mary Cornelius.
Amy⁴ m. James Mott of Richard.
Charles⁴ b. 1774, m. Mary Baldwin.
Phebe⁴ m. Petitt.
Benjamin.⁴

ABRAHAM⁴ POWELL (Solomon³ Solomon² Thos.¹) and Mary Dickerson had :

Abraham⁵ m. —— had son Abraham.⁶
Gerard.⁵
Dickerson.⁵
Jerusha.⁵
Mary.⁵
Phebe.⁵ This family lived somewhere up the Hudson river.
Elisabeth.⁵

ROBERT⁴ POWELL (Solomon³ Solomon² Thos.¹) and Mary (Cornelius) had :

Benjamin⁵ m. Phebe Carman.
Henry⁵ m. Ruth Post.
Ann⁵ n. m.
Abraham⁵ m. Eliza dau. of Noah Seaman.²
Jerusha⁵ m. Jeremiah Jackson.
Elisabeth⁵ n. m.
Solomon⁵ m. Almy dau of Willet Seaman.
Mary⁵ m. Charles Powell.
John⁵ m. Mary Ann Seaman of Benj. This family lived near Jerusalem, L. I.

BENJAMIN[5] POWELL (Robert[4] Solomon[3] Solomon[2] Thos.[1]) and Phebe Carman had:

Susan[6] John Tredwell[6] (single) William.[6]
Mary Jane[6] m. —— Smith.
Ellen.[6]
Phebe Ann[6] m. Andrew Bryant.
Coles.[6]
Robert.[6]

HENRY[5] POWELL (Robert[4] Solomon[3] Solomon[2] Thos.[1]) and Ruth (Post) had:

Iantha[6] m. Joseph W. Clark.
Charlotte[6] m. Richard Hart.
Sarah Elisabeth[6] m. Andrew Foster.

ABRAHAM[5] POWELL (Robert[4] Solomon[3] Solomon[2] Thos.[1]) m. 1st Eliza Seaman, dau. of Noah and Martha and had:

Ellison.[6]
Rebecca[6] m. Henry Justan.
Margaretta[6] m. Sylvester Smith.
m[2] —— —— and had
Thophilus.[6]

SOLOMON[5] POWELL (Robert[4] Solomon[3] Solomon[2] Thos.[1]) m. Alma Seaman, dau. of Willet and Letitia (Seaman), children:

Emily C.[6] b. 6, 2, 1842, m. Gilbert B. Allen and had Solomon and others.
Henry[6] b. 3, 2, 1846, m.[1] Mary E. Monfort, m.[2] 1872 Livia L. Remsen, no children.
Mary Letitia[6] b. 4, 3, 1849, she d. 1863.

HENRY POWELL[6] (Solomon[5] Robert[4] Solomon[3] Solomon[2] Thos.[1]) and Mary E. (Monfort) had:

Percey[7] b. Nov. 20, 1868.

Mary E. (Monfort) Powell died, and Henry m. 1872 Livia L. Remsen, she died very soon, and in

1877 he married her sister, Jennette M. Remsen, they had children:

Alma S.[7] b. July 8, 1879, she d. June 28, 1880.
Mabel R.[7] b. Oct. 19, 1882.

JOHN[5] POWELL (Robert[4] Solomon[3] Solomon[2] Thos.[1]) m. Mary Ann, dau. of Benjamin and Jemima (Seaman), children:

Julia[6] died early.
Robert[6] m. Fannie Douglass.
Solomon[6] died in youth.
Phebe[6] m. William S. Kitchell.
Albert[6] died.
Adelbert[6] died in youth.
Annie[6] m.

CHARLES[4] POWELL (Solomon[3] Solomon[2] Thos.[1]) m. Mary Baldwin, dau. of John and Esther, children:

Robert[5] m. Catharine Vandewater and had Mary Esther[6], Phebe[6], Laura[6], Prudence[6], Jerusha[6] and Charles[6] Powell.
John[5] m. Ann Petitt and had Matilda[6] and John.[6]
Esther[5] m. Robert Hilliard.
Charles[5] m. 1st Eliza Smith, dau. of Joseph and Harriet Smith, had one child, Mary,[6] m. Gilbert Smith. Charles m. 2d Mary Powell, dau. of Robert, and had Annie, m. Jesse Tyrrell.

WILLETS FAMILY.

RICHARD WILLETS, said to have come from the west of England, was at Hempstead, L. I., in 1657, probably he was there at a much earlier date, as he then had 6 gates, 6 cattle, 6 milch cows, and 28 acres of land. Only 12 men in the town paid more taxes for public charges than he did, and none paid twice as much. He died 1664 or 5.

1657. Richard Willets was present, with the widow Jane, at the reading of the Will of William Washburn, by John James, Town Clerk.

At Hempstead at the Court holden April 18, 1658.

Richard Gildersleeve, Magistrate. Richard Willets, John Hicks and Robert Forman, Assistants.

Mary, wife of Joseph Scott and the wife of Francis Weeks, fined 20 guilders and cost, each. Offence, attending a Quaker meeting.

1659. Richard Willets was surveyor of highways.

1662. Richard Willets was chosen Townsman by vote.

24 day of March, 1666 or 7, widow Willets lately of Hempstead, now of Oyster bay, sells unto Joseph Williams of Hempstead, the home lot and housing next to the lot of Joseph Langdon on the north side of it, "said home lot and housing I did lately dwell in."

Willets Family.

Previous to 1650 R. W. married Mary, dau. of W^m and Jane Washburne. Their children were:

Thomas born in 3 mo. 1650, m. Dinah Townsend, he d. 1710.
Hope b. 7 mo. 1652, m. Mercy.
John b. 5 mo. 1655, single.
Richard b. 12 mo. 1660, m. 1st 1686 Abigail Bowne, she d. 1688; m. 2d 15, 3 mo. 1690, Abigail Powell, Richard Willets d. 1703.
Mary b. 2 mo. 1663, m. 1686 John Fry, she d. 1687.

June 10, 1665, widow Mary Willets made returns, six horses.

1667. Mary, widow of Richard^1 Willets, bought a portion of her brother in law Robert Williams' Oyster Bay Patent or Purchase, and settled at Jericho, where she and some of her children resided the rest of their lives. She joined the Society of Friends, became a minister, had meetings at her house, suffered distraint of property at the hands of the Authorities on account of her nonpayment of Ministers' and Church Rates.

The youngest son, Richard^2 Willets, died at Jericho 14, 3 mo. 1703, his widow lived till 1757, "having seen her granddaughter's grand child, and having her understanding and memory to admiration to the last." Richard^2 Willets and wife Abigail (nee Powell) were both active members of the Society of Friends, and great unanimity seems to have subsisted between the two widows, mother in law Mary and daughter in law Abigail in their long continued widowhood.

William and Jane Washburne were among the earliest settlers of the Town of Hempstead. Their children were:

John m. Mary Butler, dau. of Richard, he d. 30, 8, 1658; widow m. Thomas Hicks.

Mary b. 1629, m. Richard Willets, she d. 17, 12, 1713.
Martha m. Edmond Titus, she d. 17, 2, 1727.
Sarah m. Robert Williams, died about 1695.
Agnes m. Robert Jackson.
Hope single, and perhaps other sons.
Phebe m. John Ashman, had dau. Phebe, she d. 1665.

THOMAS[2] WILLETTS (Richard) married Dinah, dau. of Richard Townsend and Deliverance Cole, dau. of Robert and Mary (Hawkhurst) Cole, he d. 1710 at Secatague, L. I., children:

Isaac[3] m. 1st, 1716, Clement Hallock, both died at Islip in 4th mo. 1736.
Amos[3] m. 1st 1713, Mary Hallock, m. 2d 1719, Rebecca Whitson, he d. 1748.
Richard[3] m. 1st Sarah Hallock, m. 2d Margaret (Hallock) widow of John Powell.
Thomas[3] b. 1683, m. 1st 1706, Catharine Hallock, m. 2d Rachel Powell, dau. of Thomas.[1]
} Daughters of John and Abigail Hallock.

Mary[3] m. 1691 Thomas[2] Powell, son of Thos[1] she d. 1739.

Elisabeth[3] m. John Underhill
Hannah[3] m. Samuel Underhill
} Sons of John & Mary (Prior) Underhill.

Sarah.[3]

Dinah[3] perhaps m. William Hallock.

In 1673 Thomas Willets bought land at Jericho of Robt Williams; but most of the families lived at Secatague now (Islip).

ISAAC[3] WILLETS (Thomas[2] Richard[1]) and Clement, had children:

Dinah[4] m. Abraham Underhill.

Willets Family.

Sarah.⁴

Catharine⁴ & Zebulun⁴ both d. 1736 of small pox.

David⁴ m. 1742 Deborah Willets, his cousin and had Ezra,⁵ died young; Charity⁵ m. 1770, Job Willets, no children, she d. 1846.

JONAH⁵ b. 1762, m. 1784, Mary, dau. of Samuel Willets, she d. 1821, he d. 1837. They had children:

David⁶ b. 1785, m. 1818, Deborah Whitson, dau, of Amos, he d. 1837.

Abraham⁶ m. Henriette, dau. of Caleb Frost.

Samuel⁶ b. 1789, died 1820.

Deborah⁶ b. 1791, unm., she d. 1846.

Isaac.⁶

Amy⁶ m. Zebulun Pinkham, no children.

DAVID⁶ WILLETTS (Jonah⁵ David⁴ Isaac³ Thos.² Richard¹) and Deborah Whitson, had:

Isaac⁷ m. Mary, dau. of Oliver Cromwell.

Wm.⁷ m. a Mitchell.

Jonah.⁷

ABRAHAM⁶ WILLETS (Jonah,⁵ David,⁴ Isaac,³ Thos.² Richard¹) and Henrietta, had children:

Mary.⁷

Elizabeth.⁷

Leonard.⁷

Isaac.⁷

Edward.⁷

Sarah.⁷

AMOS³ WILLETTS (Thos.² Richard¹) and 1st wife Mary Hallock, had:

Samuel,⁴ m. 1742, Jane, dau. of Wait³ Powell and Mary (Mudge).

Ruth⁴ m. 1743, Richard Willets, son of Jacob of Jericho.

Mary,⁴ perhaps of the first children.

Amos³ m. 1719 Rebecca Whitson, dau. of Thos. and Martha, children of 2d marriage:
Catharine⁴ m. Jacob Underhill.
Sarah⁴ m. John Willis, was his 2d wife, no children.
Jacob⁴ b. 19, 2, 1723, m. 1744, Hannah, dau. of John Powell and Margaret.
Amos⁴ m. 1754 Rebecca, not in meeting.
Joseph⁴ b. 1728 (m. 1752 Phebe Williams), m. 7, 5, 1755 Hannah Titus, dau. of William.
Jemima⁴ m. William Jervis.
Martha⁴ m. 13, 11, 1755, Thomas, son of Samuel Prior and Mary (Powell).
Hannah⁴ b. 1734, m. Wait Powell.
Thomas⁴ b. 1738, m. 1762, Leah b. 1744, dau. of Zebulun Seaman, both d. 1813.

SAMUEL⁴ WILLETS (Amos³ Thos.² Richard¹) and Jane, had children:
Jemima⁵ m. 1773, Amos Powell, son of Joshua.³
Ann⁵ m. 1773, Zebulun Powell, son of Isaac.³
Twins { Mary⁵ m. 1784, Jonah Willets, son of David, she d. 1821.
Amy⁵ m. 1782, Daniel Titus, son of Henry and Sarah (Birdsall).
Wait⁵ m. Mary Post, dau. of John.

WAIT⁵ WILLETS (Samuel⁴ Amos³ Thos.² Richard¹) and Mary, had children:
Samuel⁶ m. Hannah Carpenter.
John⁶ m. Elisabeth Horton.
Henry⁶ m. —— Tompkins.
Sarah.⁶
Phebe.⁶
Amy⁶ m. Eleazar Thrall.
Mary.⁶
Jane.⁶

JACOB[4] WILLETS (Amos[3] Thos.[2] Richard[1]) and Hannah (Powell) had:

John[5] b. 3, 9, 1745, m. children: Jacob[6], Rhoda[6], Phebe[6].

Job[5] b. 10, 7, 1748, m. 1733, Deborah, dau. of Joseph Udal.

Jacob[5] b. 20, 11, 1750, m.

Daniel[5] b. 24, 5, 1753, m. Martha, dau. of Zebulun Seaman, he d. 1825.

Henry[5] b. 13, 10, 1755, m.

James[5] b. 1, 5, 1758, m. 1784, Johanna Titus, dau. of Henry.

Thomas[5] b. 12, 9, 1760, m.

Samuel[5] b. 1, 1, 1763, m. Hannah Seaman, b. 1776, dau. of William.

Phebe[5] b. 14, 6, 1765, m. 1st Stephen Titus, son of Stephen; m. 2d George Townsend, had dau. Mary m. Obadiah Titus, of Dutchess county.

George[5] b. 10, 5, 1769, m. Mary, dau. of Jacob Mudge.

JOB[5] WILLETS (Jacob[4] Amos[3] Thos.[2] Richard[1]) and Deborah, had:

Amy[6] m. Wm. Griffin.
George[6] m. Jemima Secor.
Jacob[6] m. Susan Clark.
Rachel[6] m. Job Freeland.
Ann[6] m. Isaac Secor.
Phebe[6] m. Samuel Lewis.

JACOB[5] WILLETS (Jacob[4] Amos[3] Thos[2] Richard[1]) m. and had:

George.[6]
Jacob[6] m. Deborah Rogers.
Rachel,[6] Ann,[6] Phebe[6] and Amy.[6]

DANIEL[5] WILLETS (Jacob[4] Amos[3] Thos.[2] Richard[1]) and Martha, had children :
Charles[6] m. —— Lawrie.
Seaman[6] m. Ann Pearsall, dau. of Samuel, he d. 1827.
Thomas.[6]
Libni.[6]
SEAMAN[6] WILLETS (Daniel[5] Jacob[4] Amos[3] Thos.[2] Richard[1]) and Ann, had children :
Thos. S.[7] m. Rebecca Leggett.
Mary[7] m. Jordan Wright (once Cox).
Margaret Ann[7] m. Robert Willets, son of Samuel and Sarah.
JAMES[5] WILLETS (Jacob[4] Amos[3] Thos.[2] Richard[1]) and Johanna, had :
Jacob,[6] Henry,[6] Stephen,[6] Samuel,[6] John,[6] Sarah,[6] Mary,[6] Johanna.[6]
THOMAS[5] WILLETS (Jacob[4] Amos[3] Thos.[2] Richard[1]) m. and had children :
Edmond,[6] Mary,[6] Charity,[6] Ann,[6] Hannah.[6]
SAMUEL[5] WILLETS (Jacob,[4] Amos,[3] Thos.[2] Richard[1]) and Hannah (Seaman), had children :
Isaac[6] m. Amy Underhill, dau. of Daniel.
Mary[6] m. Samuel J. Underhill, son of Daniel.
William[6] m. Phebe Prior, no children.
Jane[6] unm.
Henry[6] b. 6, 10, 1812, m. Sophia Underhill, no children.
Andrew.[6]
Esther[6] unm., Hannah,[6] b. 21, 1, 1818.
ISAAC[6] WILLETS (Samuel[5] Jacob[4] Amos.[3] Thos.[2] Richard[1]) and Amy, had children :
William[7] m. Mary Valentine.
John[7] m., had one son.
Daniel[7] m. Lydia Moore, and had three daughters.

Mary[7] m. Thomas Whitson.
Phebe[7] m. William Frame.
Hannah[7] m.
Amy[7] m.
GEORGE[5] WILLETS (Jacob[4] Amos[3] Thos.[2] Richard[1]) and Mary (Mudge), had:
Henry[6] died young.
David[6] m. Jane Hutchings.
Eliza[6] m. John Burtis.
Mary,[6] Martha,[6] Elizabeth,[6] Edwin,[6] Deborah,[6] Johanna,[6] John Henry.[6]
AMOS[4] WILLETS (Amos.[3] Thos.[2] Richard[1]) m. 1754 Rebecca, and had:
Phebe.[5]
Jemima[5] m. Wm. Jarvis.
Amos[5] m. Mary Platt, dau. of Jonas.
Platt[5] m. Amy Buffet.
John,[5] Elisha,[5] Lott.[5]
Samuel[5] m. Mehitable Jennings, dau. of Hezakiah.
Kesia[5] m. Cornelius Stadge.
Isaac[5] m. Catharine Edwards.
Mary[5] m. —— Mobrey.
Ruth[5] m. Jesse Bryant, no children.
ISAAC[5] WILLETS (Amos[4] Amos[3] Thos.[2] Rich'd[1]) m. 1792 Catharine, dau. of John and Sarah Edwards, of Sayville, and had:
Mary Mowbray[6] m. Josiah R. Smith.
Sarah.[6]
Charlotte[6] m. 1818, William T. Brown.
Jemima.[6]
Isaac[6] m. Phebe Williams, dau. of —— and Sarah (Rock Smith) Williams.
Samuel[6] m. 1st ——, 2d ——, 3d Henrietta ——.
Platt,[6] Eliphalet,[6] John Edwards,[6] all died.
Gilson.[6]

Edmond[6] S.

Mehitable Catharine,[6] m. 1833, Benj. Lewis Penny of Cutchogue.

AMOS[5] WILLETS (Amos[4] Amos[3] Thos.[2] Rich'd[1]) and Mary (Platt), had:

Platt,[6] Kesia,[6] Eliphalet,[6] Rebecca,[6] Oliver,[6] Ruth,[6] Mary.[6]

JOSEPH[4] WILLETS (Amos[3] Thos.[2] Richard[1]) and Hannah (Titus), had:

Phebe[5] b. 1756, d. 1760.

Amy[5] b. 1758, m, 1774, Amos Whitson.

Elizabeth[5] b. 1761, m. Benjamin Baldwin.

William[5] b. 1763, m. Letitia Valentine, dau. of Charles.

Catharine[5] b. 1766, m. Edmond Post, she d. 1844.

Robert[5] b. 1768, m. 1790, Mary Robbins, dau. of Stephen.

Richard[5] b. 1772.

Joseph[5] b. 1775, d. 1777.

Rachel[5] b. 1777, m. Benjamin Hicks.

WILLIAM[5] WILLETS (Joseph[4] Amos[3] Thos.[2] Richard[1]) and Letitia, had:

Joseph[6] m. Phebe Smith.

Charles[6] died young.

Valentine[6] m. Jane Rushmore.

Jacob[6] m. —— Underhill.

George,[6] Benjamin,[6] Stephen.[6]

Mary[6] m. Gideon Frost.

Perhaps, as some records say, Wm.[5] Willets had 2d wife, Amy Bedell.

ROBERT[5] WILLETS (Joseph[4] Amos[3] Thos.[2] Richard[1]) and Mary (Robbins), had:

Amos[6] b. 1792, m. 1814, Annie Titus, dau. of Daniel and Amy.

Samuel[6] b. 1795, m. Sarah Hicks.

Stephen[6] b. 1797, m. 1822, Maria Titus, dau. of John and Sarah (Post).
Edmund[6] b. 1800, m. Martha Whitson, dau. of Thos.
Robert R.[6] b. 1802, m. Lydia Titus, dau. of John and Sarah(Post).
Phebe[6] b. 1805, m. 1823, William Titus, dau. of Daniel and Amy.
William[6] b. 1808, m. 1st 1835, Ann Whitson, m. 2d Elisabeth P. Titus, dau. of Samuel and Mary (Powell) Titus.

AMOS[6] WILLETS (Robert[5] Joseph[4] Amos[3] Thos.[2] Richard[1]) and Annie Titus, had:
Daniel[7] m. Elisabeth Bowne, dau. of Sidney.
Mary[7] m. Aaron Wright.

SAMUEL[6] WILLETS (Robt.[5] Joseph[4] Amos[3] Thos.[2] Richard[1]) and Sarah, had:
Jacob[7] m. Sarah Powell.
Robert[7] m. 1st Margaret Ann Willets, dau. of Seaman, m. 2d —— Nicol.
Amelia[7] m. Edward Merritt.
Edward[7] m. Cornelia Crossman.

STEPHEN[6] WILLETS (Robt.[5] Joseph[4] Amos[3] Thos.[2] Richard[1]) and Maria, had:
Stephen[7] Lydia[7] Sarah.[7]

EDMUND[6] WILLETS (Robt.[5] Joseph[4] Amos[3] Thos.[2] Richard[1]) and Martha, had:
Joseph[7] m. Griffin.
Anna[7] unm.
Mary.[7]
Sarah M.[7] m. Caleb Shepherd.
Martha H.[7]
Thomas[7] m. —— Keese, dau. of John.
Daniel,[7] Edward.[7]

ROBERT[6] R. (Robt.[5] Joseph[4] Amos[3] Thos.[2] Richard[1]) and Lydia, had:
John[7] T. m.
Elisabeth.[7]
William H.[7] m.
Maria[7] Robert R. jr.[7]
Cornelia[7] m. John J. Carle, son of John.

WILLIAM[6] WILLETS (Robert[5] Joseph[4] Amos[3] Thos.[2] Richard[1]) m. 1st 1835, Ann Whitson, had:
Thomas[7] died an infant.
m. 2d Elizabeth P. Titus, dau. of Samuel and Mary (Powell) and had:
Mary[7] b. 1737, m. Isaac H. Cocks.
Ann T.[7] b. 1839.
William W.[7] b. 1843, m.

THOMAS[4] WILLETTS (Amos[3] Thos.[2] Richard[1]) and Leah (Seaman), b. 1744, had:
Charles[5] b. 1764, m. 1789, Esther Powell, dau. of Richard, no children, she d. 1828.
Mary[5] b. 1768.
Phebe[5] b. 1770, m. Richard Eldred, she d 1830.
Rachel[5] b. 1773, m. 1794, Edmond Pearsell, she d. 1830.
Rebecca[5] b. 1776, m. Benjamin Prince.
Joseph[5] b. 1778, m. Abigail Lyon, dau. of Walker.
Sarah[5] b. 1784, m. 1806, Benjamin Albertson, she d. 1871.
Zebulun[5] b. 1786, m. and had: Edmond,[6] Lawrence,[6] Mary,[6] Henry,[6] Elizabeth,[6] Charlotte,[6] he d. 1827.

JOSEPH[5] WILLETS (Thos.[4] Amos[3] Thos.[2] Richard[1]) m. Abigail Lyon, dau. of Walker and Senor (Van Wycke Lyon), their children were:
Benjamin.[6]

Thomas[6] m. Catharine, dau. of David and Rachel (Acker) Stillwaggon.
Charles.[6]
Joseph.[6]
Scena.[6]
Anna[6] m. Henry Valentine.
Mary[6] m. —— Kirk.
THOMAS[6] WILLETS (Joseph[5] Thos.[4] Amos[3] Richard[1]) and Catharine, had:
David[7] m. —— Field, family live in Flushing.
There were other children.
Abraham Acker m. Catharine Van Wart. Their dau. Rachel Acker b. 18, 9, 1785, at Tarrytown, m. 1810, David Stillwaggon of Flushing, she d. 11, 1, 1891, at Flushing, L. I., aged 105 years, 3 mos. 23 days. Rachel's mother saw Benedict Arnold go on board the British ship and sail down the river after betraying his country. The captors of Andres, —— Williams and Van Wart were both her relatives.
The children of David and Rachel Stillwaggon were:
Catharine m. Thomas Willets.
Cornelia, single.
George m. lives at Flushing, has dau. Minnie.
RICHARD[3] WILLETS (Thos.[2] Richard[1]) m. Sarah Hallock, dau. of John and Abigail of Brookhaven, children:
Thomas[4] died single in 1756.
Richard[4] m. 1736 Hannah, dau. of Selah Strong.
Daniel[4] m. 1742 Phebe, dau. of Joseph Carpenter, she died in 1744, m. 2d Amy, dau. of John Powell and Margaret.
Sarah[4] m. about 1734, Wm. Kirbie, died before her father.
Jane[4] she d. 1776.
Phebe.[4]

Deborah[4] m. David Willets.

In 1740 Richard[3] Willets, widower, married Margaret (nee Hallock), widow of John Powell and sister of his first wife Sarah Hallock.

Clement Willets says of her Aunt Margaret, "She was, I think, a "mother in Israel." I lived with her more than two years, and the meeting was kept at her house and she often appeared very ably therein, I thought she was the wisest woman I ever lived with." Richard and Margaret each secured his or her property to his or her own children previous to their marriage.

RICHARD[4] WILLETS (Richard[3] Thos.[2] Rich'd[1]) and wife Hannah, had children:

Ann[5] m. Samuel Underhill.
Deborah[5] m. 1774 Andrew Underhill.
Isaac.[5]
Samuel[5] b 1740, d. 1768.
Hannah.[5]

DANIEL[4] WILLETS (Richard[3] Thos.[2] Richard[1]) m. Phebe Carpenter, dau. of Joseph and had:

Jacob[5] b. 1743, m. 1766, Hannah Powell, dau. of Joshua[3], m. 2d, Catherine (Seaman) widow Powell.
Daniel[4] m. 2d 1745, Amy Powell, dau. of John[1] and Margaret, and had:
Phebe[5] b. 1746, 12, 14, m. Adonijah Underhill.
Charity[5] not m.

Children of JACOB[5] and Hannah Willets:

Daniel[6] m. Kitty, dau. of Henry Smith.
Joshua[6] b. 1769, m. Phebe, dau. of Elias Hicks, no children.
Richard[6] not m.
Phebe[6] m. Elijah Seaman.
Ann[6] m. 1804 Thomas Whitson, son of Henry.
Rebecca[6] d. 1778.

Willets Family.   85

DANIEL[6] WILLETS (Jacob[5] Daniel[4] Richard[3] Thos.[2] Richard[1]) and Kitty (Smith) had:
Hannah[7] m. Richard Udall.
Jacob[7] m.

Thomas[3] Willets, son of Thomas and Dinah lived at Sectague, L. I., till 1736, when he removed with his second wife and some of his children to Pennsylvania. His home was at a place called Lebanon. He was born in 1683, married 1706, Catharine Hallock, dau. of John and Abigail (Swezey) Hallock, of Brookhaven. They had five children. She died 1718 and in 1719 he married Rachel Powell, daughter of Thomas[1] Powell of Bethpage and his second wife Elizabeth (Phillips).

THOMAS[3] WILLETTS (Thos.[2] Richard[1]) m. 1704 Catharine Hallock, dau. of John and Abigail (Swezey), had children of both m.

Clement[4] b. 15, 9, 1709, at Islip, d. 1772, after being confined to her bed with rheumatism 39 years. For 20 years she could not see her hand, she died at Thomas Jackson's of Jericho, was buried at Westbury. She was remarkably patient under her sufferings. The Record of her life, painful as it is, is also very interesting.

Hannah[4] b. 1712, m. 1743, Thomas Seaman, son of Nathaniel, she d. 1755.

Jesse[4] b. 1714, m. 1751 Elisabeth ——, removed to Pennsylvania 1762, had children: Richard[5] b. 25, 4, 1753; Martha[5] b. 16, 9, 1755.

Amy[4] m. 1738, William Hughes, she d. 1760.

John.[4]

Isaiah[4] m. in Pennsylvania.

Elisabeth[4] b. 1725, m. 1747, Samuel Hughes, had son Ellis, dau. Rachel Hughes b. 28, 1, 1748, m. 1768, John Willets of Bucks county, Penn.

86   *Willets Family.*

Great grandson of Hope² Willets and Mercy. And perhaps others.

Children of AMY⁴ (Willets) and William Hughes: Amy⁵ m. Moses Roberts.

JOB⁵ b. 1741, m. Eleanor Lee, and had: Amos,⁶ Samuel,⁶ Job,⁶ Joel,⁶ Sarah,⁶ Rachel,⁶ Abigail,⁶ Amy⁶ m. 1812, Stephen Bowman from Dutchess county, N. Y. At the time of their marriage, he was a resident of Prince Edward county, Ontario, Canada. Job and Moses were at one time in Lancaster jail. Removed to Canada after the Revolution.

HOPE² WILLETS (Richard¹) m. Mercy Langdon, dau. of Joseph. They had children:

Joseph³ b. 1677, m. 1702, Deborah Seaman, dau. of Solomon.

Mary³ b. 1679, m. 8, 9, 1702, Richard Ridgeway at Jerusalem, he was of West Jersey.

Elisabeth³ b. 1681, m. 1701, Jervis Ffaro.

Richard³ b. 1683, m. 15, 7, 1704, Elisabeth Ridgeway at Springfield Meeting.

Esther³ b. 1686.

Timothy³ b. 1687.

Hope³ b. 1689.

Phebe³ b. 1690.

James.

Three b. 3, 8, 1696 { Hannah³ / Patience³ / Abigail³ m. 1716, Thomas Cranmer.

Hope² Willets had grist-mill at Jerusalem, lived and died there. Widow Mercy was selling land there in 1706.

About 1706 Joseph³ and Richard³ Willets removed from farms at Jerusalem and settled on farms at Egg Harbor, N. J. The other members of the family soon followed.

Willets Family.

JOSEPH[3] WILLETS (Hope[2] Richard[1]) and Deborah, had:
  Solomon[4] b. 1703.
  Mary[4] b. 1705.
  Hope[4] b. 1707.
  Joseph[4] b. 1710, m. 1734, Sarah Beck, dau. of Henry. Out of Meeting, repented and was reinstated.
  Deborah[4] b. 1712, m. 1732, at Chesterfield, Samuel Wilson, son of Samuel.
  Henry[4] b. 1714, m. 1746, Sarah Lee b. 1717, dau. of Anthony. She d. 1754, he d. 1755. Family removed to Haddonfield in 1730.

HENRY[4] WILLETS (Joseph[3] Hope[2] Richard[1]) and Sarah (Lee), had children:
  Samuel[5] b. 19, 11, 1746, m., went to Deer Creek, Fayette county, Pa.
  John[5] b. 1748, m. 1772, Rachel Hughes, dau. of Samuel of Exeter, he d. 1826.
  Jesse[5] b. 1750, m. 1779, Phebe Hutton, dau. of John of Maiden Creek, he d. 1817.
  Amos[5] b. 1753.

Children of JESSE[5] and Phebe b. 1762, were:
  John H.[6] b. 1782, d. 1861, Sarah[6] b. 1784, d. 1809, Mary[6] b. 1785, d. 1786, Mary[6] b. 1786 m. John Starr.
  William[6] b. 1789, m. Esther Lightfoot.
  Elisabeth[6] b. 1791, d. 1869, Henry[6] b. 1793, Esther[6] b. 1795.
  Phebe[6] b. 1797, m. Thomas Pearson, she d. 1865.
  Susanna[6] b. 1799, d. 1831, Jesse[6] b. 1802, Deborah[6] b. 1805, she d. 20, 7, 1841.

RICHARD[3] WILLETS (Hope[2] Richard[1]) and Elisabeth Ridgeway, had children:
  Mercy[4] b. 1705.

Willets Family.

Richard[4] b. 1707, m. Sarah Barton.
Elisabeth[4] b. 1709, Amos[4] b. 1711, Mary[4] b. 1713, Deliverance[4] b. 1715.
Micajah[4] b. 1718, m. Elizabeth.
Cornelius[4] b. 1720, Sarah[4] b. 1724.
Children of RICHARD[4] WILLETS and Sarah (Barton):
Micajah[5] m. Hannah Parker.
Richard.[5]
Deliverance[5] m. Stephen Birdsall.
MICAJAH[5] and Hannah Willets had children:
Micajah[6] m. Judith Cranmer, and went west.
Richard[6] m. Rachel Birdsall.
Mercy[6] m. Jesse Andrews.
Deliverance[6] m. Samuel Cranmer.
MICAJAH[4] WILLETS (Richard[3] Hope[2] Rich'd[1]) and Elisabeth, had:
Elisabeth[5] b. 1742, Mary[5] b. 1743, Richard[5] b. 1746, Sarah[5] b. 1748, Deliverance[5] b. 1751, Micajah[5] b. 1753, Hannah[5] b. 1756, Mercy[5] b. 1760.
RICHARD[2] WILLETS (Richard[1]) m. 1st 25, 1, 1686 Abigail, dau. of John and Hannah Bowne, and had:
Hannah[3] b. 24, 11, 1687, m. 1710, Job Carr, son of Samuel, she d. 1727.
Abigail d. 16, 4, 1688. Richard m. 2d 15, 3, 1690 Abigail b. 1668, dau. of 1st Thomas Powell, and they had:
Abigail[3] b. 27, 12, 1690, m. 1714 John Willis, she d. 1777.
Mary[3] b. 16, 1, 1692, m. 1710 Henry Scudder, he d. 1715, she m. 2d 1717 Thos. Williams, she d. 1750.
Martha[3] b. 24, 11, 1694, m. 1715, Obadiah Valentine.

Jacob[3] b. 6, 4, 1697, m. 1717, Mary Jackson, dau. of James and Rebecca, he d 1722.
Phebe[3] b. 14, 2, 1699, m. 1731 Adam Mott, he d. 1738, she m. 2d Tristram Dodge, he d. 1760, she d. 7, 9, 1782.
Elisabeth[3] b. 27, 4, 1701, she d. 1722.

Carr Family.

CALEB[1] CARR b. 1624, came to Rhode Island 1635, d. 1695 (had brother Robert Carr), m. 1st Mercy Easton b. 1631, d. 1651; m. 2d Sarah Clarke, sister of Gov. Walter Clarke. CALEB and Mercy had:

Samuel[2] Carr b. 1650, m. unknown, had son Job[3] m. Hannah Willets.
Nicholas[2] and Mercy[2] died young.
Caleb.[2]
CALEB[1] and second wife Sarah Clarke had:
Mercy[2] John[2] Edward[2] Francis[2] James[2] Sarah[2] and Elisabeth.[2]

JOB[3] CARR (Samuel[2] Caleb[1]) and Hannah (Willets), dau. of Richard and Abigail Bowne Willets, had:

Mary[4] b. 1712.
Samuel[4] b. 1714, d. 1743.
Hannah[4] b. 1716, m. Jeremiah Robbins of ———-.
CALEB[4] b. 1719, m. 1746 Sarah Ridgeway, dau. of T. Ridgeway, jr., and had: Mary[4] b. 1747, Job b. 1750, Joseph, Samuel b. 1754, Catharine and James.

1714 or 15 Job Carr and Hannah to George Townsend, 500 acres in Bucks county, Penn., by Neshaming Creek, formerly laid out to John Bowne, dec. in 1688 and conveyed by his son Samuel Bowne in 1696 to Hannah Carr.

"In 1717 Laid out to Job Carr 58 acres on Rights that were Wm. Washburne's dec. West side of road from Lusum to Matinecock near the ridge of hills that lies on the north side of the level Land so called. Several courses given, last course being N. E. by the south side of the ridge of hills to the road aforesaid.

"1718, Job Carr of Jericho to Ebenazer Dodge of Cold Spring Land adjoining John Ireland. "In 1750, Nathaniel Dodge (house Carpenter) & Ann (his mother) son of Ebenezer dec. to Solomon Weeks, place described as farm where I now live near Cold Spring in O. B. bought by my father of Job Ireland and Job Carr."
"Witnessed by Job Carr in 1750."

JACOB[3] WILLETS (Richard[2] Richard[1]) m. 1717, Mary Jackson, dau. of James of Flushing, and Rebecca (Hallett), children:

    Richard[4] b. 28, 9, 1718, m. July 7, 1743, Ruth b. Oct. 16, 1718, dau. of Amos Willets, he d. Dec. 9, 1787.

    Mary[4] b. 1721, m. 1737, David Seaman, son of David.

RICHARD[4] WILLETS (Jacob[3] Richard[2] Richard[1]) and Ruth, had:

    Jacob[5] b. 8, 6, 1744, m. Martha Williams, dau. of John and Elizabeth. he d. Feb. 20, 1823.

    Mary[5] b. 27, 6, 1746, died in youth.

    Richard[5] b. 20, 6, 1748, m. Abigail Seaman, dau. of Samuel and Martha (Valentine).

    James[5] b. 21, 2, 1751, died in infancy.

    Amos[5] b. 21, 4, 1754, m. Phebe Powell, dau. of Joshua and Phebe, he d. Dec. 21, 1831.

    Thomas[5] b. 7, 4, 1757, d. 1758.

Sarah⁵ b. 23 Oct. 1759, d. Jan. 27, 1779.

Richard⁴ Willets m. 2d 1786, Phebe, widow of Joshua Powell, he d. 1787.

JACOB⁵ WILLETS (Richard⁴ Jacob³ Richard² Richard¹) and Martha, dau. of John, son of Thos. Williams and Mary (nee Willets) widow Scudder, dau. of Richard² Willets and Abigail² (Powell), and Elisabeth, dau. of Obadiah Valentine and Martha (nee Willets), dau. of Richard² and A. (Powell), had children:

Mary⁶ b. 22, 8, 1768.

Ruth⁶ b. 24, 6, 1770.

Elizabeth⁶ b. 25, 12, 1771, m. —— Rushmore, no children, she d. 1836.

Martha⁶ b. 19, 7, 1774, m. Obadiah Willets, his 3d wife.

Williams⁶ b. 10, 10, 1780, m. 1835, Phebe Underhill, dau. of Richard, no children.

Jacob⁶ b. 14, 6, 1784, m. Abigail Willets, dau. of Obadiah and Elisabeth (Robbins).

Phebe⁶ b. 10, 9, 1788, m. David Ketchum, son of David and Jane.

JACOB⁶ WILLETS and Abigail, had children:

William⁷ m. Fannie Hewlett, dau. of Israel, had: Elisabeth, Frederick, Annie, Mary, Alice, Martha.

Elisabeth⁷, Martha⁷ m. Townsend Jackson; Ruth,⁷ Caroline,⁷ Phebe,⁷ Mary.⁷

Mary⁸, dau. of William and Fannie Willets, is a graduate of Swathmore College, Pa. These families spell their name Willits.

RICHARD⁵ WILLETS (Richard⁴ Jacob³ Richard² Richard¹) m. Abigail Seaman, b. 1749, dau. of Samuel and Martha, and had:

James⁶ b. 3, 10, 1770, d. 8, 11, 1776.

Willets Family.

Obadiah[6] b. 28, 2, 1772, m. 1st Elisabeth Robbins, dau. of Jacob, b. 20, 8, 1788, she d. 1815, he d. 1842.

Richard[6] b. 28, 5, 1774, m. 30, 4, 1800, Mary, b. May 10, 1783, d. Dec. 30, 1805, dau. of Gideon Seaman.

Martha[6] b. 21, 11, 1776, m. Simeon Loines, she d. 18, 4, 1850.

OBADIAH[6] WILLETS (Richard[5] Richard[4] Jacob[3] Richard[2] Richard[1]) m. 1807, Elisabeth Robbins b. 20, 8, 1788, d. 11, 4, 1815, dau. of Jacob, and had:

Richard R.[7] b. 26, 2, 1808, m. and has children:

Abigail[7] b. 3, 11, 1809, m. Jacob Willets, dau. of Jacob and Murtha.

Mary R.[7] b. 26, 2, 1812, m. Edmond Kirby.

Elisabeth[7] b. 28, 3, 1814, m. William Robbins of Willet.

Married 2d Aug. 20, 1820 Widow Phebe Dodge, formerly Downing, and had:

Hannah[7] m. Jordan Underhill.

Jacob[7] m.

Charles[7] b. 17, 5, 1826, m. 1st   m. 2d

RICHARD[6] WILLETS (Richard[5] Richard[4] Jacob[3] Richard[2] Richard[1]) and Mary Seaman, had:

Edward S.[7] b. 22, 9, 1803, m. 1st Esther, and 2d Amy, dau's of Abraham Whitson.

Ann[7] b. 18, 7, 1806, d. small.

Married Dec. 4, 1812, 2d Mary b. 1783, dau. of Samuel and Abigail (Robbins) Titus, and had:

James[7] b. 6 10, 1813.

Henry[7] b. 22, 11, 1815.

Martha[7] b. 16, 1, 1819.

Mary[7] b. 10, 2, 1822.

AMOS[5] WILLETS (Richard[4] Jacob[3] Richard[2] Richard[1]) m. 1774 (Phebe Powell), dau. of Joshua and Phebe (Post) of Bethpage), b. 17, 9, 1749, and had:
   Hannah[6] b. 26, 8, 1775, m. 1797, Thomas Whitson, no children.
   Joshua[6] b. 21, 10, 1780, m. Sarah, dau. of Henry Robbins, and had: Phebe,[7] William,[7] Amos,[7] Sarah[7] and Joshua.[7]
   Sarah[6] m. Dr. Morris M. Rogers, and had:
      Charles m. Sarah Hicks, dau. of Benjamin, of Great Neck, and had two children, d. small.
      Amos m. Caroline Hicks, dau. of Benjamin of Great Neck.
      Martha m. Isaac Sherwood.
   Amos[5] Willets m. 2d Elisabeth Birdsall, dau. of Thomas (she m. 1st Parmenas Jackson, m. 2d James Downing) Downing, widow of James.
   The will of Phebe Willets of Jericho, 1691, says: daughters Hannah and Phebe, granddaughters Phebe Seaman and Ann Whitson, dau's of Jacob Willets and Hannah Powell, Hannah and Sarah, dau's of Amos Willets and Phebe Powell.
   Phebe was widow of Richard,[4] father of Amos.[5]

WILL OF ABIGAIL WILLETS OF JERICHO, DATED 12, 6, 1757. PROVED 25 OCT. 1757.

I will and bequeath unto my three daughters, Abigail Willis, Martha Valentine and Phebe Dodge my wearing apparel of all sorts to be equally divided between them.

I will and bequeath unto my daughter Abigail Willis three of my silver spoons,—to Martha Valentine three of my silver spoons. I will to my granddaughters Elisabeth Hewlett, Phebe Doty and Ann

Williams each of them one silver spoon. To my grand-daughter Elisabeth Willis the wife of John Willis of Oyster Bay one silver spoon — to my two grand-sons Adam Mott and Stephen Mott each of them one silver spoon. To my grandson Richard Willets of Jericho my couch and my great table at Jericho in his possession. Unto my grand-daughter Mary Seaman the wife of David Seaman, my great iron pot, one pair of Andirons and my spit all in her possession.

I will to my four grand-daughters, to wit, Elisabeth the wife of Jonathan Seaman, Elisabeth Willis the wife of John Willis, Esther the wife of Samuel Way and Ann Williams dau. of Thomas Williams dec. to each of them one silver spoon. I will to my grand children that is the children of my deceased daughter Mary Williams as much of my Estate, as to be equal in value, with the fourth part of the value of my close, and the value of one of my silver porringers, to be equally divided amongst them all, as fully as if named.

I will unto my daughter Abigail Willis one of my silver porringers. I will to my daughter Martha Valentine one of my silver porringers. I will to my three grand children Elisabeth Willis, Adam Mott and Stephen Mott the other of my silver porringers. To my dau Martha Valentine my Bible and pye pan. I will and bequeath all the remainder of my estate, that is, my silver tankard and all the money I have out at interest, and all debts due to me and all other of my Estate whatsoever to be equally divided, that is, to my daughter Abigail 1 fourth part,— to my daughter Martha 1 fourth part,— to the children of my deceased daughter Mary Williams the equal fourth part to be equally divided amongst them,—and the other fourth part I will, to my three grand children Elisabeth Willis, Adam Mott and Stephen Mott, to be equally divided amongst them.

Appoint my two sonsinlaw Obadiah Valentine and John Willis to be my Executors of this my last Will and Testament.
ABIGAIL WILLETS.

Witnesses Nathaniel Seaman jnr, Richard Townsend, Richard Townsend jnr.

Nathaniel Seaman a Quaker was duly affirmed, Rich'd Townsend jnr was duly sworn.

HALLOCK FAMILY.

Tradition says that Peter[1] Hallock came with twelve other heads of families to New Haven in 1640; same season crossed the sound and landed at Southold, Peter being the first to step on shore at a spot still called Hallock's Neck. Also, that having bought a large tract of land of the Indians, he went back to England for his family. Wife was unwilling to come, but Peter promised to give her two daughters (by a former husband) considerable land, and the family all came over in two or three years; meantime the Indians had resold his land, and another party had possession. The records of this period are lost. In 1654, according to Southold records, Wm.[2] Hallock was in possession of a large property there, and was quite a man of business in the town. He died in 1688 or 1689. Will makes his wife Margaret executrix. The children named in the will were:

John[3] 1679 m. Abigail Sweezey, dau. of John, he d. at Westbury 25, 5, 1737.

Thomas,[3] Mary,[3] Martha,[3] Sarah.[3]

Peter,[3]   William, wife named Mary.

Elisabeth[3] m. 1st Harrud, m. 2d 1675 Richard Howell.

Abigail[3] m. David Horton.

The Sweezey's were Friends from Salem, Mass., and Wm. Hallock, who was a strong Church of England man, disiniherited his son John, and any others of the family to all time, if they married or contracted with any Quaker or any son or daughter of a Quaker. Years afterwards a grandson of this disinherited John Hallock who lived in Westchester county gave very small portions to any of his children who married those not Quakers.

JOHN[3] HALLOCK (William[2] Peter[1]) of Southold, m. 1679, Abigail, dau. of John Sweezey, he d. 25, 5, 1737, she d. 23, 1, 1737, both at Westbury, their children were:

    John Jr.[4] b. 1680, m. Hannah, lived at Setauket, L. I.
    Margaret[4] b. 1682, m. 1704, John[2] John Powell, son of Thomas.[1]
    Benjamin[4] m. Sarah.
    Catharine[4] m. 1706, Thomas Willets ⎫
    Sarah[4] m. Richard Willets.   ⎬ sons of Thomas and Dinah.
    Mary[4] m. 1713, Amos Willets.   ⎪
    Clement[4] m. 1716, Isaac Willets. ⎭
    Abigail[4] b. 1688, unm.
    Peter[4] m. 1723, Abigail Powell, dau. of Thomas[2] and Mary (Willets).
    William.[3] ?

Children of JOHN Jr.[4] and Hannah Hallock, were:

    John[5] b. 1701, m. 1731, Martha Quimby of Mamaroneck, he d. 1757.
    Sarah[5] b. 1702, m. 1727, Caleb Hunt.
    Abigail[5] b. 1705, m. 1724, Thomas[3] Powell, son of Thomas[2] and Mary (Willets).
    Hannah[5] b. 1707, m. Saterlys.
    Catharine[5] b. 1712, m. 1732, Moses Powell, son of Thomas[2] and Mary (Willets).
    Edward[5] b. 1717, m. 1737, Phebe Clapp, dau. of John and Dorcas (Quimby), he d. 1810.

Phebe[5] b. 1720, m. 1746, Abraham Underhill, son of Abraham of White Plains.

Clement[5] b. 1723, m. 1752 Caleb Powell, son of Caleb and Sarah.

Samuel[5] b. 1725, m. 1754.

Almy[5] b. 1727, m. 1747, Jacob Underhill, son of Abraham of White Plains.

PETER[4] HALLOCK (John[3] William[2] Peter[1]) and Abigail, had removal certificate to Nine Partners Monthly Meeting in 1755, their children appear to have been:

Moses, Jesse, Thomas, John, Peter, Jr., Zebulun and perhaps others.

PETER, Jr.[5] and wife Ann, had:

Isaac[6] b. 1754, Israel b. 1755, Abigail b. 1757, Robert b. 1759, he d. 1762, 29, 12, Ann, b. 1762.

Peter settled north of Washington Hollow on the Main road to Stanford, others lived around that part of the country.

JOHN[5] HALLOCK (John[4] John[3] William[2] Peter[1]) and Martha Quimby, had:

John[6] eldest, by his father's will in 1757 had £300.

James[6] 2d, by his father's will in 1757 had £250.

Daniel[6] } not 21. { had £200.
Samuel[6] }   { had £200.

Martha[6] m. Joseph Sands, £80.

Phebe when 21, £80.

Martha (Quimby) Hallock, wife of John, to have use of £100 during widowhood, £35 if she marry.

EDWARD[5] HALLOCK (John[4] John[3] William[2] Peter[1]) and Phebe (Clapp), b. 11, 7, 1719, had certificate to Nine Partners in 1764. Their children were:

Hannah[6] b. 4, 10, 1740, m. Nathaniel Smith.

Dorcas[6] b. 21, 1, 1744, m. —— Young.

Clement[6] b. 24, 4, 1746, m. David Sands.

Mary⁶ b. 30, 3, 1748, m. Richard Carpenter.
Catharine⁶ b. 31, 3, 1750, m. Obadiah Palmer.
Phebe⁶ b. 30, 3, 1752, m. Gardner Earl.
Edward⁶ b. 22, 4, 1754, m. 1st Susanna Smith, m. 2d Anna Jones.
Amy⁶ b. 27, 4, 1756.
Philena⁶ b. 11, 7, 1757, m 1st Jeremiah Bedell, m. 2d Joseph Wheeler.
Martha⁶ b. 1759, m. James Thorne.
James⁶ b. 1, 12, 1761, m. Elisabeth Townsend.
Sarah⁶ b. 27, 4, 1763, m. Henry Hull.

Children of EDWARD⁶ and Susannah Smith Hallock:

Rebecca⁷ b. 13, 11, 1780, m. 29, 3, 1821, John⁵ Powell, son of Moses⁴ and Hannah Wheeler.
Silas,⁷ Dorcas,⁷ Phebe,⁷ Villetta,⁷ Epenetus,⁷ Sarah,⁷ Jonas.⁷

Second wife, Anna Jones, had:
Arrabella,⁷ Mary,⁷ Ann,⁷ Susan.⁷

JAMES⁶ HALLOCK (Edward⁵ John⁴ John³ William² Peter¹) m. Elisabeth Townsend, dau. of Nicholas and Philadelphia (Doughty) and had:

Nicholas⁷ m. 1st Elisabeth, dau. of Samuel Titus, m. 2d Phebe Smith.
John Townsend⁷ m.¹ 1817, Ann Everett, dau. of Thomas and Susanna.
Edward⁷ m. 1st Annie Sherman, m. 2d Sarah Hull.
William⁷ m. Phebe Ann Hull, dau. of John and Annie.
Nathaniel⁷ m. Phebe Ann Burling, dau. of Thos. and Elisabeth (Hull).
Phebe⁷ m. John Mann, son of John and Freelove (Hull).
Philadelphia⁷ m. James Sherman.

Martha T.⁷ b. 1801, m. David Ketcham, had 3 sons, 2 grew to manhood and died in the war of the Rebellion.

EDWARD⁷ HALLOCK and Annie (Sherman) had:
Nicholas⁸ m.
Valentine⁸ m. Henrietta Burling, dau. of Thos.
Isaac⁸ m.

Mann Family.

MATTHIAS¹ MANN m. Sarah Stansbury, had:
JOHN² m. Freelove Hull b. 1790, and had:
JOHN³ m. Phebe Hallock and had:
James Mann m. Belle ———.
Townsend m.
Sarah m. Isaac Ketchum.
Martha m. John Hicks.

Hull Family.

JOSEPH HULL m. Phebe ——— and had:
James b. 1772, m.
John b. 1776, m. Annie.
Wager b. 1779 m.
Phebe b. 1781, m. William Renouf.
Freelove b. 1790, m. John Mann.
Joseph d. 1791 aged 2 years.

NICHOLAS⁷ HALLOCK (James⁶ Edward⁵ John⁴ John³ William² Peter¹), m. 1st Elisabeth, b. 1785, dau. of Samuel Titus and Abigail (Robbins), and had:
Elisabeth⁸ died young.
Robert⁸ b. 26, 11, 1806, m. ——— Barret.
Ann⁸ b. 24, 2, 1808.

Hallock Family.

James[8] b. 1809, m. Mary Rathbun, had Elisabeth, m. Calvin G. Alvord.
Samuel[8] jr b. 1811, m. a Baylis.
Sarah[8] m. a Scram.
Nehemiah[8] m. a Wood.
Martha[8] m. a Falkner.
David[8] m. Martha S. Ketcham, dau. of John and Rebecca.
Mary[8] m. an Allen.
William[1] Quimby the Immigrant, John[2], Josiah[3] m. Mary Mullinieux, their dau. Dorcas[4] m. John Clapp.

CLAPP FAMILY.

Dr. GEORGE[1] GILSON CLAPP b. in England 1650, had son
Capt. John[2] Clapp who m., and had son
JOHN[3] b. 1690, who m. Dorcas Quimby, and had:
Phebe[4] b. 1719, m. Edward Hallock, dau. of John and Hannah.
Dorcas b. 1738, m. 1st William Sutton, son of Joseph and Mary Sands Sutton, m. 2d Francis Nash.
Alice Sutton, dau. of Wm. and Dorcas, m. Benjamin Cornell, and had:
Silas Cornell b. 1789, m. Sarah Mott.
Phebe Cornell b. 1791, m. Stephen Underhill.

Will of William Hallock, of Brookhaven, 1748, says:
Wife Dinah and children Jesse m., Wm., Richard, David, Mary m. Wm. Long, Dinah, Sarah (she m. 1751 Joseph Dickinson and had Henry and Isaac), Elisabeth.
Witness JESSE WILLETS.

1770, Mary Hallock cert. to Purchase, Monthly Meeting.

David Hallock m. Grace Burling, moved to Purchase, was there in 1775.

Richard Hallock of Brookhaven 1769, m. 1773. 1785 moved near Purchase. Richard Hallock m. 1st Amy Horton, had George, m. 1834 Mary Pierce, dau. of Isaac and Sarah, and Joseph m.

John Swazey's children, John jr, Joseph (m. Mary Betts, dau. of Capt. Richard of Newton), Abigail, Mehitable, Sarah and Mary.

Bertha Sweezey, dau. of Joseph, m. William Coleman.

TITUS FAMILY.

Silas Titus d. 1637; Constatia d. 1667.

Robert Titus of St. Catharines, came to New England in 1635. He was born 1600, wife, Hannah b. 1604, she died in Huntington, L. I., in 1679. They came in the "Hopewell" with children, John aged 7, and Edmond aged 5 years; other children: Samuel, b. 1635, Susanna, Abial, Content b. at Weymouth, Mass., 1643.

Robert Titus signed a Covenant with others and settled at Seakunk in 1644.

In 1653 Robert Titus, his son John and one other son settled at Oyster bay, L. I.

Edmond Titus came to Long Island in 1650, married Martha, dau. of Wm. and Jane Washburn, she b. 1637, d. 1727. They settled at Westbury, L. I. He died 1715.

EDMOND[2] TITUS (Robert[1]) and Martha had children:

Samuel[3] b. 1658, m. 1691, Elisabeth Powell, dau. of Thos.[1], she d. 1704, he d. 1732.

Phebe[3] b. 1660, m. 1st Samuel Scudder (son of John), he d. 1688; m. 2d Robert Field.

Martha[3] b. 1663, m. Benjamin Seaman, son of Capt. John.

Mary[3] b. 1665, m. William Willis, she d. 1747.

Hannah[3] b. 1667, m. Benjamin Smith.

Jane[3] b. 1670, m. James Denton.

Titus Family.

John[3] b. 1672, m. 1st 1695, Sarah Willis; m, 2d 1732, Mary, widow of John Smith, he d. 1781.

Peter[3] b. 1674, m. Martha Jackson, dau. of John, he d. 23, 10, 1753, she d. 10, 12, 1753.

Silas[3] b. 1676, m. Sarah Haight, dau. of Samuel and Sarah, he d. 1750.

Patience[3] b. 1678, m. 1704, Nicholas Haight, dau. Hannah m. Isaac Thorne.

Temperance[3] b. 1681.

SAMUEL[3] TITUS (Edmond[2] Robert[1]) and Elisabeth (Powell), had:

Phebe[4] b. 1693, m. 1716, John Haight.

Temperance[4] b. 1695, she d. 15, 2, 1704.

Martha[4] b. 1696, m. Epenetus Wood.

Samuel[4] b. 1704, m. 1725, Mary Jackson, dau. of John and Elisabeth (Hallett), he d. 19, 2, 1750.

Samuel[3] Titus m. 2d Elisabeth (Bowne), widow Prior.

SAMUEL[4] TITUS (Samuel[3] Edward[2] Robert[1]) and Mary (Jackson), had:

Stephen[5] b. 24, 12, 1737, m. 1750, Sarah Mott, dau. of Samuel.

Elisabeth[5] b. 16, 8, 1729, m. John Keese, son of John and Mary of Flushing.

Mary[5] b. 7, 6, 1732, m. Samuel Titus, son of Jacob.

Samuel[5] b. 4, 9, 1734, m. 1761, Ruth Townsend, dau. of John, son of Richard.

Richard[5] b. 16, 11, 1736, m. 1770, Abigail Weeks, dau. of Samuel and Deborah (Valentine).

Phebe[5] b. 15, 11, 1739, m. Nicholas Holmes.

Jemina[5] b. 16, 1, 1742, m. 1765 William Thorne, son of Isaac and Hannah (Haight), she was dau. of Nicholas Haight and Patience Titus.

Thorne Family.

WILLIAM THORNE came from Sandwich in 1642, was in Flushing in 1645, one of the first settlers with wife Sarah, they had children:

William[2] m. Winifred[2] Linnington, dau. of Henry of Hempstead.
John[2] b. 1643, m. Mary.
Joseph[2] m. Mary Bowne.
Samuel[2] and Susanna.
Children of JOHN[2] and Mary, were:
William[3] m. 1708, Meribah Allen.
John[3] m. Catharine.
Joseph[3] 1695, m. Martha Joanna Bowne.
Mary,[3] Elisabeth.[3]
Hannah[3] m. Richard Cornell, b. 1675.
Sarah[3] m. Joshua.
Children of JOSEPH and Mary m. 1680:
Hannah[3] b. 1680, Joseph[3] b. 1682, William[3] b. 1683.
Mary[3] b. 1686, m. 1709, John Shotwell, son of John.
Hannah[3] b. 1688, John[3] b. 1690.
Thomas[3] b. 1693, m. 1725, Penelope Coles.
Benjamin[3] b. 1694, Abraham[3] b. 1696, Isaac[3] b. 1698, Jacob[3] b. 1700.
Sarah[3] b. 1702, m. 1725 (one record says 1716), James Jackson.
Isaac[3] m. 1722, Hannah Haight, and had William,[4] m. Jemima Titus, and nine more.
WILLIAM[4] THORNE and Jemima, had:
Samuel[5] m. Phebe Dean.
Nicholas.[5]
Phebe[5] m. Nehemiah Merritt, and William.[5]
SAMUEL[5] THORNE and Phebe Dean, had:
Jonathan[6] m. Lydia Ann Corse.
Mary[6] m. Peter Keese.
Anna[6] m. Anson Lapham.

STEPHEN[5] TITUS (Samuel[4] Samuel[3] Edmond[2] Robert[1]) and Sarah Mott, and had :

Stephen[6] m. Phebe Willets, dau. of Jacob and Hannah (Powell).

Samuel[6] m., son Obediah, m. Mary Townsend.

John[6] m. 1st Thorne, m. 2d Haight, m. 3d a Vincent.

Anne[6] and Mariam.[6]

Stephen's[5] will says, Joseph Hicks, my wife's brother, presumably his 2d wife.

STEPHEN[6] TITUS (Stephen[5] Samuel[4] Samuel[3] Edmund[2] Robert[1]) and Phebe (Willets), had :

Hannah[7] m. Samuel Underhill, dau. of Israel.

Samuel[7] b. 1788, m. 1810, Mary Powell, dau. of Joshua and Phebe, he d. 1823.

Stephen[7] m. Hannah Underhill, dau. of Israel, and had Sarah b. 1817 and Elisabeth b. 1820.

Stephen[6] Titus d. 1762, widow Phebe (Willets) m. 2d George Townsend, and had Mary m. Obadiah Titus of Dutchess county.

SAMUEL[7] TITUS b. 1788 and wife Mary Powell, had :

Elisabeth P.[8] b. 18, 11, 1815, m. 1835, William Willets, b. 1808, son of Robert.

Stephen[8] b. 1813, m. Sarah Saterthwaite.

Samuel[8] m.

JOHN[6] TITUS (Stephen[5] Samuel[4] Samuel[3] Edmund[2] Robt.[1]) and 1st wife —— Thorne had:

Jacob.[7]

Second wife Sarah Haight had:

Margaret[7] Richard[7] Stephen, Nicholas.[7]

Elisabeth[7] m. Stephen Sweet.

Elias,[7] third wife —— Vincent, had:

Daniel[7] Stephen[7] and Samuel.[7]

Children of Elisabeth and Stephen Sweet, George and others.

SAMUEL[5] TITUS (Samuel[4] Samuel[3] Edmund[2] Robt.[1]) and Ruth Townsend had:
Samuel[6] m. Mary Townsend, no ch.
Stephen[6] m. Betty Holmes, and had:
Ruth.[7]
Phebe[7] m. Thomas Tabor.

RICHARD[5] TITUS (Samuel[4] Samuel[3] Edmund[2] Robt.[1]) m. 1760, Abigail Weeks, she d. 1820, dau. of Samuel and (Deborah Valentine, dau. of Richard) Weeks, and had:
Mary[6] b. 1770, m. 1795, Joseph Lundy, son of Thos. of Hardwick.
Phebe[6] b. 1772, m. Wicks Seely.
George[6] b. 1774, m. Jemima Downing.
Deborah[6] m. Azariah Howland.
Abigail,[6] Amelia and Richard d.
Jemima[6] b. 1780, m. Wm. Paul Osborne.
Miriam[6] b. 1782.
Children of Mary and Joseph Lundy:
Mary m. a Barnard, lived in Philadelphia, had ch.

JOHN[3] TITUS (Edmund[2] Robt.[1]) m. 1695, Sarah Willis, dau. of Henry and Mary (Peace) had children:
Mary[4] b. 1696, m. 1717, Henry Pearsall, son of Thomas and Mary (Seaman).
John[4] b. 1698, m. 1721, Sarah Pearsall, dau. of George, he d. 1757, she d. 28, 1, 1753.
Philadelphia[4] b. 1700, m. Thomas Seaman, son of Richard and Jane.
Jacob[4] b. 1703, m. Margaret Gormon.
William[4] b. 1705, m. 18, 9, 1730, Elisabeth Seaman, dau. of Thomas of Jerusalem, he d. 18, 4, 1750.
Sarah[4] b. 1708, m. 1st Edmund Titus, m. 2d Isaac Doty.
Phebe[4] b. 1710, m. John Ridgeway.

Titus Family.

JOHN[4] TITUS (John[3] Edmond[2] Robert[1]) and Sarah Pearsall, had:

Henry[5] b. 1722, m. Sarah Birdsall, his will 1749.
Mary[5] b. 1724, m. 1751, John Mott, son of James of Rockaway.
James[5] b. 1730, m. Annie Cox, dau. of Samuel and Martha.
Elisabeth[5] b. 1733, m. 1757, Samuel Cock.
Sarah[5] b. 1737.
Jonathan[5] b. 1743, m. 1767, Mary Whitson.
HENRY[5] TITUS and Sarah Birdsall, had children:
Sarah[6] b. 1753, 2, 2, m. Charles Clement.
William[6] b. 1754, 10 mo., m. Mary Birdsall.
John[6] b. 1757, m. Elisabeth Mugglesford.
Samuel[6] b. 1760, m. 1st Mary Field, m. 2d Mary Pearsall.
Daniel, b. 1762, m. 1783, Amy Willets, dau. of Samuel and Jane (Powell).
Johanna[6] b. 1765.
DANIEL[6] TITUS and Amy (Willets), had:
Henry[7] b. 1784, m. Phebe b. 1786, dau. of Joshua and Hannah (Titus).
Annie[7] b. 1785, m. Amos Willets, son of Robert and Mary (Robbins).
Mary[7] b. 1786, d. 1821, Sarah b. 1788, d. 1819, Phebe d. 1818.
William[7] b. 1799, m. Phebe Willets, dau. of Robert and Mary.
HENRY[7] TITUS and Phebe, had:
James[8] m. Caroline Valentine, dau. of Elwood.
Anne[8] m. James Willets, son of Richard and Mary.
JAMES[5] TITUS (John[2] John[3] Edmond[2] Robert[1]) m. Annie Cox, dau. of Samuel and Martha, and had:
Martha[6] m. Thomas Powell, son of Isaac[3] and Martha.

Titus Family. 109

John[6] m. Phebe Titus, dau. of Thomas and Martha (Powell) Titus.

Joshua[6] m. 1785, Hannah Titus, dau. of John and Sarah (Robbins).

Willet,[6] Sarah.[6]

JOHN[6] TITUS (James[5] John[4] John[3] Edmond[2] Robert[1]), and Phebe, dau. of Thos. and Martha Titus, had family and went to Cornwall on the Hudson.

JOSHUA[6] (James[5] John[4] John[3] Edmond[2] Robert[1]), and Hannah, had:

Phebe[7] b. 1786, m. Henry Titus, son of Daniel[6] & Amy.

Mary[7] b. 1788, Sarah[7] b. 1704, and Joshua[7] b. 1797.

JACOB[4] TITUS (John[3] Edmond[2] Robert[1]) and Margaret Gormon, had:

Timothy[5] m. Charity, dau. of Simon Losea, he d. 1804.

Phila[5] m. Adam Carman.

Phebe[5] m. Silas Rushmore.

Jacob[5] m. Martha Keen, dau. of Francis and Martha, he d. 1808.

Margaret[5] m. Charles Titus.

Sarah[5] m. Joseph Doty.

Elisabeth[5] m. Sampson Crooker.

Samuel[5] m. Mary, dau. of Samuel Titus.

TIMOTHY[5] TITUS (Jacob[4] John[3] Edmund[2] Robt.[1]) and Charity had:

Timothy[6] m. Margaret Titus, dau. of Jacob and Martha (Keen).

Henry[6] m. Jane Smith.

Isaac[6] Edmund[6] Jacob[6] Willis.[6]

Margaret[6] m. a Robbins.

Sarah[6] m. a Dickinson.

Ruth.[6]

Jemima[6] m. a Van Cott.

JACOB[5] TITUS (Jacob[4] John[3] Edmund[2] Robt.[1]) and Martha Keen had:
  Margaret[6] m. Timothy Titus.
  Rowland[6] m. Sarah b. 1779, d. 1844, dau. of Richard Weeks.
  Mary b. 1781, m. George Van Cott, she d. 1852, he d. 1868.
  One m. David Nostrant.
  Children of ROWLAND[6] Titus and Sarah Weeks:
  Isaac.[7]
  Phebe[7] m. George Valentine.
  Silas[7] m. Mary Titus.
  Robert[7] m. Eliza Chapman.
  Richard[7] W. m. Mary P. Plummer.
  Elisabeth[7] m. Sidney Alley.
  Rachel[7] m. Edward Robbins.
  Lydia[7] m. Samuel Mosier.

WILLIAM[4] TITUS (John[3] Edmund[2] Robert[1]) m. 1730, Elisabeth Seaman, dau. of Thomas of Jerusalem, and had:
  Elisabeth[5] b. 1731.
  Hannah[5] b. 1733, m. Joseph Willets, son of Amos.
  Phebe[5] b. 1735, m. Stephen Loines.
  Thomas[5] b. 1738, m. 1756, Martha[4] Powell, dau. of Isaac.[3]
  John[5] b. 1743, m. 1765, Sarah Robbins, dau. of Jeremiah.

THOMAS[5] TITUS and Martha (Powell) had:
  Kesia[6] b. 23, 2, 1757, m. Samuel Seaman, son of Samuel.
  William[6] b. 4, 3, 1759, m. Mary b. 1761, dau. of Henry Cock and Elisabeth (Robbins).
  Phebe[6] b. 29, 7, 1761, m. John Titus of Cornwall-on-the-Hudson, son of James.
  Isaac[6] b. 26, 4, 1764, m, 1st a Coles, m. 2d Mary Betts.

Martha⁶ b. 28, 7, 1778, m. Jabez Green.
WILLIAM⁶ TITUS and Mary (Cock) had:
Martha⁷ b. 1789, m. David Irish of Oblong.
ISAAC⁶ TITUS, m. 1st —— Coles, had Daniel⁷ who m. and d. young.
Married 2d Mary Betts, had son Samuel⁷ B., after the death of the father his mother changed his name to Isaac⁷ B., he m. and had a family. All these went from L. I. to Cornwall.

JOHN⁵ TITUS (William⁴ John³ Edmund² Robert¹), m. Sarah Robbins, and had:
- Hannah⁶ b. 1766, m. Joshua Titus, son of James and Annie (Cox) Titus.
- Elisabeth⁶ b. 1768.
- Mary⁶ b. 1769, m. 1788, James Underhill, son of Jacob, no children.
- Richard⁶ b. 1771.
- Jane⁶ b. 1773, m. 1793, Samuel Post, m. 2d Lewis Valentine.
- David⁶ b. 1775.
- Phebe⁶ 1777.
- John⁶ b. 1779, m. Sarah Post, dau. of Henry.
- Sarah⁶ b. 1782, m. Alvan Hyatt.
- Oliver.⁶

Children of JOHN⁶ and Sarah:
- Henry⁷ m. a Conklin.
- Maria⁷ m. Stephen Willets.
- Lydia⁷ m. Robert R. Willets.
- Wm. P.⁷ m.

JOHN³ TITUS (Edmund² Robert¹) m. 2d, 1732, Mary (widow of John Smith, son of Richard) and had son:
RICHARD⁴ who m. 1st ——, m. 2d Elisabeth Palmer, and had:
- Margery⁵ b. 1762, Samuel⁵ b. 1765.
- Elisabeth⁵ b. 1767, m. 1786, Jordan Wright.

Titus Family.

PETER³ TITUS (Edmond² Robert¹) m. Martha Jackson, he b. 1674, d. 1753, their children were:

Sarah⁴ m. a Barnes.

Hannah⁴ m. (? Thomas) Seaman.

Daniel⁴ d. 1756, gave property to brothers, sisters, E. Townsend, and Mary wife of James Titus for her daughters Parafine and Sarah.

Richard⁴ m. 1736, Mary Peters, dau. of Dr. Charles, he d. 1784.

Peter⁴ m. Mary Scudder.

Elisabeth⁴ m. Henry Townsend.

James⁴ m. Mary, he d., left son James⁵ who m. Jane Seaman.

John⁴ m. Amy Barker, dau. of Samuel.

Mary⁴ m. Jecamiah Scott.

RICHARD⁴ TITUS (Peter³ Edmond² Robert¹) and Mary Peters, had:

Charles⁵ m. Margaret Titus.

Peter⁵ m. 1765, Elisabeth Mudge.

Mary⁵ m. Richard Townsend.

Zipporah⁵ unm.

PETER⁵ TITUS (Richard⁴ Peter³ Edmond² Robert¹) and Elisabeth (Mudge), had:

Mary⁶ b. 1765, m. 1784, Leonard Seaman, she d. 1788, and had: Zebulun Seaman m. Amelia Clussman, and Mary Elizabeth b. 1786, m. Silas Carle.

Sarah⁶ b. 1767, d. 1829, m. Oliver Hewlett and had Mary, Elisabeth, Oliver, Peter, Joseph, Charles, Robert, Susan, Mary and Charlotte.

Phebe⁶ b. 1770, m. Jacob Carle and had Ann, Mary, John, Elisabeth and Edward.

Michael⁶ b. 1772, m. Alice Hicks.

Margaret⁶ b. 1774, m. 1795, Whitehead Hicks, d. 1836.

Titus Family. 113

George⁶ b. 1776, m. 1806 Mary Carle, b. 1781, dau. of John and Phebe.

Robert⁶ b. 1779, Susan b. 17—, Zipporah, b. 1786.

MICHAEL⁶ TITUS (Peter⁵ Richard⁴ Peter³ Edmond² Robert¹) and Alice (Hicks) had:
Phebe,⁷ Peter,⁷ Robert,⁷ Wm. H.,⁷ George⁷ and Allen.⁷

GEORGE⁶ TITUS (Peter⁵ Richard⁴ Peter³ Edmond² Robert¹) and Mary (Carle) had:
Robert⁷ and Silas.⁷

Margaret⁶ and Whitehead Hicks had Gilbert, Robert,⁷ Mary, Elisabeth, Jane, Margaret, Susan, Ann, Catharine and Henrietta.

PETER⁴ TITUS (Peter³ Edmond² Robert¹) m. Mary Scudder and had:
Samuel⁵ b. 1748, m. 1773, Abigail Robbins, dau. of Jeremiah and Hannah (Carr) he d. 1809.
Jacob⁵ not m., Robert⁵ not m.
Henry⁵ m. Martha Seaman.
Phebe⁵ m. John Van De Water.

SAMUEL⁵ TITUS (Peter⁴ Peter³ Edmond² Robert¹) and Abigail (Robbins) had:
John⁶ b. 1774, d., Stephen⁶ b. 1776, d., George b. 1778, d. 1780.
Rosetta⁶ b. 1779, m. Daniel Post.
Hannah⁶ b. 1781, m. Jacob Mudge.
Mary⁶ b. 1783, m. Dec. 4, 1812, Richard Willets.
Elisabeth⁶ b. 1785, m. Nicholas Hallock, she d. 1838.
Samuel B.⁶ b. 1787, m. Phebe Frost, dau. of Charles and Mary (Rushmore).
David⁶ b. 1788, m. Jane Collins.
Martha⁶ b. 1790, m. Jacob Valentine, son of Lewis.
Peter⁶ b. 1792, m. Sarah Reynolds.
Ann⁶ b. 1794, m. Stephen Valentine, son of Lewis,

To our dear friends and brethren at Flushing:

This is to Certify that Silas Titus hath given us good Satisfaction concerning his buying his brother's goods when took from him on Truth's account having condemned the act, desiring our forgiveness for the same.

Signed at the Monthly Meeting of Westbury held 29, 9, 1704, by

Edmond Titus, Benjamin Seaman, Richard Seaman, Thomas Powell, John Titus, Nathaniel Seaman, Thomas Pearsall, Thomas Powell, jun., William Willis, John Hallock.

SILAS[3] TITUS (Edmond[2] Robert[1]) b. 1676, m. Sarah Haight, dau. of Samuel and Sarah of Flushing, and had:

    Edmond[4] b. 1705, m. Sarah Titus, dau. of John and Sarah (Willis), he d. 1756.

    Temperance[4] b. 1707, m. 1730, Thomas Hicks, son of Jacob.

    Silas[4] b. 1709, m. Sarah Townsend, dau. of Thomas, and went to Pennsylvania.

    Sarah[4] b. 1712, m. Wm. Walmsley, went to N. J.

    Hannah[4] b. 1714, d.

    Phebe[4] b. 1717, m. 1736, Benjamin Hicks, son of Jacob.

    David[4] b. 1719, m. 1741, Hannah, dau. of Jacob Hicks, he d. before 1747.

    William[4] b. 1722, m. 1747, Sarah, dau. of Samuel Bowne and lived on the old place at Westbury.

    Mary[4] b. 1725, m. 1754, Thomas Walton, son of Jeremiah and Elisabeth of Pennsylvania.

EDMOND[4] TITUS (Silas[3] Edmond[2] Robt.[1]) and Sarah had:

    Phebe[5] b. 22, 4, 1733, m. 1753, Joseph Prior, son of Samuel and Mary (Powell).

Titus Family.

Sarah[5] b. 27, 8, 1735.
Martha[5] b. 24, 1, 1737, she d. 1769.
Mary[5] b. 17, 7, 1740, m. 1761, Henry Post, son of Richard and Mary.
Hannah[5] b. 12, 7, 1745, m. 1764, Willets Kirby, son of William and Sarah (Willets).

WILLIAM[4] TITUS (Silas[3] Edmund[2] Robert[1]) and Sarah (Bowne) had:
Abigail[5] b. 1755, Elisabeth b. 1758, Sarah b. 1760, Silas b. 1765 and Mary b. 1769.

SAMUEL[2] TITUS (Robert[1]), of Huntington, says, in 1683, My father and two of my brothers were freely admitted as inhabitants and Townsmen of Oysterbay about 30 years ago.

Children of SAMUEL[2] Titus, of Huntington:
Hannah[3] b. 1669, Rebecca b. 1675, Patience b. 1679, Experience b. 1680.

Children of Abial,[2] son of Robert[1]:
Mary[3] b. 1673, Rebecca[3] b. 1676, Abial[3] b. 1678, Henry[3] b. 1681, John[3] b. 1684.

CONTENT[2] TITUS, son of Robt.[1] b. 1643 at Weymouth, Mass., m. Elisabeth, dau. of Rev. John Moore and Margaret (Howell). Children:
Robert[3] lived in Deleware.
Silas[3] m. 1715, Sarah, dau. of Ephraim Hunt, lived at Newton, L. I.
John.[3]
Timothy[3] lived at Hopewell, N. J.
Hannah[3] unm.
Phebe[3] m. Jonathan Hunt.
Abigail m. George Furness.

Children of Silas[3] and Sarah (Hunt) Titus:
Ephraim[4] b. at Hopewell, N. J.
Edward[4] John[4] Sarah[4] and Susanna.[4]

Titus Family.

Will 1725. Henry Titus of Huntington says, bro Johns son Henry, bro Abials sons Abial and Timothy. Wife Rachel, Executor bro John Pugsley of Westchester.

Will 1754. John Titus of Huntington wife Martha; children Platt Jonathan, Zebulun, Israel, Joseph, John, Abial, Elisabeth Titus, and Mary Hugens, Grandsons, John and Jonas.

Will 1754. Henry Titus of Huntington says, wife Sarah, and son Henry. He mentions three brothers, Jonathan, Platt and Zebulun, Loving uncle Amos Platt and brother Isaac Smith Executors.

Will 1750. Philip Titus, wife Charity eldest son Philip and son Samuel, daughters, Rebecca, Mary and Martha quite young, bro Abial of Huntington. Ex.

ALMY FAMILY.

WILLIAM[1] ALMY, b. 1601, m. Audrey ———, their son Christopher Almy m. Elisabeth Cornell, dau. of Thomas and Rebecca. Thomas and Rebecca Cornell came to L. I. Job Almy, son of Christopher and Elizabeth, m. Mary Unthank, dau. of Christopher and Susanna Unthank, Rebecca Almy b. 1671, dau. of Job and Mary, m. 1792, John[4] Townsend, of (Thomas[3] John[2] Thomas[1]), Audrey Almy, dau. of Job and Mary, b. 1669, m. James Townsend, son of John and Susanna.

Job Almy d. 1684, his widow Mary (Unthank) became the second wife of Thomas[3] Townsend, father of John.[4]

TOWNSEND FAMILY.

In 1638 THOMAS[1] TOWNSEND was a farmer at Lynn, Mass., with sons John[2] d. 1669, Thomas,[2] Henry[2] and Richard,[2] he d. 1660.

JOHN[2] TOWNSEND (Thomas[1]) m. ? Elisabeth Montgomery, ? perhaps dau. of Robert Cole, they had children:

    John[3] m. 1st Susanna Harcourt, dau. of Richard, m. 2d Phebe, he d. 1709.

    Thomas[3] m. 1st ——, m 2d Mary Almy, widow of Job.

    James[3] m. 1st Elisabeth Wright, m. 2d Jane Ruddock, m. 3d Delivered Pratt.

    Elisabeth[3] m. Gideon Wright.

    Anne.[3]

    Rose[3] m. 1st John Wicks, m. 2d Samuel Hayden.

    Sarah.[3]

    George[3] m. 1684 Mary Hawxhurst, had George[4] b. 1687, m. 1711 Rosanna Coles.

    Daniel.[3]

JOHN[3] TOWNSEND (John[2] Thomas[1]) and Susanna, had:

    James[4] m. Audrey Almy, dau. of Job and Mary (Unthank).

    Thomas,[4] Nathaniel,[4] Hannah.[4]

    Elisabeth[4] m. 1st Theophilus Phillips, m. 2d Thomas[1] Powell.

Solomon,[4] in Rhode Island in 1707.
One more daughter.

JAMES[4] TOWNSEND (John[3] John[2] Thomas[1]) and Audrey, had:

Mary[5] m. Thomas Jackson, son of James.
Deborah[5] m. Abraham Seaman.
JACOB[5] b. 1692, m. Phebe Seaman, dau. of Benj. and Martha, and had:
BENJAMIN[6] b. 1723, who m. Betty Frost, and had six children, he d. 1789.

Frost[7] b. 1749, d. James[7] d. at sea 1790.
Elisabeth[7] m. Henry Mitchell.
Phebe[7] m. Samuel Talman.
Benjamin[7] m. Martha Powell, dau. of Henry and Mary.
George[7] m. Elizabeth Bowne.
Nancy[7] m. Abraham Franklin.

BENJAMIN[7] TOWNSEND (Benjamin[6] Jacob[5] James[4] John[3] John[2] Thomas[1]) m. Martha (Powell), and had:

Benjamin[8] m. Lucy Buckley.
Nancy[8] m. Johannes Jenkins.
Jacob Powell[8] m. Mary A. Barrett.
Elisabeth.[8]
Mary[8] m. Nathaniel Harcourt.

JACOB P.[8] TOWNSEND (Benjamin[7] Benjamin[6] Jacob[5] James[4] John[3] John[2] Thomas[1]) m. Mary A. Barrett, and had:

Elisabeth B.[9]
William Henry[9] m. Theophiler Handly, dau. of Jacob.
Thomas Powell[9] m. Mary Clark.
Caroline[9] m. Dr Quick.
Mary Powell[9] died a young woman.
Louisa P.[9] m. L. P. Hait.

James Augustus[9] m. Elisabeth Marvin.
Amelia[9] m. F. H. Laing.
Harriet[9] m. George Reynolds.
Mary Ann[9] died a young woman.
George W.[9] m. 1st Susan Underhill, m. 2d M. Louisa (Seaman) widow Carle.

GEORGE[9] W. TOWNSEND and Susan, had:
Harriet Reynolds.[10]
Anna Louisa[10] m. Howe Thornton.
Mary Rushmore[10] m. John Gorham.

The Jacob Powell Townsend family lived at Milton, Ulster county, N. Y.

THOMAS[3] TOWNSEND (John[2] Thos.[1]) m. 1st unknown, children:
Temperance and Sylvanus died small.
John[4] b. 1672, m. 1st April, 1692, Rebecca Almy, m. 2d Rose Wright, dau. of Peter, he d. 1709.
Freelove[4] b. 1674, m. Thomas Jones, from Rhode Island, settled at Massapequa, L. I.
Sarah[4] b. 1679, m. Abraham Underhill.
Phebe[4] b.— she d. 26, 12, 1726.

Married 2d Mary (Unthank) widow of Job Almy and went in 1686 to Rhode Island to reside. On the death of his son John in 1709 he came back to Oyster bay. The last time he was on the Records was 1712. There is reason to suppose that he returned to Rhode Island and died there. In 1693 he bought Massapequa of the Indians and gave it to his daughter Freelove and her husband.

JOHN[4] TOWNSEND (Thomas[3] John[2] Thos.[1]) called Rhode Island John and 1st wife Rebecca (Almy), had:
Thomas,[5] of Oblong, Philena[5] and John.[5]
Second wife, Rose Wright, had:
Penn[5] m. 1739, Esther Parrish.

Townsend Family, 121

Rose[5] m. Zebulun Dickinson, son of Joseph and Rose (Townsend).
Children of Rose and Zebulun :
Townsend and Henry.

GEORGE[3] TOWNSEND (John[2] Thos.[1]) m. 1684 Mary Hawxhurst, and had:

Sarah[4] m. Thomas Weeks.
George[4] b. 1687, m. 1711, Rosanna Coles, dau. of of Nathaniel.
Richard[4] b. 1690, m. Susanna Weeks.
Samuel[4] b. 1692, m. Sarah Cooper, dau. of Robt., son of Simon.

Children of GEORGE[4] Townsend and Rosanna :
Rosanna[5] b. 1712, m. Hezekiah Cock.
George[5] b. 1713, m. 1743, Rosanna Youngs, he d. 1802.
William[5] b. 1715, m. Elisabeth, dau. of Henry Cock and Mary Feaks.

Children of SAMUEL[4] and Sarah (Cooper):
Joseph[5] m. 1st Hannah Youngs, dau. Judith m. James Fleet.

JAMES[3] TOWNSEND (John[2] Thos.[1]) m. 1st Elisabeth Wright, dau. of Peter, m. 2d, 1677 Jane Ruddock, dau. of Henry, m. 3d Delivered Pratt, he d. 1698. Children :

Job[4] Alice[4] Daniel[4] Thomas[4] Ruddock[4] Joseph.[4]
Joshua[4] m. Meribah Cock (she m. 2d Micajah Townsend).
REUMOURN[4] b. 1698, d. 1740, m. 1728, Mary Allen b. 1701, d. 1769. Children :
Mary[5] b. 1729, m. William Willis b. 1721, son of John and Abigail.
Restore.[5]
Sarah[5] b. 1736, m. 1751, John Hewlett b. 1731, d. 1812, had son Divine.

16

JOSHUA⁴ TOWNSEND (James³ John² Thos.¹), son of James and Delivered Pratt, m. Miribah Cock, and had:
    Noah⁵ b. 1765, m. Margaret Wright, and had Joshua, d. single.
Widow m. 2d Daniel Thorne, m. 3d John Jackson.
John Townsend of Westchester m. Eliza Platt Horton, he d. 1862. Children:
Josephine.
Dorinda m. Stephen Hyatt.
Melissa m. Reuben W. Flowers.
Caroline m. Thomas Wilson.
John jr. m. Mary E. Adonis.
Leander b. 1810, m. Ann Elisa Wood, dau. of Joseph, and had Mary Elma m. Oct. 4, 1866, James M. Coleman.
John Townsend of Queens county, L. I., m. 1768 Susanna Shotwell of Elizabeth, N. J.

HENRY² TOWNSEND (Thomas¹) m. Annie Cole, dau. of Robert and Mary (Hawxhurst), had children:
    Henry³ m. Deborah Underhill, dau. of Capt. John.
    John³ m. 1693, Esther Smith.
    Mary³ m. John Wright, son of Nicholas.

HENRY³ and Deborah (Underhill) Townsend, had:
    HENRY⁴ m. Eliphal Wright, dau. of John and Mary (Townsend), and had:
        Henry⁵ m. Elisabeth Titus, the beautiful Quakeress, dau. of Peter and Martha (Jackson) Titus.
        Abraham,⁵ Absalom.⁵

HENRY⁵ TOWNSEND (Henry⁴ Henry³ Henry² Thomas¹) m. Elizabeth (Titus) had:
    Nicholas⁶ m. Philadelphia Doughty.
    Martha.⁶

Elisabeth[6] m. John McCoun, and went to Troy.
Phebe.[6]
Sally[6] m. Elisha Tibbetts.
Henry,[6] Peter[6] and Absalom.
NICHOLAS[6] and Philadelphia Townsend, had:
Elisabeth[7] m. James Hallock.
Hannah[7] m. Jacob Cock.
Philadelphia[7] m. Wm. Cock.

JOHN[3] TOWNSEND (Henry[2] Thomas[1]) m. Esther Smith, and had:

Zerviah[4] m. Dr. Matthew Parish, and had: Townsend[2] Parish, who m. Freelove Dodge, and had son Jacob[3] Parish, who m. Freelove Powell, dau. of Henry[4] and Mary (Keen), and had Henry[4] m. Susan M. Delafield, Daniel[4] b. 10 Nov. 1796, m. Mary Ann Harris, Martha[4] m. Allen M. Sherman.

Daniel[4] Parish (Jacob[3] Townsend[2] Dr. Matthew[1]) and Mary Ann had: John,[5] Sarah, Elisabeth, m. Robert J. Dillon.

Mary Powell[5] m. John J. Kingsford, and had nine children.

Henry[5] m. Elisabeth Wainright, and had seven children.

Martha[4] and Allen M. Sherman, had: Margaret,[5] Ann,[5] Thomas[5]

Richard[2] Townsend (Thomas[1]) was a farmer, his 1st wife was Deliverence, dau. of Robert and Mary Cole. They were all residents of Warwick, R. I., in 1655. The children of Richard and Deliverance, were:

Dinah m. Thomas Willets, son of Richard and Mary.

Leah m. John Williams, son of Robert and Sarah.

In 1657, Richard Townsend and his older brothers were all living at Jamaica, L. I., but in 1658 Richard settled at Pawtucket, where he married 2d Elizabeth, dau. of John Wicks, one of the original settlers of Warwick who had changed his place of abode on account of persecution for not joining the authorities against Quakers and others. Richard[2] Townsend died at Jericho, L. I., about 1671. He and his family, and the brother and sisters of both his wives having all removed and settled with their families in Queens Co., L. I. The children of Richard[2] and his 2d wife Elisabeh Wicks, were:

    John[3] m. 1st Phebe, dau. of Robert Williams, m. 2d Mercy ——, he d. 1721.
    Richard[3] m. Ruth Marvin, dau. of John and Hannah (Smith).
    Hannah,[3] Mary,[3] Deliverance.[3]

Richard[2] Townsend's widow m. John Smith of Hempstead, whose first wife was a dau. of Richard and Experience (Gildersleeve), Smith died in 1694. Will gives some property to Richard[3] Townsend, he to provide for his mother and sister Elisabeth Smith.

RICHARD[3] TOWNSEND (Richard[2] Thomas[1]) was living at Hempstead, L. I. in 1693. was married there — bought a farm at Cedar Swamp in 1717, where he died in 1737. His wife was Ruth Marvin, dau. of John and Hannah (Smith). Children:

    Richard[4] b. 1706, died single 1797.
    John[4] b. 1708, m. 1732 Phebe, dau. of Thomas Carman, he d. 1797, she d. 1798.
    Mary[4] m. 1738, Samuel Jackson.
    Timothy[4] m. 1738, Sarah Hewlett.
    Sylvanus[4] m. 1st Susanna Jackson, m. 2d Letitia Hedges.

JOHN[4] TOWNSEND (Richard[3] Richard[2] Thos.[1]) m. Phebe Carman, lived at Westbury, had children:
    Ruth[5] m. Samuel Titus.
    Samuel[5] m. Elisabeth Smith.

Townsend Family.

Thomas[5] b. 1732, m. Mary Loines b. 1734, he d. 1779.
Mary[5] m. Richard Hewlett.
Richard[5] b. 1740, m. 1st 1761 Mary Titus; m. 2d 1770 Rosetta Seaman.

Children of THOMAS[5] Townsend and Mary Loines, dau. of William:

William[6] b. 1756, m. Elisabeth Doughty, went to Cornwall, had children: Mary[7] Elisabeth[7] and Townsend.[7]
Anna[6] b. 1759, m. 1777, Thomas Hanford, went to Nova Scotia.
Jervis[6] b. 1761, and John b. 1765, both died.
Pamela[6] b. 1763, m. 1784 Richard Underhill.
Phebe[6] b. 1767, m. Stephen Rushmore.
John[6] m. Sarah Townsend.
Obadiah[6] m. Phebe Lawrence, dau. of Joseph.
Mary[6] m. Joseph Wood.

OBADIAH[6] and Phebe (Lawrence) Townsend had: Mary[7] Sally[7] Lydia[7] Thomas[7] Effingham[7] and

JOSEPH[7] m. 1st Margaret Sherman, dau. of Isaac no ch.; m. 2d Hannah Whitson, and had:

William[8] m. 1st   m. 2d Anna Willets, dau. of Thomas S. and Rebecca.
Joseph[8] Mary[8] m. George Titus.
Phebe[8] and Lydia.[8]

RICHARD[5] TOWNSEND (John[4] Richard[3] Richard[2] Thos.[1]) and 1st wife Mary Titus had:

Richard[6] b. 1762, m. 1781 Mary Hewlett, he d. 1813.
Mary[6] m. Samuel Titus, son of Samuel and Ruth.
Second wife Rosetta Seaman had:
Thomas S.[6] b. 1771, m. Margaret Nostrant.
John S.[6] Jacob S.[6] Wm. S.[6] and Jackson S.

WILLIS FAMILY.

HENRY[1] WILLIS, a native of England, lived in Wiltshire where his six children were born, m. ———— ————, he d. 1675. Children were :

Sarah[2] b. 1626.

Henry[2] b. 1628, Sept. 14, m. 1654, Mary Peace, b. July 12, 1632; she d. April 23, 1714; he d. July 11, 1714.

Alice[2] b. 1630, Catharine[2] b. 1632, Elisabeth[2] b. 1636, Margery[2] b. 1638.

Henry[2] and Mary lived at town of Devizes until 1667. Elder children born there. The year after the great fire they removed to London, where several children were born. About 1675 Henry and his family (except dau. Mary who came later), emigrated to America, apparently stopped at Philadelphia From thence found a temporary home in Oysterbay. Afterward bought land of Capt. John Seaman and made a home at Wood Edge, now Westbury.

In 1683 Henry Willis bought of Capt. John Seaman 50 acres at the south west end of the great plains at a place called Foster's Meadow. Joseph Petit on the north, on the west Foster's river, on the south a lot of Edmond Titus, east the Common.

"In the house of Henry Willis, Westbury, the 27th of the 9th mo., 1678, George Masters of New York, tailor, married Mary Willis, dau. of Henry and

Willis Family.

Mary." Henry was fined for allowing his dau. to be married by Friends ceremony.

Children of Mary and George Masters were: Mary b. 1679, m. 1702, William Haig, merchant of Antigua; Philadelphia b. 1684, m. Jeremiah Williams, of New York, she d. 1715. Mary and William Haig had daus. Mary b. 1704, and Sarah. Parents both d. 1718 at Pasquotank, North Carolina.

HENRY[2] WILLIS (Henry[1]) m. Mary Peace and had:

Mary[3] m. 1678, George Masters, he d. 1686, she d. 18, 7, 1702.

Elisabeth[3] m. Robert Zane, from Ireland.

William[3] b. 1663, m. 1687, Mary Titus, dau. of Edmond, he d. 3, 7, 1736.

Henry[3] b. 1666, d. 1675.

Rachel[3] m. 8, 9, 1695, Nathaniel Seaman, she d. 1739.

Sarah b. 1671, m. 8, 9, 1695, John Titus, son of Edmond, she d. 1, 1, 1730.

Hester b. at Westbury, 1677, m. 1695, Wm. Albertson, son of William of Newtown, West New Jersey.

WILLIAM[3] WILLIS (Henry[2] Henry[1]) and Mary Titus had:

William[4] b. 1688, m. 1712, Hannah Powell, dau. of Thomas[1] and Elisabeth, he d. 1750.

Henry[4] b. 1690, m. 1712, Phebe Powell, dau. of Thomas[1] and Elisabeth, he d. 1744.

John[4] b. 1693, m. 1715, Abigail Willets, dau. of Richard and Abigail (Powell), he d. 1777.

Jacob[4] b. 1695.

Silas[4] b. 1700.

Samuel[4] b. 1704, m. 1728, Mary Fry b. 1713, she d. 1800, he d. 1790.

Mary[4] b. 1707.

WILLIAM[4] WILLIS (William[3] Henry[2] Henry[1]) and Hannah (Powell), she born 1691, had:

    Mary[5] b. 11, 4, 1713, m. Wm. Bedell, had Mordecai, Rachel, Jehiel, and others.
    Hannah[5] b. 27, 12, 1715, m. Micah Spragg.
    Elisabeth[5] b. 1716, m. Richard Post, widower.
    Rachel[5] b. 5, 7, 1718, she d. 12, 7, 1738.
    Jacob[5] b. 5, 5, 1720, m. Elisabeth (Denton), dau. of James, widow Dusenbury.
    Samuel[5] b. 27, 12, 1721, m. Mary Wright, dau. of Joseph, of Westbury.
    Amy[5] b. 1723, d. 1729.
    Mordecai[5] b. 14, 10, 1725, m. 1752, Mary Clements.
    Silas[5] b. 5, 7, 1727, he d. 1750, Martha[5] b. 29, 7, 1729.
    William[5] b. 5, 12, 1730, m. 1756, Sarah Clements, dau. of Joseph.
    Joseph[5] b. 15, 4, 1734, m., had several children.

HENRY[4] WILLIS (William[3] Henry[2] Henry[1]) and Phebe (Powell), had:

    Mary[5] b. 22, 2, 1713, m. 1732, Richard Post, son of Richard, she d. 13, 5, 1744.
    Silas[5] b. 4, 1, 1715, m. 1741, Ann Pearsall, dau. of Henry, he d. 1745.
    Phebe[5] b. 1, 1, 1718, m. Benjamin Downing, and had Silas, b. 1747, m. Phebe Rushmore, dau. of Isaac, and had son Stephen Downing.

JOHN[4] WILLIS (William[3] Henry[2] Henry[1]) and Abigail, had:

    Phebe[5] b. 1715, m. John Post.
    Richard[5] b. 1716, m. Elisabeth Pine, dau. of James.
    Elisabeth[5] b. 1718, m. Jonathan Seaman, she d. 1777.
    William[5] b. 1720, m. Mary Townsend of Reumourn.
    John[5] b. 1726, m. Margaret Cornell, dau. of Caleb, he d. 1813.
    Stephen[5] b. 1730, m. Sarah Smith, dau. of Jonathan.

Willis Family.

SAMUEL[4] WILLIS (William[3] Henry[2] Henry[1]) and Mary Fry, had:
Mary[5] b. 1731, m. 1st 1748, Thomas Jackson, son of Samuel of Jerusalem, m. 2d, Thomas Jackson of Jericho.
John[5] b. 1734, m. 1755, Elisabeth Mott. } Ch. of Adam Mott & Phebe Willets, dau. of Richard & Abigail (Powell) Willets.
Sarah[5] b. 1736, m. 1755, Adam Mott.
Amy[5] b. 1738, m. 1762, Stephen Mott.
Jane[5] b. 1740, m. a Parsons.
Fry[5] b. 1744, m. Anna Seaman.
Kesia[5] b. 1747, Henry[5] b. 1749, did not marry.
Edmond[5] b. 1752, m. 1778, Abigail Titus, dau. of William and Sarah.
Phebe[5] b. 1756, m. 1779, Edmond Prior, son of Joseph and Phebe.

JACOB[5] WILLIS (William[4] William[3] Henry[2] Henry[1]) and Elisabeth (Denton), had:
Amy,[6] Mary[6] Jane[6] and Abigail.[6]

MORDECAI[5] WILLIS (William[4] William[3] Henry[2] Henry[1]) and Mary Clement, had:
Silas,[6] Oliver,[6] Sarah,[6] Daniel,[6] Betsy,[6] Polly[6] and Jane.[6]

SILAS[5] WILLIS (Henry[4] William[3] Henry[2] Henry[1]) and Ann Pearsall, had:
Jordan[6] b. 15, 2, 1752.
Phebe[6] b. 25, 3, 1745, m. 1766, Solomon Whitson, son of David and Clement (Powell).

WILLIAM[5] WILLIS (John[4] William[3] Henry[2] Henry[1]) and Mary Townsend, had:
Ruth[6] b. 1751, m. Samuel Hewlett.
Sarah[6] b. ——, d. 1787.
Abigail[6] b. 1755, m. 1775, Richard Townsend.
Townsend[6] b. 1757, m. 1783, Hannah Bowne.
Mary,[6] Esther.[6]

JOHN[5] WILLIS (John[4] William[3] Henry[2] Henry[1]) and Margaret Cornell, had:
    Cornell[6] m. Elisabeth Hicks, dau. of ——.
    John[6] m. Sarah Jones.
    Richard[6] died early.
    Charles[6] m, Hannah Whitson.
    William[6] Joshua[6] Elisabeth[6] m. Hewlett Cornell.
    Mary[6] m. a Cornell.

CHARLES[6] WILLIS (John[5] John[4] William[3] Henry[2] Henry[1]) and Hannah Whitson had:
    Charles[7] m. Abigail Albertson, he d. 1894.
    Elisabeth[7] m. Hicks Albertson.

TOWNSEND[6] WILLIS (Wm.[5] John[4] William[3] Henry[2] Henry[1]) and Hannah Bonwe had:
    Mary[7] b. 1783, m. John J. Hewlett.
    Sarah[7] m. William Simonson.
    Townsend[7] m. Mary Coles.
    Hannah.[7]
    Abigail[7] m. 1st Samuel Jones, no ch.; m. 2d Robert Seaman, no ch.
    Jacob[7] m. Phebe Hewlett.
    William[7] m. Letitia Downing.

TOWNSEND[7] WILLIS (Townsend[6] William[5] John[4] William[3] Henry[2] Henry[1]) and Mary Coles had:
    Townsend[8] m. Mary Jackson, dau. of Jacob and Phebe.
    Ethelinda[8] m. Timothy Jackson, son of Obadiah.
    Esther[8] m. Thomas Jackson, son of Obadiah.
    Hannah[8] m. a Whitson.

JOHN[5] WILLIS (Samuel[4] William[3] Henry[2] Henry[1]) m. 1st Elisabeth Mott, and had:
    Adam[6] b. 13, 7, 1757, died in youth.
    Samuel[6] b. 7, 3, 1759, m. 1785, Rachel Pearsall, dau. of Thomas, he d. 1838.

Willis Family. 131

Phebe[6] b. 5, 4, 1761, m. Joshua[4] Powell, son of Joshua.[3]

Elizabeth[6] d. 1683.

SAMUEL[5] WILLIS (John[4] Samuel[3] William[2] Henry[2] Henry[1]) and Rachel Pearsall had:

    Henry[7] b. 1786, m. 1813 Phebe Post, dau. of Edmond, he d. 1865.

        Phebe[7] b. 1787, m. James Post, son of Henry, she d. 1883.

    John[7] b. 1793, m. Mary W. Kirby, dau. of Jacob and Mary.

    Amy[7] b. 1797, m. Townsend Rushmore, son of Isaac and Phebe.

HENRY[7] WILLIS and Phebe Post had:

Samuel[8] m. Catherine Post, dau. of Joseph.

Edmond P.[8] m. 1st ——, m. 2d Sarah (Kirby), widow of Jeffries Hallowell.

Catherine[8] unm.

Isaac[8] m. Mary H. Seaman, dau. of Robert.

Samuel[8] and Catherine had Mary, m. Augustus Albertson, and Phebe.

Isaac[8] and Mary H. had Henry and Robert S.

JOHN[7] WILLIS (Samuel[6] John[5] Samuel[4] William[3] Henry[2] Henry[1]) and Mary (Kirby) had:

    Edward[8] m. Elisabeth H. Seaman, dau. of Robert.

    Mary F.[8] m. Isaac Hicks, son of John and Sarah.

    Rachel W.[8] b. 1820, m. Samuel Hicks, son of John and Sarah.

    Lucretia Mott[8] died small.

Edward[8] and Elisabeth H. (Seaman) Willis had:

Sarah.[9] 2 ch. died.

    Henrietta[9] m. Stephen Underhill, son of Jordon and Hannah.

Willis Family.

FRY[5] WILLIS (Samuel[4] William[3] Henry[2] Henry[1]) m. 1746, Annie Seaman, dau. of Thomas and Hannah (Willets) Seaman and had :
Isaac[6] died.
 Thomas[6] b. 1771, m. 1st 1795, Phebe Searing ; 2d Phebe Young, dau. of —— Young and Dorcas Hallock, had Mary[7] m. Samuel Smith.

EDMOND[5] WILLIS (Samuel[4] William[3] Henry[2] Henry[1]) m. 1778 Abigail Titus and had :
William[6] m. Annie W.

Hutton says : May, 1638, shipped for New England from Southampton, John Fry, of Basing (wheelwright), his wife and three children.

Westbury Monthly Meeting Records give us the m. 1707, of Mary, dau. of Wm. and Tamison Fry (she d. 1758), from Old England, and William Gladding, by Friends' ceremony. Wm. Fry died 1717.

In 1686 John Fry, jr., son of John and Frances Fry, came from England. m. Mary, dau. of Richard and Mary Willets. She died 1687. Son John b. 1687, m. 1711, 10, 19, Mary, dau. of John Urquhart. Their little dau. Mary b. 1712, was left an orphan by the death of both parents in 1714. John Urquhart and the elder John Fry had both removed to New Jersey and the little one was brought up by the executors of her father's will. Wm. Willis was one of the executors and she was often cared for in his family. A Bible given to the little one by Francis Fry, her great grandmother, has a name written in it three times by Samuel Willis. First, Mary Fry, her book ; years afterwards, Mary Willis, her book ; still later, Samuel Willis, his book.

Fry Willis' house stands on land adjoining the fence and upon the hill in the line of the division between the town of Oyster bay and Robert Wil-

Willis Family. 133

liams, his patent, northeastly course by William Kirby's cow yard east 28 degrees till it comes to Wm. Jones' Round Swamp, between my land and Jeremiah Robbins his land.   SAMUEL WILLIS.

ZANE, Elisabeth Willis and Robert Zane had: Esther, Rachel and Robert Zane.

In 1677 Robert Zane came from Ireland with friends named Thompson and settled first at Salem, removed in 1682 to Newtown with Thomas Sharpless and others.

SEAMAN FAMILY.

Capt. JOHN¹ SEAMAN m. 1st Elisabeth, dau. of John Strickland, and had :
John² m. Hannah Williams.
Jonathan² m. Jane.
Benjamin² m. Martha Titus, dau. of Edmund and Martha (Washburne).
Solomon² m. Elizabeth Linnington, dau. of Henry, he d. 1733.
Elisabeth² m. John Jackson, son of Robert and Agnes (Washburne).
Capt. JOHN m. 2d Martha Moore, dau. of Thomas and Martha (Youngs), and had :
Thomas² m. Mary?
Samuel² m. Phebe Hicks, dau. of Thomas.
Nathaniel² m. 1695, Rachel Willis, dau. of Henry and Mary (Peace).
Richard² b. 1673, m. 1693, Jane Mott, dau. of Adam² and Mary (Stillwell), he d. 1749.
Sarah² m. John Mott, son of Adam¹ and Jane Hewlett.
Martha² m. Nathaniel Pearsall, son of Henry.
Hannah² m. a Carman.
Deborah² m. a Kirk.
———² m, a Carman, d. before 1694.
Mary² m. Thomas Pearsall, of Henry.
One² did not marry.

JOHN[2] SEAMAN (Capt. John[1]) and wife, had :
John[3] died.
Joseph[3] m. and had Joseph and others.
Hannah[3] m. William Mott.
JONATHAN[2] SEAMAN (Capt. John[1]), m. Jane and had :
  David[3] m. Temperance, dau. of John and Leah (Townsend) Williams, he d.
  Jonathan[3] m. Elisabeth Denton, and went to Kakiat.
  John[3] m. Hannah, dau. of John and Leah (Townsend) Williams.
  Joseph[3] went to Kakiat.
  Caleb[3] m.
DAVID[3] SEAMAN (Jonathan[2] Capt. John[1]) was a judge of the Court of Common Pleas in 1732, m. Temperance Williams, and had :
  David[4] b. 1709, m. 1737, Mary Willets, b. 1721, dau. of Jacob and Mary (Jackson), they had 15 children.
  Zebulun[4] b. 1718, m. Phebe Valentine, dau. of Obadiah and Martha (Willets). He was in the Assembly at Albany from 1769 to 1775. The Assembly offered a premium for the best linen that the Assemblymen could produce. They to raise the flax, the wives to spin and (perhaps weave) the cloth. Zebulon raised the flax, Phebe spun the thread, and they took the premium. A piece of the *homespun* linen is in the hands of the compiler of this.
ZEBULUN[4] and Phebe, had :
Leah[5] b. 1744, m. Thomas Willets.
Mary[5] b. 1745, m. Jordan Seaman, son of Giles and Letitia (Onderdonck), she d. 1790.
Zebulun[5] b. 1747, m. Jane Jackson, he d. 1806.

Seaman Family.

John W.⁵ b. 1749, m. Rebecca Demilt, he d. 1826.
Martha⁵ b. 1755, m. Daniel Willets she, d. 1816.
Leonard⁵ b. 1762, m. 1784, 1st Mary Titus, 2d Leah Simonson he d. 1821.
Phebe⁵ Esther⁵ Rachel⁵ and George all died small.
²Phebe⁵ m. Samuel Searing.

ZEBULUN⁵ SEAMAN (Zebulun⁴ David³ Jonathan² Capt. John¹) and Jane (Jackson) had :
Richard⁶ m. 1st Margaret Simonson, 2d Mary Allen.
Jacob⁶ m. a Conklyn.

The children of RICHARD⁶ and Margaret were
Jane⁷ m. Timothy Boerum.
Zebulun⁷ m. Jane Cornwell.
Leonard⁷ m. Mary Ann Allen.

JOHN W.⁵ SEAMAN (Zebulun⁴ David³ Jonathan² Capt. John¹) m. Rebecca Demilt and had .
George⁶ m. Sarah Wright.
Phebe⁶ m. Robert Mitchell.
Mary⁶ m. Simeon Searing she d. 1815.
Rebecca⁶ m. Simeon Searing she d. 1871.
Martha⁶ m. Luther Anthony.

The children of GEORGE⁶ and Sarah (Wright) were :
Jane⁷ m. John Gray.
Elisa⁷ d. John⁷ W. d.

LEONARD⁵ SEAMEN, (Zebulun⁴ David³ Jonathan² Capt. John¹) and 1st wife Mary (Titus) had :
Mary E. ⁶ b. Oct. 19, 1786, m. Silas Carle.
Zebulun⁶ b. July 12, 1788, m. Amelia Clussman, he d. 1842.
Second wife Leah (Simonson) had :
William⁶ b. Feb. 24, 1791 m. Hannah Weed March 3, 1813, he d. Jan. 19. 1832.

The children of ZEBULUN⁶ SEAMAN and Amelia (Clussman) were:
Mary E.⁷ b. Apr. 19, 1819, m. William B. Scott.
Caroline⁷ b. Dec. 29, 1820.
Catharine L.⁷ b. Nov. 14, 1822.
Amelia⁷ b. Aug. 25, 1825.
John A.⁷ b. July 24, 1827.
Wm. L.⁷ Silas C.⁷ George⁷ M.
The children of WILLIAM⁶ SEAMAN and Hannah (Weed) were:
Mary E.⁷ b. Apr. 29, 1816, m. James A. Harriman,
Margaret⁷ b. Feb. 12, 1818, m. Richard L. Schoonmaker.
Leonard W.⁷ b. May 14, 1820, d. Oct. 31, 1841.
Martha⁷ b. Sept. 12, 1822, m. Henry MacDonald.
Anna Leah⁷ b. Sept. 21, 1824, m. Gilbert Sayres, of Jamaica, L. I.
Hannah Maria⁷ b. May 26, 1827, m. James A. Henry, of Jamaica, L. I.

JONATHAN³ SEAMAN (Jonathan², Capt. John¹), m. Elisabeth Denton (his will proved, 1755; dated in Orange county, N. Y.), and had:
Jonathan⁴ went to Virginia, left one son and one daughter.
Jonas⁴ m. Jane D. Moss, went to Virginia, had seven sons and seven daughters.
Jecaniah⁴ m. Rachel Secor.
John⁴ died.
Elisabeth⁴ m. John Palmer.
Martha⁴ m. Michael Vandervort.
Phebe⁴ m. Samuel Coe.
Hannah⁴ m. William Coe.

JECANIAH⁴ SEAMAN and Rachel (Secor), had:
Jonathan⁵ m. Mary Conklin.
Jonas⁵ m. Martha Anthony.

Elisabeth[5] m. Isaac Odell. John Onderdonck is
    their grandson.
Hannah[5] m. John Monroe.
Esther[5] m. Justin Monroe.
Anna[5] m. Richard Wilks.
Phebe[5] m. Daniel Lawrence.
Martha[5] Polly[5] Catharine[5] m. Robert Cayton.
JONATHAN[5] SEAMAN and Mary Conklin, had:
Hannah.[6]
Phebe[6] m. William Furman.
Jecaniah[6] and Catharine[6] died.
Amy[6] m. William Furman.
Rachel[6] m. John Coe, live in Michigan.
William[6] m. Elisabeth Odell and had son Jonathan.
Daniel[6] m. Margaret Fritts[11] and had Thomas and
    William.
JONAS[5] SEAMAN and Martha (Anthony) had:
Rachel[6] m. Jacob Young.
Elisabeth[6] m. Jesse Baldwin.
Esther[6] and Susan[6] died.
Martha[6] m. Josiah Conklin. Sarah.[6]
Phebe[6] m. William Williams.
John[6] m. Elisabeth Fritts, and had: Charles,[7]
    Thomas,[7] Anne,[7] Elbert.[7]
JOHN[3] SEAMAN (Jonathan,[2] Capt. John[1]), m.
Hannah Williams, dau. of John and Leah (Townsend,) and had:
William[4] b. June 28, 1706, m. 1743, Martha Seaman, by Friends Ceremony.
Robert[4] m. 1743, by Friends Ceremony, Esther
    Williams, of Thos.
John[4]
Jonathan[4] m. Elisabeth, dau. of John Willis and
    Abigail (Willets).

WILLIAM[4] SEAMAN and Martha had:
Edmund[5] b. 1743, d. 1744, Micah[5] b. 1745, d. 1746.
Jane[5] b. Nov. 16, 1746, m. 1780, David Ketcham.
John[5] d. 1748, Benjamin[5] d. 1750, John[5] d. 1756.
ROBERT[4] SEAMAN (John[3] Jonathan[2] Capt. John[1]), m. Esther Williams, of Thomas and Mary (Willets), widow Scudder, and had:
William[5] m. Mary Jackson, he d. 22, 4, 1729.
Ch. of WILLIAM[5] SEAMAN and Mary Jackson were:
David[6] b. June 12, 1770, m. Sarah Kirby.
Mary[6] b. 27, 9, 1774, m. Jacob Kirby.
Hannah[6] b. 1776, m. Samuel Willets.
Esther[6] b. 30, 4, 1779, m. Willet Robbins.
DAVID SEAMAN[6] and Sarah (Kirby) had:
Robert[7] b. Oct. 31, 1792, m. Sarah Hicks, of Elias and Jemima.
Hannah[7] b. July 21, 1794, d. 1795.
William[7] b. July 21, 1796, m. Caroline Hicks, dau. of Valentine and Abigail.
Phebe[7] b. July 26, 1798, m. James C. Haviland, she d. 1863.
Lydia[7] b. Feb. 7, 1802, d. 1864.
Esther[7] b.   m. William Haviland.
ROBERT[7] SEAMAN (David[6] William[5] Robert[4] John[3] Jonathan[2] Capt. John[1]), and Sarah had:
Phebe[8] died.
Hannah[8] m. Matthew F. Robbins.
Willet[8] d.
Elizabeth[8] m. 1839 Edward Willis.
Elias H.[8] m. Phebe Underhill.
Willet[8] m. Mary Wing.
Mary[8] m. Isaac Willis, son of Henry and Phebe.

Dr. WILLIAM[7] SEAMAN (David[6] Wm.[5] Robt.[4] John[3] Jonathan[2] Capt. John[1]), and Caroline, had:

Valentine H.[8] m. Rebecca Cromwell, dau. of David and Rebecca.

Sarah[8] m. Henry Cromwell, son of David and Rebecca.

Samuel[8] m. Hannah Husband, of Philadelphia.

JONATHAN[4] SEAMAN (John[3] Jonathan[2] Capt. John[1]), and Elizabeth (Willis) had:

Jemima[5] m. Elias Hicks, the preacher, she d. 17, 3, 1829.

David[5] d. 10, 5, 1770.

CALEB[3] SEAMAN (Jonathan[2], Capt. John[1]), m. ———, and had:

Caleb,[3] Joshua.[3]

Nehemiah[3] he was drowned in the S. Bay.

ISAAC[3] m. July 5, 1763, Phebe Jackson, dau. of Thomas and Mary (Townsend), and had:

Daniel[4] b. April 21, 1766, m. Mary Duryea, b. Oct. 20, 1771, he d. Aug. 3, 1844, she d. Sept. 7, 1861.

James[4] m. Jerusha Powell, dau. of Joseph.

Children of DANIEL[4] Seaman and Mary (Duryea), were:

Phebe[5] b. May 3, 1792, m. Epenetus Fleet, Feb. 26, 1814, she d. July 30, 1853.

Jermima[5] b. Sept. 13. 1798, m. Benjamin Seaman son of Enoch, she d. Dec. 22, 1863.

Ann[5] b. Oct. 22, 1806, d. July 10, 1848.

Alfred[5] b. Sept. 12, 1809, m. Martha Powell, b. April 13, 1816, she d. Oct. 6, 1861.

ALFRED[5] SEAMAN and Martha (Powell), had:

Thomas[6] b. Feb. 22, 1835, m. ———, has Alfred[7] m. and others.

Mary E.[6] b. Oct 22, 1837, m. Elbert Smith, son of Hewlett and Nancy (Post).

Catharine[6] b. May 5, 1841, m. John Wesley Southerd.
Esther[6] b. Sept. 20, 1843, m.
Daniel[6] b. Aug. 7, 1847, d. Sept. 3, 1849.
Anne[6] b. July 13, 1850, m.
Jemima[6] b. Jan. 24, 1852, d. March 2, 1861.
JAMES[4] SEAMAN (Isaac,[3] Jonathan[2], Capt. John[1]), m. Jerusha Powell, and had :
Townsend[5] m. a Smith.
Fannie[5] m. Samuel Nichols.
Phebe[5] m. Henry Nichols.

BENJAMIN[2] SEAMAN (Capt. John[1]), m. Martha Titus, dau. of Edmond and Martha (Washburne), he d. 1733, and had :
Benjamin[3] b. 1685, m. Jane Mott, dau. of Joseph and Mary (Mott), he d. 1729.
Martha[3] m. Jonathan Rowland.
Jane[3] m. Joseph Clements.
Jacob[3] m. Mary Seaman, dau. of Samuel and Phebe (Hicks), he d. 1766.
James[3] m. Martha Seaman, dau. of Samuel and Phebe (Hicks), he d. 1781.
Phebe[3] b. 1699, m. Jacob Townsend, b. 1692, he d. 1742, she d. 1774.
Elisabeth[3] m. 1st James Worden ; m. 2d Thomas Rushmore.
Temperance[3] m. 1st a Kirk; m. 2d Joseph Wright.
Solomon, m. 1740, Hannah Seaman, dau. of Thomas.
Hannah[3] m. a Denton.

BENJAMIN[3] Seaman and Jane (Mott), had :
Elisabeth[4] b. 1710, m. Amos Underhill, they lived at Flushing.
Martha[4] b. 1711, m. 1743, William Seaman, b. 1706, son of John and Hannah (Williams).

Jane[4] b. 1713, m. 1731, John Robbins.
Miriam[4] b. 1716, d. 1729. Hannah, b. 1718, d.
Benjamin[4] b. 1719, m. Elisabeth Mott, dau. of Adam, of Staten Island.
Ann,[4] Phebe,[4] Mary,[4] Edmond,[4] all d. early.
SOLOMON[3] SEAMAN (Benj.[2] Capt. John[1]) and Hannah had:
Thomas[4] he was a Schoolmaster, d. single.
David[4] he was a Saddler, d. single, Almy[4] d single.
Martha[4] m. a Vandewater.
Israel[4] m. Sarah Rowland of Jonathan[2] and Hannah (Marvin.)
Mary[4] m. Joshua Buffett.
Deborah[4] m. June 20, 1773, Samuel Jackson, son of Thomas and Mary (Townsend.)
ISRAEL[4] SEAMAN and Sarah (Rowland) had:
Solomon[5] d.
Benjamin[5] m. Jane Rhinehart.
Almy[5] m. William D. Jones, son of David and Elisabeth (Seaman).
Benjamin[6] Seaman and Jane Rhinehart had:
Israel[6], Sarah[5] not m. Almy[5] not m. Mary Jane[5] not m.
Benjamin[6] not m. David[5] d. an infant.
John F.[6] m. F. Jeanette Rogers.
J Milton[6] m. Sarah L. B. Goodwin.
Martha Ann[6] m. Samuel L. St. John.
JOHN F. SEAMAN and Jeanette had:
Agnes Gertrude[7] Henrietta V. W.,[7] and Adae[7] d. an infant.
J. MILTON[6] SEAMAN and Sarah had:
Tullius G.[7] Alma[7] George[7] John[7] and Milton[7].
Benjamin[5] and Jane and their families are of Canada.

SOLOMON[2] SEAMAN (Capt. John[1]) m. Elisabeth, dau. of Henry Linnington and Catherine. They had two sons who went to Maryland besides:
Solomon[3] m. 1705, Mary Mott.
Henry[3]
Deborah[3] m. 1702, Joseph, son of Hope Willets.
Mary.[3]
Abigail.[3]
SOLOMON[3] SEAMAN and Mary Mott had son SOLOMON[4], who m. Hannah and had:
Samuel[5] b. 1741 m. a Hall, he d. Dec. 11, 1837, aged 96 years.
Martha[5] m. Epenetus Burtis.
Jacob[5] m. had Phebe[6] Elisabeth[6] Joseph[6] James[6] and Jane[6] m. an Underhill.
Thomas[5] m. and had 11 children Adam[6] m. Phebe Post Wm.[6] m. Abigail Bedell, Thomas[6] m. Ann Smith and Elisabeth Mott, Parmenus[6] m. Sarah Post, Susan[6] m. Jackson Post, Sally m. Isaac Post.
BENJAMIN[5] m. 1st Mary and 2d Hannah Denton and had:
Mary[6] m. Daniel Hewlett.
Rhoda[6] m. a Campbell.
Jane[6] m. Samuel Clowes.
Cornelia[6] m. Oliver Hewlett.
BENJAMIN[4] SEAMAN (Benjamin[3] Benjamin[2] Capt. John[1]) m. Elizabeth Mott, and had:
Edmond[5] m. and had Catharine,[6] Robert,[6] and John.[6]
Benjamin[5] m. and had George[6] and Catharine.
William[5] m. and had Henry John,[6] Benson,[6] Elizabeth,[6] Harriet,[6] Julia,[6] William,[6] Rebecca,[6] ——,[6] Fannie,[6] Susan M.[6]
John[5] died.
Henry[5] b. 1761, m. 1784, Sarah Billop, b. 1765, and

had Billop,[6] (she d. 1811, he d. 1799), who m. and had Henry J.,[7] Hester M.,[7] Catharine,[7] and Edmond.[7]

Jasper F.[6]

Edward.[6]

Frances J.[6] b. 1797, m. 1817, Wm. Wilmot Townsend, b. 1795, he d. 1827, she d. 1851.

Henry J.[6]

JACOB[3] SEAMAN (Benjamin[2] Capt. John[1]) and Mary (Seaman) had:

Jane[4] m. Richard Jackson.

Amy[4] m. Obadiah Jackson.

Deborah[4] m. 1755, Thomas Williams.

Jacob[4] m. Margaret Birdsell, no ch.

JAMES[3] SEAMAN (Benj'n[2] Capt. John[1]), and Martha, had:

Phebe[4] m. John Birdsall.

Mary[4] m. 1st, a Hunt, m. 2d, Jordan Seaman.

Benjamin[4] m. 1758, Letitia Allen, dau. of Thomas and Elizabeth (Seaman).

Martha[4] m. Benjamin Drake.

BENJAMIN[4] SEAMAN and Letitia, had:

Enoch[5] m. Mary Smith, dau. of

Esther[5] m. Almy,[5] m. Braddock Seaman, son of Thomas and Martha (Jackson).

Martha[5] m. John Althouse.

ENOCH[5] SEAMAN and Mary (Smith) had:

James[6] m. E. Nichols, and had Mary,[7] she m. Stephen Jackson.

Elisabeth[6] d. Benj'n,[6] John,[6] Silas[6] and Willet,[6] all d.

Jacob[6] m. Dorothy Haff, and had Enoch,[7] m. E. Box, and Wm.,[7] m. E. Smith.

Benjamin[6] m, Jemima Seaman, dau. of Daniel and Mary (Duryea).

Letitia⁶ m. Willet Seaman, son of John and Mary (Whitson).

BENJAMIN⁶ Seaman and Jemima, had:

Elizabeth⁷ d. small, another Elizabeth⁷ b. much later, an interesting young woman, d. single.

Phebe⁷ m. John Jackson Seaman.

Mary Ann⁷ m. John Powell, son of Robert and Mary (Cornelius).

Martha⁷ m. Edward H. Seaman, son of Ardon and Elizabeth (Merritt).

Letitia⁷ m. Wm. S. Hicks, son of Whitehead and Mary Ann (Merritt).

Charlotte⁷ m. Daniel Valentine.

Almy⁷ m. William Henry Jones, son of Elbert and Mary (Seaman).

Benjamin B.⁷ m. Rosena N. Lyle, Sept. 19, 1865.

SAMUEL² SEAMAN (Capt. John¹) m. Phebe Hicks and had:

Samuel³ m. and had several children.

Mary³ m. Jacob Seaman.

Martha³ m. James Seaman.

Hicks³ m. 1726, Elisabeth Barnes. Went to live in Westchester co.; had a farm in 1764 near Croton river.

SAMUEL³ SEAMAN, "a freeholder in 1685 living with his father," had children:

Phebe,⁴ Charity,⁴ Samuel,⁴ Deborah.⁴ There were three later children:

Amelia⁴ m. Jonathan Smith.

Margaret⁴ m. Ambrose Seaman.

Anna⁴ m. Peter Perbasco.

THOMAS² SEAMAN (Capt. John¹) and wife Mary ? had:

John³ m. Sarah Allen, he d. May 11, 1757. She d. Nov. 11, 1775.

Samuel[3] m. Ann Pratt.
Nathaniel[3].
Thomas[3] m. Hannah. His will proved March 29, 1762.
Mary[3] m. a Smith.
Elizabeth[3] m. (? Thomas) Alling.
Richard[3] m. Hannah Jackson, dau. of John and Elizabeth (Seaman).
Sylvanus[3] m. Rebecca Jackson, dau. of James and Rebecca.
Abigail[3] m. Samuel Jackson, son of John and Elizabeth (Seaman).
Hannah[3] m. 1732, Samuel Totton.
JOHN[3] SEAMAN (Thomas,[2] Capt. John[1]) and Sarah Allen had :
Elisabeth[4] b. 1774, m. Benjamin Smith.
Zebulun[4] b. 1726, m., he d. 1782.
Mary[4] b. 1731, m. Silas Smith.
John[4] b. 1734, m. Elisabeth Carman, he d. 1778.
Thomas[4] b. 1739, m. 1761, Martha Rowland b. 1741, dau. of Jonathan and Hannah (Marvin).
JOHN[4] SEAMAN and Elisabeth Carman had:
Mary[5] b. 1757, m. James Birdsall.
John[5] b. 1761, m. Mary Stephens.
David[5] b. 1764, m. —— Conklin, dau. of Jacob.
Elisabeth[5] b. 1766, m. Jeremiah Terry.
Sarah[5] b. 1771, m. Elisha Post.
JOHN[5] SEAMAN and Mary Stephens had :
Mary[6] m. a Pearsall.
William[6] m. Cornelia Y. Briggs.
Edward[6] m. a Brown.
Jane[6] m. a Tredwell.
John[6] and Hannah[6] d.
DAVID[5] and wife had :
Conklin,[6] John,[6] Carman,[6] Elisabeth[6] m. a Stewart.

Seaman Family. 147

THOMAS[4] SEAMAN (John,[3] Thomas,[2] Capt. John[1]) and Martha (Rowland) had:

Jacob[5] b. 1761, m. Anna Van Cott, no ch.
Zebulun[5] b. 1764, m. 1st Charlotte Birdsall, no ch.; m. 2d Martha Combs.
Almy[5] b. 1768.
Mary[5] b. 1774, m. Zebulun Seaman, son of Jordan and Mary, he d. 1838, she d. 1861.
Rowland[5] b. 1777, m. 1st Esther Smith, dau. of Dorcas, and had Esther, m. Obediah Wells Rowland; m. 2d Ruth Buffett; m. 3d Ann Rowland.

ZEBULUN[5] and Martha Combs had:

Allen[6] b. 1791, m. Mary Bryant, no ch.
Ann[6] b. 1795, m. James Shirley.
Thomas[6] b. 1797, m. Almenia Vail, had son William and others.
Esther[6] b. 1800, d. 1828.
Jacob[6] b. 1803, m. Elisabeth Brush, no ch.
Mary[6] b. 1805.
Hannah[6] b. 1808, m. James Rowland.

SAMUEL[3] SEAMAN (Thomas,[2] Capt. John[1]) m. Ann Pratt and had:

Obadiah[4] m. 1st Deborah Smith; 2d Sarah Carman.
Elijah[4] d.
Samuel[4] b. Jan. 11, 1738, m. Mary Birdsall July 18, 1762, she b. Sept. 21, 1746, dau. of John and Elisabeth (nee, Coe) (widow Pearce) Birdsall.

OBADIAH[4] and Deborah had:

Catharine[5] m. 1st Willet Powell; 2d Jacob Willets.
Isaac[5] m. Sarah Mowbray.
Jonathan[5] m. Rebecca Douglas.
Deborah,[5] Ann,[5] Silas[5] and Stephen[5].

SAMUEL[4] SEAMAN (Samuel,[3] Thomas,[1] Capt. John[1]) and Mary (Birdsall) had:

Samuel[5] b. 1763, m. 1785, Charity Tredwell, she d. 1846, he d. 1850.
Jemima[5] b. 1766, m. John Jackson Seaman, son of Thomas and Martha (Jackson).
John[5] b. 1769, m. Mary Whitson, dau. of Silas, b. Jan. 14, 1772, he d. 1849.
Elijah[5] b. 1772, m. Phebe Willets, dau. of Jacob.
Elisabeth[5] b. 1774, m. 1808, William Bunting, she d. 1833.
Thomas[5] b. 1777, m. Sarah (Smith, widow Williams), dau. of Amos Smith.
James[5] b. 1779, d. 1837, Mary[6] b. 1787, she d. 1849, David Sands b. 1791, d. 1793.

SAMUEL[5] SEAMAN (Samuel,[4] Samuel,[3] Thomas,[2] Capt. John[1]), m. Charity and had:

Tredwell[6] b. 1787, m. 1807, Hannah Hewlett, b. Oct. 20, 1789.
John[6] m. Maria Carman, dau. of Joseph, had S. Carman.[7]
Mary[6] m. Jacob Townsend.
Phebe[6] m. Benjamin Smith.
Elijah[6] m. a Chichester.

TREDWELL[6] Seaman and Hannah Hewlett had:
Mary Ann[7] b. June 10, 1822.
Charity[7] b. Aug. 10, 1824.
Sarah Elisabeth[7] b. March 17, 1827, m. Gideon Searing.
Hannah[7] b. June 27, 1831, d. 1832, Sept. 9. Sarah.[7]
Benjamin[7] b. May 26, 1835, m. Elisabeth Helen Townsend.

ELIJAH[6] Seaman m. a Chichester and had:
Mary Elisabeth[7] and Samuel.[7]

Seaman Family. 149

JOHN SEAMAN[5] (Samuel,[4] Samuel,[3] Thomas,[2] Capt. John[1]) and Mary Whitson, had:

Willett[6] b. April 9, 1791, m. Letitia, dau. of Enoch Seaman.

Sarah[6] b. Sept. 31, 1763, m. Thomas Elwood Althouse.

Jemima[6] b. June 5, 1794, m. Samuel Seaman.

Maria[6] b. Oct 6, 1796, m. Walter Powell, son of Benjamin.

David Sands[6] b. Sept. 3, 1798, m. Feb. 19, 1829, Ann Maria Bunting, she was b. Dec. 21, 1808.

Esther[6] b. Jan 1, 1803, m. Gelston Smith, son of James.

Ann[6] b. Jan. 12, 1809, m. John B. Post, she d. July 18, 1849.

John Gilbert[6] b. Sept. 9, 1813, m. Dec. 5, 1834, Jane Althouse, dau. of Jackson.

WILLET[6] SEAMAN and Letitia had:

Almy[7] m. Solomon Powell, son of Robert.

Maria[7] m. Arnold Fleet.

Gulielina,[7] Mary Louisa,[7] Amanda,[7] 1st d.; Amanda,[7] 2d d.; Adelia[7], d.

John Enoch[7] m. a Totton.

James[7] m. 1st Susan Duryea; m. 2d her sister.

Gilbert[7] m. Mary Jackson.

DAVID SANDS[6] SEAMAN (John[5] Samuel[6] Samuel[3] Thomas[2] Capt. John[1]), m. Ann Maria Bunting, and had.

William B.[7] b. Nov. 30, 1829.

Mary Elizabeth[7] b. March 8, 1831, m. William Jagger.

Ellen Althouse[7] b. Sept. 22, 1832, d. May 29, 1857.

Maria Louisa[7] b. March 15, 1834, m. Abraham Willits.

Sarah Jane[7] b. Dec. 25, 1835, d. April, 1864.

Frances Forbes[7] b. April 12, 1837, m. William Laurie.

Charles Lowell[7] b. Oct. 28, 1839.

John Whitson[7] b. Feb. 16, 1843, m. 1st,   m. 2d, Ellen.

JOHN GILBERT[6] SEAMAN (John[5] Samuel[4] Samuel[3] Thos.[2] Capt. John[1]) and Jane (Althouse) had:

John Jackson[7] b. Oct. 27, 1840.

William Henry[7] b. June 23, 1844, m. Sarah Maria Post, dau. of John.

Helen Louisa[7] b. Dec. 2, 1850, died.

ELIJAH[5] SEAMAN (Samuel[4] Samuel[3] Thomas[2] Capt. John[1]), and Phebe, had :

Avis C.[6] m. James Birdsell, she d. March 26, 1865.

Jacob W[6] m. Mary B. Seaman, dau. of Thomas, had Samuel.[7]

Hannah[6] m. Samuel Underhill.

Samuel[6] m. Charlotte English, and had Emma,[7] Amelia[7] and Charlotte.[7]

Richard W[6]., m.

THOMAS[5] SEAMAN (Samuel[4] Samuel[3] Thos.[2] Capt. John[1]) and Sarah (Smith) dau. of Amos, had :

Thomas[6] b. July 9, 1809, m. Hannah Allen, she b. 1804.

James M.[6] b. Jan. 2, 1811, m. 1st, 1838, Martha, m. 2d, Jemima Seaman.

Elizabeth[6] b. Sept. 5, 1814, m. Israel S. Jones.

Mary B.[6] m. Jacob Seaman.

THOMAS[6] SEAMAN m. Jan. 8, 1829, Hannah Allen, and had :

Elbert W.[7] b. Jan. 7, 1835. Henry F.[7] b. Feb. 2, 1838. Thomas W.[7] b. Jan. 1, 1840. Wm. A.[7] b. Feb. 19, 1844, and Sarah Elisabeth[7] b. Dec. 18, 1847.

JAMES M.⁶ SEAMAN and wife Martha, dau. of Samuel and Jemima Seaman (d. April 5, 1840), had:
Sarah⁷ b, Dec. 22, 1835, m. Sidney L. Seaman, son of Lawrence, he m. 2d, Jemima, dau. of Thomas and Deborah Seaman, and had:
Martha⁷ b. June 16, 1846.
Agnes D.⁷ b. Nov. 19, 1848, m. a Towner.
Thomas⁷ and James,⁷ twins, b. July 26, 1853, both m.
Amelia⁷ b. 1857, d. 1860.
Ella G.⁷ b, June 20, 1860, m. Frederick Kropp.
RICHARD³ SEAMAN (Thos² Capt. John¹) and wife Hannah Jackson had:
Thomas⁴ m. Martha Jackson, dau. of John and Kesia (Mott.)
Richard⁴ m. and moved to Dutchess County.
THOMAS⁴ SEAMAN and Martha (Jackson) had:
John Jackson⁵ m. Jemima, dau. of Samuel⁴ and Mary (Birdsall) Seaman.
Braddock⁵ m. Almy Seaman, dau. of Benjamin and Letitia, no children.
Rosetta⁵ m. a Townsend.
Mary⁵ m. Townsend Jackson.
Elisabeth⁵ m. David Jones.
JOHN JACKSON⁵ SEAMAN and Jemima had:
Thomas⁶ b. Oct. 10, 1786, d. Nov. 10, 1829, m. Deborah Birdsall, dau. of Joseph and Mary (Clowes) b. Oct. 10, 1784, d. Nov. 21, 1862.
Samuel⁶ m. Jemima Seaman, dau. of John and Mary (Whitson).
Martha⁶ } both lived single.
Mary⁶ }
THOMAS⁶ SEAMAN and Deborah Birdsall had:
Mary Ann⁷ b. July 6, 1810.
Elisabeth⁷ b. Oct. 6, 1812, d. Nov. 3, 1815.

Braddock[7] b. Feb. 13, 1815, m. Maria Smith, dau. of James, he d. Sept. 24, 1848.

Amelia[7] b. Feb. 28, 1818, d. 1864.

John Jackson[7] b. May 27, 1821, m. 1st Phebe b. 1723, dau. of Benjamin Seaman, 2d Sarah Dean.

Jemima[7] b. March 12, 1823, m. James M.[6] Seaman, son of Thomas and Sarah.

Elisabeth[7] b. Oct. 18, 1826.

JOHN JACKSON[7] SEAMAN and Phebe had:

Braddock[8] b. Feb. 3, 1852.

Benjamin[8] b. March 28, 1854.

Edgar[8] and 2d wife Sarah, dau. of Daniel Dean had:

Gertrude[8]

SAMUEL[6] SEAMAN (John J.[5] Thos.[4] Richard[3] Thos.[2] Capt. John[1]) and Jemima had:

Martha[7] m. James M.[6] Seaman.

Mary[7] m. Elbert Jones, son of Wm. D. and Almy (Seaman).

John Jackson[7] m. Esther, dau. of Andries Seaman and had:

Mary Ann[8] Elbert J.[8] Horace[8] Edgar[8] Antoinette[8]. Adelia[8] Elmira[8] Samuel[8] Alice[8] Sylvester.[8]

NATHANIEL[2] SEAMAN (Capt. John[1]), m. 9, 8, 1695, Rachel Willis, dau. of Henry and Mary (Peace) Willis, she d. Aug. 20, 1759, he d. Oct. 9, 1759. Their children were:

Rachel[3] b. 1696, died.

Nathaniel[3] b. 18, 11, 1699, m. 1722, Sarah, dau. of Thomas[1] Powell and Elisabeth, he d. 1774.

Hester[3] b. 8, 9, 1701, m. John Whitson, son of Thomas and Martha (Jones).

Jacob[3] b. 10, 6, 1703, m. Mercy Powell, dau. of Thos.[1] and Elizabeth, he d. April 4, 1759, she d. March 13, 1759.

Seaman Family. 153

Abraham[3] b. 10, 11, 1706, m. Deborah Townsend, dau. of James.
Rachel[3] b. 7, 1, 1708, m. 1738, Jeremiah Elfreth, son of Phila.
Hezekiah[3] b. 4, 3, 1711.
Thomas[3] b. 2, 11, 1713, m. 1741 Hannah Willets, dau. of Thomas and Catharine (Hallock).
Samuel[3] b. 13, 9, 1715, m. Martha Valentine, dau. of Obadiah and Martha (Willets).

NATHANIEL[3] SEAMAN (Nathaniel,[2] Capt. John[1]) and Sarah Powell, had:
Nathaniel[4] b. 1724, m. Sarah, dau. of Richard Smith, d. Nov. 21, 1816, aged 92 years.
Kesia[4] m. Jacob Mott.
Ambrose[4] m. Margaret Seaman, dau. of Samuel,[2] son of Samuel.[1]
Stephen,[4] Rachel.[4]
William[4] went to Penn'a.
Thomas.[4]

NATHANIEL[4] SEAMAN (Nathaniel,[3] Nathaniel,[2] Capt. John[1]) and Sarah Smith, had:
Richard[4] b. June 17, 1753, m. 1770, Elizabeth Lawrence, b. Oct. 8, 1751, he d. 1799, she d. 1842.

AMBROSE[4] SEAMAN (Nathaniel,[3] Nathaniel,[2] (Capt. John[1]) and Margaret, had:
Samuel[5] died.
Noah[5] m. 1st had William;[6] m. 2d Martha Totten.
Sarah[5] m. Daniel Weeks.
Nathaniel[5] died.   Hicks,[5] died.
Ibbe[5] m.
Ambrose[5] m.
William[5] m.

NOAH[5] SEAMAN and Martha (Totten), had:
Margaret[6] m. George Vanderwater, she d. 1864.
Jacob[6] m. Letitia Nostrant.

20

Fanny[6] m. George Nostrant
Noah[6] m. 1st an Underhill; m. 2d a Titus.
Martha.[6]
Hannah[6] m. Zebulen Powell.
Andries[6] m. Ann Nostrant.
Gideon[6] m. Elisabeth Lewis.
Eliza[6] m. Abraham Powell, son of Robert.
JACOB[6] SEAMAN and Letitia Nostrant, had:
Susan[7] m. Jordan Seymour.
Henry[7] m. a Post.
Elizabeth[7] m. a Vanness.
Noah[7] m. a Post.
NOAH[6] SEAMAN and his 1st wife m. Underhill, had:
Martha[7] m. a Samis.
Abigail[7] m. H. Lewis.
Royal[7] m.
Esther m. an Underhill.
NOAH[6] and 2d wife Titus, had:
Emma[7] m. a Conklyn.
Samuel[7] m.   d.
Rosanna Cecillia[7] m.
ANDRIES[6] SEAMAN and Ann (Nostrant), had:
Esther[7] m. John Jackson Seaman, son of Samuel.
Andries[7] m.   Gideon[7] m.
THOMAS[4] SEAMAN (Nathaniel[3] Nathaniel[2] Capt. John[1]), m. Phoebe Hinton and had:
Jacob[5] m. Sarah Hewlett and had Elizabeth.[6]
Eliphalet.[5]
Gideon.[5]
Stephen[5] m. and had Thomas[6] and Oliver.[6]
Benjamin[5] m. and had George[6] and Sarah.[6]
Isaac[5] m. and had Conklyn,[6] Selah,[6] Henry.[6]
Sarah[5] m. a Snedecker.
Phoebe[5] b. March 17, 1775, m. Dec. 17, 1894, Eb-

enezer Rogers, she d. Jan. 12, 1854, they had 10 children.

David[5] m., had Gideon[6] and Eliphalet.[6]

Amy sometimes called Abbie m. John Abbott.

Ebenezer Rogers and family removed from L. I. to Indiana about 1812 or 1814.

OLIVER[6] SEAMAN and Hannah (Dodge) had: John D.[7] m.

Mary E.,[7] Henry T.,[7] Susan J.,[7] Chas. W.,[7] Elizabeth J.,[7] Platt,[7] Hannah[7] d, Hannah M.[7]

JACOB[3] SEAMAN (Nathaniel[2] Capt. John[1]) m. 1726, Mercy Powell, (d. 1759), dau. of Thomas[1] and Elizabeth, and had:

Jacob[4] and Jemima[4] b. Feb. 20, 1732, Jemima[4] d. Jacob[4] m. 1752, Ann Kirk.

Amy[4] m. Jacob Kirby, she d. 16th of 6th month, 1759.

Gilbert[4] and probably others.

ABRAHAM[3] SEAMAN (Nathaniel[2] Capt. John[1]) and Deborah (Townsend) had:

James,[4] Peleg,[4] Stephen,[4] Almy[4] and Abraham.[4]

HEZEKIA[3] SEAMAN (Nathaniel[2] Capt. John[1]) and wife, dau. of Isaac Doughty had:

Thomas[4] Jacob[4] Stephen[4] and Almy.[4]

THOMAS[3] SEAMAN (Nathaniel[2] Capt. John[1]) and Hannah (Willets) had:

Simeon[4] b. Aug. 31, 1743, d. 1751.

Gideon[4] b. Dec. 5, 1744, m. Elizabeth Keese.

Anna[4] b. 25, 12, 1746, m. Aug. 1, 1770, Fry Willis.

Hannah[4] b Aug. 3, 1749, m. William Jackson of Penn.

Rachel[4] b. March 30, 1752 m. March 5, 1783, Jacob Smith.

Phebe[4] b, May 9, 1755, m. John Loines.

GIDEON[4] SEAMAN and Elisabeth (Keese) had:
Mary[5] m. 1800, Richard Willets, son of Richard and Abigail.
Rachel[5] b. 1789, m. 1815, Abraham Hicks.
SAMUEL[3] SEAMAN (Nathaniel[2] Capt. John[1]) m. Martha Valentine, she was a dau. of Obadiah Valentine and Martha (Willets,) dau. of Richard and Abigail (Powell) Willets. Their children were:
Willet[4] m. Mary, dau. of Dr. Searing.
Valentine.[4]
Obadiah[4] m. Deborah Valentine, dau. of Obadiah.
Rachel[4] b. 1742, m. Feb. 3, 1762, Silas Hicks, she d. 1797.
Martha[4] m. Henry Titus, had Peter S. and Martha.
Phebe[4] m. Samuel Hicks, had Isaac and Samuel.
Miriam[4] m. Stephen Robbins, had Willet, Stephen and others.
Samuel[4] m. Kesia Titus b. 1757, dau. of Thomas and Martha (Powell).
Esther[4] m. Samuel Sands.
Abigail[4] m. Richard Willets, son of Richard and Ruth.
Marmaduke.[4]
WILLET[4] SEAMAN and Mary Searing had:
Elisabeth[5] m. Isaac Cock.
Martha.[5]
John[5] m. Charity Jackson.
James[5] d. Galielma[5] d. Samuel[5] died.
Valentine[5] b. April 2, 1770, m. July 11, 1794, Ann, dau. of John Ferris d. June 1817.
Mary[5] m. William Thurston.
Rachel.[5]
Willet.[5]
Benjamin.[5] m. Amy Cock.
James.[5]

JOHN[5] SEAMAN and Charity (Jackson) had:
Margaret.[6]
Edward[6] m. Mary Valentine, he d. March 14, 1825, aged 26.
Samuel.[6]
Sidney[6] b. 1800, m. Phebe Valentine, he d. June 14, 1827.

VALENTINE[5] SEAMAN (Willett[4] Samuel[3] Nathaniel[2] Capt. John[1]) and Ann Ferris, had:
William Ferris[6] m. Elizabeth Hicks, dau. of Isaac and Sarah.
Elizabeth,[6] Mary Anna,[6] d, Eliza,[6] Anna,[6] Percival.[6]
John Ferris[6] m. a Drake.
James Valentine[6] m.
Willet[6] m. a Jenkins.
Mary Anna.[6]
Eliza[6] m. Augustus Leggett.

OBADIAH[4] SEAMAN (Samuel[3] Nathaniel[2] Capt. John[1]) and Deborah Valentine, had:
Sarah,[5] Samuel,[5] Peter,[5] Phebe,[5] Martha,[5] Keturah,[5] all died early.

SAMUEL[4] SEAMAN (Samuel[3] Nathaniel[2] Capt. John[1]) m. Kesia, dau. of Thomas Titus and Martha Powell, and had:
Thomas[5] m. Sarah Brown.
Silas[5] m. a Green, and had Willet,[6] Phebe,[6] Wm.,[6] Valentine.[6]
Martha[5] m. Josiah Hazard.
John[5] m. Amy Pearsall, dau. of Wait, son of Rowland and Anna (Powell).
William[5] d., Isaac[5] died.
Rachel[5] m. a Marshall.
Samuel[5] m. 1st, Anna, m. 2d, Phebe Pearsall, both daus. of Wait, had 12 children.

THOMAS[5] SEAMAN and Sarah Brown, had:
Jacob[6] m. Hannah Cock.
Kesia[6] m. a Cornell.   Martha.[6]
Ketura[6] m. Peter S. Titus.

JOHN[5] SEAMAN and Amy (Pearsall) had:
Henry[6] m. a Thorburn, and had Avis Robbins,[7] Adria Allen.[7]
Wait[6] died.
Rachel[6] m. a Bogart, lives in Plainfield, New Jersey.
Hannah[6] m. Alfred Underhill, lives at Chappaqua.
Martha K.[6] m. George Brinkerhoff of Jamaica, L. I.
Avis[6] m. 1st, a Mosier, m. 2d, Laing, of Plainfield, N. J.

RICHARD[2] SEAMAN (Capt. John[1]), youngest son of Capt. John, m. 1695, Jane Mott, dau. of Adam[2] and Mary (Stillwell). He was a minister in the Society of Friends and travelled extensively in the service, with Samuel Prior for a companion, and a minute of unity from the monthly meeting at Westbury; he visited, in 1725, the Friends in New Jersey, Maryland, Pennsylvania and Virginia; in 1740 Henry Pearsall accompanied him, with a minute, to visit Friends towards Carolina, and, in 1745, he had a minute to visit Friends westward; born in 1673; he d. 25, 7, 1749; she d. 21, 8, 1759. Their children were:

Richard[3] b. 1694, m. Sarah.
Thomas[3] b. 1696, m. 1722, Philadelphia Titus, dau. of John and Sarah.
Tamar[3] b. 1699.
Jane[3] b. 1701, m. James Titus.
Adam[3] b. 1704, m. 1730, Hannah Pine, R's will gave him £10.

Sarah[3] b. 1706, m. Henry Dusenberry, some rec. say Benjamin Dusenberry.

Hannah[3] b. 1710, m. 1733, Isaac Doty, she d. 1753.

Giles[3] m. 1735, Lititia Onderdonk, he d. 1782.

Elisabeth[3] m. a Townsend.

Phebe.[3]

Mary[3] m. 1749, William Mott, son of James of Mameroneck.

RICHARD[3] SEAMAN (Richard,[2] Capt. John[1]) and Sarah, had:

Richard[4] m. 1751, Sarah Searing, he d. 1784.

Mary[4] m. Richbell Mott.

Sarah[4] m. a Lake.

RICHARD[4] SEAMAN and Sarah (Searing), had:

Richard[5] b. Jan. 31, 1745, m. Sarah Searing, d. Oct. 6, 1843.

Jacob[5] m. and had Solomon, who went to Maryland.

Benjamin, m. Jane Willis.

John[5] m. and had Christina,[6] Wm. R.[6] and Sarah Maria,[6] m. a Curtis.

RICHARD[5] SEAMAN and Sarah (Searing), had:

Martha[6] b. 1779, m. James Walters.

Mary[6] b. 1781, m. Josiah Purdy.

Eliza[6] b. May 1, 1783.

Richard[6] b. April 28, 1785, m. Susan Keese.

John[6] b. Dec. 31, 1786, died.   Jacob[6] b. Oct. 2, 1788, died.   Susan[6] b. May 23, 1790.   James[6] b. 1794, died.   Sarah, died.

Samuel[6] b. Feb. 25, 1792, m. Phebe Ann Pratt, and had Samuel Augustus.[7]

Richard,[7] Elisabeth C.,[7] Sarah Jane,[7] James Alfred,[7] Caroline Amelia,[7] Mary.[7]

THOMAS[3] SEAMAN (Richard[2] Capt. John[1]) m. 1722, Philadelphia, b. 1700, dau. of John[3] and Sarah (Willis) Titus, and had:

Sarah[4] b. 1724, m. Daniel Hauxhurst, and had Seaman who m. a Carpenter and had Philadelphia m. Reuben Haight, Sarah m. a Talcot, Phebe m. a Field.

Obadiah[4] b. Feb. 17, 1729, m. 1754, Maria Pearsall, and had Walter,[5] James,[5] Thomas[5] and Richard.[5]

Phebe[4] b. 1733, m. 1753, John Wright, son of Joseph.

Mary[4] b. 1737, m. Henry Franklin.

ADAM[3] SEAMAN (Richard[2] Capt. John[1]) was Supervisor at North Castle, Westchester Co.-in 1739, Will dated at Rye, Aug. 20, 1757, m. Hannah Pine, dau. of James and had :

Adam,[4] James,[4] Israel,[4] Richard,[4] Samuel.[4]

Letitia[4] m. a Doughty.

Jane,[4] Hannah[4] and Mary.[4]

GILES[3] SEAMAN (Richard[2] Capt. John[1]) m. 1735, Letitia, dau. of Hendrick and Mary (Foster) Onderdonk, and had :

Jordan[4] b. Feb· 17, 1743, m. 1764, by Rev. Samuel Seabury, Mary, dau. of Zebulun and Phebe Seaman.

Giles[4] b. 1748, m. Lydia Mott, had dau. Letitia[5] m. Elisha Carpenter, no children.

Richard[4] m. 1789, Sarah Smith, dau. of Edmond. No children.

Mary[4] m. Jacob Hawxhurst.

Hannah[4] m. Henry Oakley.

Zipporah.[4]

JORDAN[4] and Mary Seaman, dau. of Zebulun and Phebe (Valentine) Seaman had:

Jane[5] b. 1764, m. Garret Layton.

Esther[5] b. 1766, m. Peter Willets, she d. Sept. 14, 1834.

Henry O.[5] b. 1769, m. Almy b. 1773, dau. of Richard and Rosetta Jackson, she d. 1852, he d. 1825.

Zebulun[5] b. Jan, 31, 1771, m. 1794, Mary, dau. of Thomas Seaman (of Jerusalem), and Martha (Rowland).

Andries[5] b. 1780, m. 1804, Sarah Underhill, dau. of Israel, b. 1780, d. 1864, he d. 1825.

Rachel[5] b. 1782, m. Isaac Underhill, son of Israel, she d. 1829.

Jordan[4] Seaman was a Justice of the Peace at Jericho many years.

HENRY[5] O. SEAMAN and Almy (Jackson) had:

Jordan[6] b. Jan. 30, 1790, m. Elizabeth Mills, no children.

Jane[6] b. Oct. 22, 1792, d. 1793, another Jane C.[6] b. Aug. 28, 1804, lived single.

Alanson[6] b. Sep. 23, 1793, m. July 15, 1818, Elisabeth Underhill, dau. of Israel.

Rosetta[6] b. Jan. 5, 1796, m. Coe S. Downing, she d. Sept. 6, 1824.

Henry[6] b. Jan. 11, 1798, d. Sept. 30, 1820, Jacob[6], b. Dec, 30, 1799, d. Oct. 21, 1839.

Richard J.[6] b. Oct. 12, 1806, m. Ann Duryea, d. Aug. 12, 1857.

Thomas J.[6] b. Sept. 5, 1808, m. 1827, Phebe Ann Robbins, he d. July 14, 1856.

Alexander Warren[6] b. Jan. 21, 1811, d. May 19, 1846.

Mary Almy[6] b. Jan. 7, 1817, m. Sept. 12, 1836, William M. Valentine, d. 1838.

ALANSON[6] SEAMAN (Henry O.[5] Jordan[4] Giles[3] Richard[2] Capt. John[1]) and Elisabeth, had:

Caroline Elisabeth[7] b. Jan. 27, 1827, d. Nov. 23, 1827.

Mary Louisa[7] b. Sept. 12, 1829, m. Sept. 18, 1850, Timothy Carle.

RICHARD[6] J. SEAMAN (Henry O.,[5] Jordan,[4] Giles,[3] Richard,[2] Capt. John[1]) and Ann (Duryea), had:

Caroline Elisabeth[7] b. Feb. 20, 1829, m. D. Conklin.
Jane[7] m. a Van Nostrand.
Thomas,[7] Alanson,[7] Emila,[7] Warren.[7]

THOMAS[6] J. SEAMAN (Henry O.,[5] Jordan[4] Giles[3] Richard[2] Capt. John[1]) and Phebe Ann (Robbins) had:

Emma R.[7] b. March 7, 1842, d. March 11, 1845.
Henry O.[7] b. June 18, 1845.
Thomas Edward[7] b. Aug. 18, 1847.

ZEBULUN[5] SEAMAN (Jordan[4] Giles[3] Richard[2] Capt. John[1]), b. Jan. 31, 1771, m. Dec. 14, 1794, Mary, dau. of Thomas Seaman of Jerusalem, b. Aug. 11, 1774, she d. Sept. 19, 1861, he d. Sept. 7, 1838. Their children were:

Ardon[6] b. Sept. 5, 1795, m. 26, 3, 1817, Elisabeth Merritt, dau. of Jesse.
Mary L.[6] b. May 11, 1799, m. June 4, 1818, Isaac Wigham.
John G.[6] b. Nov. 20, 1802, m. 31, 10, 1835, Ann R. Wall.
Charlotte B.[6] b. Oct. 31, 1805.

ARDON[6] Seaman, b. 1795, m. 1817, Elisabeth Merritt, he d. 2, 4, 1875, she d. 3, 2, 1875. Children:

Ann M.[7] b. Feb. 19, 1818, m. 1838, Adam Emeigh. she d. 26, 5, 1864, he d. 1883.
Mary P.[7] b. Feb. 27, 1820, m. 17, 10, 1839, Alexander C. Bunker.
Edward H.[7] b. March 8, 1822, m. Jan. 18, 1848, Martha A. Seaman, dau. of Benjamin, he d. 12, 2, 1891.
Caroline E.[7] b. Feb. 20, 1829, m. Oct. 19, 1852, William Garner, he d. 10, 1873.

Seaman Family.

JOHN G.[6] Seaman and Ann R. Wall had:
William Henry[7] b. Nov. 1, 1836, m. Marianna Clark.

ANDRIES[5] SEAMAN (Jordan,[4] Giles,[3] Richard,[2] Capt. John[1]) and Sarah (Underhill), had:
Mary[6] b. Nov. 1806, m. Townsend Bailey.
Lydia[6] b. March 8, 1812, m. March 3, 1831, Jonathan G. Fleet.

CARMAN FAMILY.

JOHN[1] CARMAN, of Roxbury, came to Lynne, Massachusetts, in 1631, settled at Sandwich, Mass., wife Florence. Children :
John[2] b. 1633, m. Hannah.
Abigail[2] b. 1635, m. Benjamin Coe.
Caleb[2] died.
Joshua,[2] a minor in 1661.
Caleb[2] b. Jan. 9, 1645. The first white child born in Hempstead, was blind. In 1641 John Carman was at Stamford, Conn, removed to Hempstead in 1644. " Hempstead was bought of the natives in 1643 by Rev. Robert Fordham and Mr. John Carman." As it was under Dutch jurisdiction, they also obtained a patent from Governor Keift in 1644. John[1] Carman died about 1658.

JOHN[2] CARMAN (John[1] Carman) m. Hannah, d. 1684. Children :
John[3] m. Hannah, dau. of Capt. John Seaman.
Caleb.[3]
Benjamin[3] m. Deliverance, he d. 1694, widow m. 2d, Jonathan Lewis, of Smithtown.
Samuel.
Thomas.
Joshua, a minor in 1684.
Joseph, a minor in 1684.

Carman Family. 165

Second JOHN CARMAN'S Will says eldest son John, Caleb², dau. Abigail, son Benjamin, sons Samuel and Thomas, to have the land that lies near Robert Jackson's younger sons Joshua and Joseph. Brother Joshua's property to be taken care of for him, he to live with John and Caleb if he wishes to. Sons John and Caleb executors.

BENJAMIN CARMAN'S Will, 1694, says father John Carman, eldest son Benjamin, mute, 2d, John, eldest dau. Sarah, 2d, Dinah, 3d, Mary, not of age.

Third John Carman died before 1759, his son John is called his heir son.

THOMAS joined in the sale of land.

Ruth, dau. of Thomas Carman, m. 1730, Solomon Powell, son of Thomas.

Phebe, dau. of Thomas Carman, m. 1732, John Townsend, he b. 1708, lived at Westbury.

Hannah, dau. of Thomas Carman, m. 1755, Baront Van Wyke.

Of JOHN CARMAN and Hannah Seaman, dau. of Capt. John, descended Great Adam Carman and Adam and Stephen Carman of Hempstead South.

James Carman's will, 1780, says wife Martha, son John, daughters Mary, Ruth, Marian, Rebecca and Priscilla.

Adam Carman m. Philadelphia Titus, dau. of Jacob.

In 1709. Thomas Carman was to make assessment of every freeholder and sojourner in Hempstead Bounds.

Thomas Carman m. Sarah Brinkerhoff, she b. 1738.

In 1682. John Carman, sen., John Carman, jnr., and Caleb Carman, agree to pay Jeremy Hobart, the minister, yearly during the time we live under his ministry: John, sen., £2, John, jnr., 10 shilling, and Caleb 10 s.

1666. Richard Latten of Huntington sells his home lot to John Carman. Lot was formerly Thomas Fosters.

1663. Caleb Carman sells to Henry Disborro a Neck of Meadow lying below the mill, which he bought of Thomas Jaycocks, bounded east by Mill river neck, west by Mill river.

1680. Richard Stiles sells lot of fifty acres at Westbury to Henry Willis. Said lot bounded by land of John Seaman, Edmond Titus, John Carman and Thomas Ellison.

1683. John Carman, John Carman, jnr., not married, and Caleb Carman had land, animals, etc.

ALBERTSON FAMILY.

William[1] Albertson was at Flatlands, L. I., in 1643. In 1655 Albert Albertson was on the records as living at the west end of the island. Eva Albertson m. 1657, Roeleff Swartwout. In 1682, Wm[1] Albertson located a tract of land at Newtown Township, New Jersey. Shortly after he gave the land to his son William and removed to Byberry, Pa. In 1672, Derick Albertson built a mill near Delaware river, half of which was claimed by William Toms. In 1691 Wm. bought a tract in Gloucester Co. for his son, William m. in 1695, Esther Willis, dau. of Henry and Mary, at Westbury.

We have this of 1696.

WILLMETT (now wife of Jauram Roots) formerly m. Albertson, and had children:

Elisabeth Albertson m. Samuel Coles.
Derrick Albertson m. Dinah Coles, Will, 1744 exs.
   John Carpenter, David Valentine.
William Albertson m. Barbara.
Garrett Albertson m.

Children of DERRICK and Dinah (Coles) Albertson:

Derrick m. Rebecca Degrove, he d. 1735.
Daniel m. Elisabeth.
Penelope m. Jacob Doughty.
Wilmarth m. a Thornycraft.
Dinah m. 1696, Benjamin Carpenter, she d. 1738.

Albert, he d. 1730.
Temperance m. Joseph Coles.
Mary m. 1726, William Dennis, of Huntington.
John m. Sarah Powell, dau. of Caleb and Sarah, he d. 1750.

The will of JOHN ALBERTSON, dated 1720, proved Aug. 3, 1750, of Islip, Miller, gives wife Sarah, and children Sylvanus, Isaac, Deborah and Crodus, all under age. Executors, Brother John Wood and Richard Willets. Witnesses, Thomas Willets, David Willets, Joseph Dow and Nehemiah Heath.

DERRICK[3] ALBERTSON and Rebecca Degrove had:

Richard b. 1736, m. 1764, Sarah Hicks, dau. of Benjamin and Phebe (Titus), he d. 1809.
Anna.
Daniel.
Mary m. Benjamin Coles.

Children of RICHARD[4] and Sarah (Hicks) Alberton were:

Hicks[5] b. 1765.
Phebe[5] b. 1771.
Derrick[5] died.
Benjamin[5] b. March 16, 1782, m. Sarah Willets, dau. of Thomas and Leah.
Silas[5] b. 1784, m. 1813, Kesia Whitson, dau. of Henry and Clementine.

Children of BENJAMIN and Sarah (Willets) Albertson:

Phebe H.[6] b. 13, 7, 1806, m. 1835, John C. Merritt, son of Jesse, she d. 13, 6, 1883.
Rebecca[6] b. 1808, m. 1844, Leonard Searing, son of Samuel and Phebe.
Richard[6] m. 1844, Phebe Prior, dau. of James.

Albertson Family.

Thomas H.[6] b. 1813, m. 1846, Harriet Townsend, he d. 6, 5, 1874.
Abigail[6] m. 1839, Charles Willis, son of Charles, he d. 10, 1894.
Mary P.[6] m. 1855, John L. Haviland.
Hicks[6] m. 1838, Elisabeth Willis, dau. of Charles.
Benjamin[6] m. 1848, 1st Elisabeth Jackson; 2d 1856, Martha Jackson, daus. of Jacob and Phebe.
Children of SILAS and Kesia Albertson:
Sarah[6] b. 1815, m. a Tuthill.
Caroline[6] b. 1816, m. Alexander Underhill.
Phebe[6] b. 1818, m. Alexander Underhill.
Silas[6] b. 1825, m. Caroline Lyons.

ANDREWS FAMILY.

October 30, 1663, Samuel Andrews, son of Edward, of Barbadoes, m. Mary Wright, dau, of Peter and Alice. Their son Edward, b. 1667, m. 1694, Sarah Ong —— and Alice eldest dau. of Edward and Sarah, m. 1st Edward Higbie, m. 2d John Matthews. They went from L. I. to Eggharbor, N. J. in 1714, and their son Micajah Matthews, b. 1717, m. 1747, Mercy, dau. of Joshua and Jane Shreve. Benjamin, son of Micajah Matthews, m. Anne Merritt and their dau's. Mercy, m. Isaac Powell, and Eliza, m. Jacob Powell. The children of Jacob and Eliza Powell were Jacob, Benjamin, Samuel and Annie.

The original of which this is a copy was a few years ago among the family papers of S. H. Shreve at No. 1224 Broadway, N. Y.

WHEREAS, there hath been intentions of marriage between Jarvis Ffaro of Springfield, in the county of Burlington, in West Jersey, and Elisabeth Willets, dau. of Hope and Mercy Willets of Hempstead, L. I, in the province of New York.

These are to certify the truth to all people whom it may concern : y^t Jarvis Ffaro and Elizabeth Willets having laid their intentions of marriage before two several meetings of the people of God called Quakers, and persons having been appointed to make inquiry, by s^d meeting, of their clearness from all others in relation to marriage, and at their second meeting all things being found clear, and with consent of parents and relations ye s^d meeting consented to their proceeding.

Andrews Family. 171

And att the house of Hope Willets in the bounds of Hempstead, the fourth day of ye 1st month, one thousand seven hundred and one, att a meeting of the people of God called Quakers, for the same purpose, the party as aforesaid Jarvis Ffaro and Elisabeth Willets did stand up, and solemnly declare themselves husband and wife, promising to Live together in love and faithfulness till death shall separate them,   and for further confirmation they have hereunto sett their hands, the day and year aforesaid,

in the presents of us whose names are underwritten we being witnesses thereto. } Jarvis Ffaro
Elisabeth A. (mark) Ffaro.

Thomas Powell,
Nathaniel Pearsall,
Edmond Titus,
Cenermia Seaman,
George S. Kessington,
Richard Ridgeway,
Thomas Pearsall,

Hope Willets,
Marce Willets,
Thomas Seaman,
Richard Willets,
Thomas Powell,
Mary Powell,
Thomas Whitson.

When Samuel Andrews, of O. B. married Mary Wright in 1663, by friends ceremony, among the witnesses were John and Elizabeth Underhill, Hannah Wright and others.

In 1683. Samuel Andrews and family removed to New Jersey.

In 1684. Samuel d. at Charlestown, Mass., Richard Russell and Nicholas Davison were appointed by the General Court, of Boston to administer upon the estate, and they sold Horse Neck, L. I. to John Richbell.

Samuel bought Horse Neck of Daniel Whitehead at an early period.

BEDELL FAMILY.

The will of John James of Cardiffe, county Glamorgan, Principality of Wales, dated March 13, 1660. Devises to John Beadle my Doublet and black cloth breeches and 40 shillings, (his father owes me) to keep him in school. John James was town clerk of Hempstead 1657, '58 and '59.

1667. Daniel Bedell enters an action in the case against Adam Mott, put off till next courts.

1668. Daniel Bedell enters an action of the case against Adam Mott, jr.

1674. Robert Bedell and Blanche his wife, their sons Daniel and John.

1671. Sold to Goodman Robert Bedell, the town house or the parsonage lot; at £9 in corn or in cattle, equivalent.

1673. Matthew Bedell.

1675. John Bedell declares that William Weir owes him for a borrowed bridle —— and 1682 that Joseph Langdon owes him for butchering.

1678. Mr. Seaman and Daniel Bedell are chosen to lay out the meadow, Daniel Bedell, b. 1680, son of Daniel Bedell, sr.,

1682. John Bedell, Robert Bedell, sr., and jr., Daniel Bedell and Matthew Bedell.

1710. Job Bedell, 1718, Joseph and Jeremiah were fence viewers.

Bedell Family. 173

1718. David Bedell, he was constable and collector in 1721 and in 1783.

1718. Jeremiah Bedell was church warden till 1757.

1727. Jeremiah Bedell was surveyor, 1730, lieutenant.

1763. Jeremiah Bedell, jr. had lot near the church yard in Hempstead.

1766. Silvanus Bedell and others to sell stray sheep unclaimed at parting.

1776. William Bedle substitute for Peter Titus in American Army.

—— Uriah Bedell taken prisoner by Whig soldiers.

1780. Sylvester Bedle was a sergeant under Capt. Hewlett, Loyalist.

1783. Justice Bedell, 1784, Jecamiah Bedell pender.

1802. Richard Bedell, Abraham Bedell was the first Postmaster in Hempstead, Post Office established in 1802.

1804. Hezekiah Bedell received 654 votes in the county for member of the Assembly, 1827, Daniel Bedell.

JEREMIAH[1] BEDELL of Hempstead, m. Mary, she d Aug. 1, 1791, he d. Jan. 21, 1788. Their children were:

Gilbert[2] went South.
Joseph[2] m. had Jane, John, Elisabeth, Marion and Jemima.
Jemima.[2]
Sylvester[2] m.
Jeremiah[2] b. 1751, m. 1st a Gildersleeve, 2d Philena Hallock.

Catharine[2] b. Nov. 23, 1753, m. 1776, Thomas Clowes, b. 1743, she d. March 11, 1824.
Sarah.[2]
Mary[2] m. Thomas Dorland, dau. Mary m. Phineas Baldwin.
Richard.[2]
Jacob.[2]

SYLVESTER[2] BEDELL (Jeremiah[1]) m. and had :
William[3] b. 1771, m. 1st Abigail Powell, 2d Hannah Bradbury.
Adam.[3]
John.[3]
Benjamin.[3]
Sally.[3]

WILLIAM[3] BEDELL (Sylvester[2] Jeremiah) of Coxsackie, m. 1st Abigail, b. 1773, dau. of Elisha[4] Powell and Rachel (Ham) and had :
Rachel[4] b. 1796, m. Peter Bedell.
John W[4]. b 1798, m. Martha Titus.
Daniel[4] b. 1800, m. Marion Gurney, dau. of Benj. b. 1773, and Martha, b. 1780, Gurney.
Mary[4] b. 1802, m. Jeremiah Bedell.
Elisha[4] b. 1804, m. Ann Searles.
Henry[4] b. 1806, m. Deborah Searles.
Catharine[4] b. 1808, m. Robert Nelson.
Children of 2d marriage :
William[4] b. 1813, m. Matilda Bedell.
Phebe[4] b. 1815, m. Thurston Chase.
Hannah[4] d.
Abraham[4] b. 1817, m. Sarah Sanderson.
Benjamin[4] b. 1820, m. Mary Ann Cook.
Ellen[4] b. 1821, not m.
Elisabeth[4] b. 1823, not m.

Bedell Family.

DANIEL[4] BEDELL and Marion (Gurney) had:
Abigail[5] m. Luman Powell.
  Ann C[5]. m. Isaac Stevens.
  Martha G.[5] m. Coenard Powell.
  Benjamin G[5].
  William.[5]
  Mary C[5].
  Guli Elma.[5]
  Ambrose.[5]
  Henry P[5].
  Phebe E[5]. m. a Serles.
  Daniel E[5].
  Sarah M[5]. m. a Gurney.

Children of MARTHA (BEDELL) and Benjamin Gurney, b. 1773.
  Marion Bedell Gurney, m. Daniel[4] Bedell.
  Catharine, m a Gree.
  Mary, m. a Hoag.
  Henry B. m.
  Anna, m. a Griffin.
  Jacob B.
  Jeremiah Gurney lives in New York, Photographer in Broadway.
  Peter Cooper, of Cooper's Institute, New York, m. a Bedell, her brother lived in 30th street, New York. Ex-Mayor Hewett, m. Peter Cooper's daughter.

JEREMIAH[2] BEDELL JR. (Jeremiah[1]) m. Miriam Gildersleeve, and had:
  Thomas[3] m. Esther Carman.
  Mary[3] m, Caleb Spencer.
  Jeremiah[3] m. Ruth Chase.
  Martha[3] m. Benjamin Gurney.
  Kesia[3] m. N. Golden.
  Henry.[3]
  Catharine[3] m. Thomas Nelson.

Gilbert[3] m. Zilla.
Joseph.[3]
John[3] m. Dorcas Powell.
Ann.[3]
Jacob[3] m. Hannah Cornell.
THOMAS[3] BEDELL (Jeremiah[2] Jeremiah[1]) and Esther (Carman) had:
  Peter[4] b. 1794.
  Jacob[4] b. 1797, m. Anna Wilson, dau. of Richard.
  Jeremiah[4] b. 1799.
  Hewlett[4] b. 1801, m. had Peter S. of Po'keepsie, Geneologist
  Joseph[4] b. 1803, Lewis[4] b. 1805, Thomas[4] b. 1808, Caleb[4] b. 1810, Anna[4] b. 1812, Henry[4], b. 1814, Gildersleeve[4] 1816.
JACOB[4] BEDELL and Anna (Wilson) had:
Caleb[5] m. Martha Raymond, dau. of Lewis and Maria (Bunker).
  Hewlett.[5]
Caleb[5] and Martha Bedell had:
Howard[6] and another, both died when nearly grown.
  Ada[6] m. ——
  Ella[6] m. a Partridge, has a little son.
Jacob[2] Bedell (Jeremiah[1]) m. Hannah Cornell had:
  William[3] m. 1st had children, 2d Henrietta (Hallock) widow Irish.
  About 1740, WILLIAM BEDELL, m. Mary Willis, a granddaughter of Thos.[1] Powell, had children, Mordecai, Rachel, Jehiel, m. 1782, out of meeting, and others.

BIRDSALL FAMILY.

Sylvester Baldwin, m. Sarah Ryan, he d. in 1638, while on a voyage to America with his family. His son Richard, b. 1622, m. Elisabeth Alsop. Richard was in New Haven in 1639. His dau. Temperance Baldwin between 1640-50, m. Nathan Burchell (or Birdsall), at New Haven.

In 1657, Nathan[1] Birdsall lived on the east side of B street, near the north end in East Hampton, L. I., left there soon.

1666. Mark Meggs sells to Nathan[1] Burcham five acres at Matinecock on which N. B. do now live.

1667-8. Indians sold land at Matinecock to Nathan Birdsall.

1678. Agreement that Nathan[1] Birdsall, Matthew Pryor, Christopher Hawxhurst and Samuel and Joseph Weeks shall have the great meadow and half the little meadow.

Capt. John Underhill, Nathan Birdsall, Matthew Pryor, James Cock and John Feaks formed the neighborhood of Killingworth Oysterbay, L. I.

1679. Nathan Birdsall bought of Lawrence I. Mott, land lying near a tract of land called Jerusalem, (Little Britain).

1679. Thomas Ireland sold to Nathan Birdsall land at Jerusalem, called Birdsall's Swamp.

Children of NATHAN[1] Birdsall, he d. 1696.

Samuel[2] m. 1690, Jane Langdon.

Benjamin,[2] m. Mercy Forman dau. of Samuel and Miriam (Harcourt).
Stephen[2] m. Mary.
Nathaniel[2] m. Mary.
William, m. Mary.
Henry[2] m. and had dau. Mary, m. John Dorland.
Nathan[2] m.

BENJAMIN[2] BIRDSALL (Nathan[1]) m. Mercy, dau. of Samuel Forman and wife Miriam (Harcourt), Will 1719. Children:

Elizabeth[3] b. 1683, m. a Townsend.
Susanna[3] b. 1685, m. an Underhill.
Samuel[3] b. 1687, m. 1st 1716, Rose Wright, 2d 1726, Sarah Townsend.
Judith[3] b. 1689, m. a Townsend.
Benjamin[3] b. 1691, m. Martha.
Miriam[3] b. 1693, John[3] b. 1696, Zilpea[3] b. 1699, Sarah[3] b. 1702, Nathan[3] b. 1705.
One more.

Children of Benjamin Birdsall, of O. B. and Martha:

Benjamin, Nathaniel, Phebe, Sarah, Mary, Debora, Martha and Elisabeth.

JOHN[3] BIRDSALL (Benjamin[2] Nathan[1]) d. 1764, children, of 1st wife E. Langdon.

Thomas[4] m. Rosanna Pearce, dau. of his stepmother.
John[4] m. 1750, Phebe Seaman dau. of James and Martha.
Joshua[4] m. a Sprague.
Benjamin[4] m. 1763, Freelove Jones, dau. of William and Phebe.
Joseph[4] m. Mary Clowes, dau. of Samuel and Rebecca (Dorland).
Samuel[4] m. had daughter Elisabeth.[5]

Birdsall Family. 179

2d wife, E. Coe, widow Pierce, had:

Elisabeth[4] m. 1st Wm. Smith, 2d James Downing, both of Great Neck.

Mary[4] b. 1746. m. 1762, Capt. Samuel Seaman.

Deborah[4] unm.

THOMAS[4] eldest son of John[3] and his 1st wife, m. Rosanna Pierce, dau. of Elisabeth Coe and her 1st husband, Pierce.

Elisabeth, dau. of Thomas and Rosanna (Pierce) Birdsall, m. 1st Parmenas Jackson, b. 1750, 2d m. James Downing, and had Jemima, Thomas and Coe S., 3d m. Amos Willets of Jericho. No children.

PARMENAS JACKSON, d. Jan 19, 1781, of wounds received at his house at Little Britain, from a party of plunderers, His children were:

Parmenas, m. Charity Coles, son of Benjamin Thomas, d.

Elisabeth, m. Micah Jackson.

Rosanna m. Samuel Nicholas.

John m. Margaret Cornell, dau. of Stephen.

JOHN[4] BIRDSALL, (John[3] Benj.[2] Nathan[1]) m. Phebe Seaman and had:

Seaman[5] m. Abigail Smith.

James[5] m. Mary Seaman, dau. of John and Elisabeth Carman.

Children of SEAMAN[5] BIRDSALL and Abigail:

John[6] m. a Williams.

Smith.[6]

James[6] m. a Jackson.

Charlotte[6] unm.

Phebe[6] m. 1st a Duryea, 2d a Wiggins.

JAMES[5] BIRDSALL and Mary (Seaman) had:

Benjamin[6] m. Almy and had Amy, Elisa, Harriet, m.

Seaman[5] Birdsall had home at Plain Edge, north of his uncle, Thomas[5] Birdsall's place, at Jerusalem. He sold it in 1810, to Elijah, son of Samuel Seaman. The place was on the west side of the Jerusalem road.

Joshua[4] Birdsall (John[3] Benjamin[2] Nathan[1]) m. a Sprague, and had:

John[5] called Dandy.

Others.

BENJAMIN[4] BIRDSALL (John[3] Benjamin[2] Nathan[1]) m. 1763, Freelove Jones, he d. 1799, children:

David,[5] Benjamin,[5]

Phebe[5] m. a Jackson.

Elisabeth[5] m. Jackson Althouse.

Margaret[5] m. 1st Jacob Seaman, 2d Dr. Timothy Tredwell.

Mary[5] m. a Wright.

Charlotte[5] b. 1764, m. Zebulun Seaman son of Thomas and Martha.

Thomas[5] m. Phebe Jackson, dau. of Jacob, d. previous to 1814. Children of Thomas and Phebe: Jackson,[6] Lena,[6] Timothy.[6]

JOSEPH[4] BIRDSALL (John[3] Benjamin[2] Nathan[1]) m. Mary Clowes, dau. of Samuel. They lived mostly at Jerusalem, were at Coxsackie a few years, after the war of the Revolution, children:

Elisabeth[5] b. 1767, unm., she d. 1846.

Rebecca[5] b. 1770, d. 1775.

John[5] b. 1773, unm., he d. 1850.

Anna[5] b. 1776, unm., she d. 1805.

Mary[5] b. 1779, m. Oliver Post, she d, 1828.

Catharine[5] b. 1781, she d. 1783.

Deborah[5] b. 1784, m. Thomas Seaman, she d. 1862.

Sarah[5] b. 1790, m. John Garner, she d. 1836.

SARAH BIRDSALL and John Garner had:

William m. Carolina E. Seaman, he d. 1873.

Birdsall Family.

John B.
Mary.
Elisabeth m. Luke Weeks.
Ann·

John Garner came about 1800, from Armagh, Ireland, he was a school teacher in Jerusalem several years, and subsequently a merchant. He had been steward in the Methodist Church at "*home*" and came with a good certificate from the Pastor, he d. highly respected in Jerusalem, about 1838.

Will of Elisabeth Birdsall, widow of John³ dated 1795, gave property to dau. Rosanna, son Samuel and dau. Mary, wife of Capt. Samuel Seaman. To grand children, Benjamin, Samuel and James Mott. Elisabeth Birdsall, dau. of Samuel, Elisabeth Pierce, wife of Samuel and Elijah Seaman and Thomas Seaman.

1767. Thomas and Elisabeth Allen sold to Joseph Birdsall, land bounded south by Jacob Seaman's land near the school house, west by the main road, then northerly, easterly and southerly, then westerly by land of Solomon Seaman, and Thomas and Samuel Seaman, to Jacob Seaman's land, then west by that to the road about 41 acres, 2d piece on the west side of the road, the north east corner near Samuel Seaman's barn, bounded north by Samuel's, west by Thomas's and Jacob's, south by road that leads from Jerusalem to Hempstead, 48 acres.

STEPHEN² BIRDSALL (Nathan¹) and Mary, he d. 1724, had:
Stephen³ m. 1738, Deliverance Willets.
Phebe³ m. 1st a Havens, 2d a Bartlett.
Children of Stephen and Deliverance:
Mary⁴ m. Timothy Willets.
Sarah⁴ m. Jarvis Hazelton.

Stephen[4] m. Desire Mott.

Mary, widow of Stephen[2] returned to Matinecock in 1726, and m. 2d David Allen. They went to Shrewsbury, N. J.

In 1696. Nathaniel and Benjamin Birdsall, sons of Nathan, were at New Britain, in the bounds of Hempstead.

In 1713. Nathaniel and Mary Birdsall sell the homestead on which they now dwell to George Wright.

In 1713. Moses Fforman, John Mathis, or Matthews went from Long Island, and with Nathaniel and Stephen Birdsall settled Daniel Mathis Island, Little Egg Harbor; subsequently Moses Fforman settled in Ocean County, New Jersey.

1731. Will of George Baldwin, wife was Mary, dau. of Thomas and Martha Ellison. Ch.

Ezekiel m. Rachel.

Samuel, Joseph, Thomas Doc., George, Abigail Townsend, Phebe Lewis, Eleanor Howard, Rachel Featherbee, wife of John, Martha Baldwin.

Mary, widow of —— Lines.

Grandson, William Lines.

Ex. { THOMAS PEARSALL, SAMUEL UNDERHILL, and MY SON SAMUEL.

1698. Derick Brower and Hannah, his wife, at Flushing, L. I., one son.

1701. Derick Brower, at Jamaica, Hendrick at Flatlands.

1711. Hendrick Brower, wife Maratie, sons Benjamin, Johannes, and others, perhaps Jeremiah and Peter. No children.

1767. Peter Brower's, will says son Jacob, daus. Elisabeth, m. Henry Ustick, and Ann, m. John Walker.

Richard Betts, m. and had three children viz:
Mary m. Joseph Sweezy, Joanna m. John Scudder, Martha, m. Philip Ketchum.

BOWNE FAMILY.

THOMAS¹ BOWNE b. 1595, at Mattock, Derbyshire, England, children:
  John² b. 1627, d. 1695, m. 1st in Flushing, May 7, 1656, Hannah Feeks, she d. 1677, Deborah² b. 1631.
John² Bowne, at Flushing, L. I., in 1649, bound himself to work for Mr. Phillips by the week, he to be free to do something else at the end of each week. In 1650, his store book accounts begin.

The children of JOHN² BOWNE and Elisabeth, dau. of Robert and Elisabeth (Fones), (widow Winthrop) Feaks, were:
  John³ b. 1656, d., Elisabeth³ b. 1658, m. 1st John Prior, he d. 1698, she m. 2d Samuel Titus, a widower.
  Maria³ b. 1660, m. Joseph Thorne.
  Abigail³ b. 1662, m. 1686, Richard Willets, she d. 1688.
  Hannah³ b. 1665, m. 1691, Benjamin Field.
  Samuel³ b. 1667, m. Mary Becket from England.
  Dorothy³ b. 1669, m. 1689, Henry Franklin, she d. 1690.
  Martha Joanna³ b. 1673, m. 1695, Joseph Thorne.
2d m. 1679, Hannah Bickerstaff, she d. 1690, children:
  Sarah³ b. 1680, d., b. 1681, Sarah.³

John³ b. 1683.
Thomas³ b. 1684.
John³ b. 1686.
Abigail³ b. 1688.
3d m. 1693, Mary Cock, dau. of James and Sarah, children:
Ann³ b. 1694, sometimes called Annis.
Ruth³ b. 1795.
In 1663. John Bowne was banished to Holland, for being a Quaker. The authorities there soon let him come home, and he was not molested any more.
1676. All accounts ballanced between me and my Master, John Bowne,
    (signed)
JAMES CLEMENTS.

James Clements came from Durham, England, with wife Jane.

At Flushing, 1698, James Clements and wife Sarah, children: Thomas, Jacob and Joseph, (*his* two sons, Samuel and Nathan), Mary, Hannah, Margaret and Bridget.

In 1723. Joseph Clements, m. Sarah Williams, dau. of Hope, he d. 1766.

In 1700. Thomas Clements was brother-in-law to Richard Valentine.

CLOWES FAMILY.

SAMUEL[1] CLOWES (Surveyor), b. in England, March 16, 1674, came to New York, 1697, m. July 18, 1698, Catharine Donne, he d. Aug. 27, 1760.
Children:
Gerardus[2] b. April 27, 1699, m. Oct. 19, 1719, Sarah, dau. of Major Thomas Jones, he d. 1752. Samuel,[2] John,[2] Peter,[2] Joseph,[2] Alletta,[2] Mary,[2] Catharine[2] and Mellicent.
Children of GERARDUS[2] and Sarah:
Samuel[3] b. 1722, m. Rebecca Dorlan, he was Surrogate of Queens County, several years.
Catharine[3] b. 1726, m. John Langdon.
Timothy Bagley.[3]
John[3], he d. 1758.
SAMUEL[3] CLOWES, d. May 10, 1800, wife Rebecca, d. 1787. They had:
Thomas[4] b. 1743, m. 1762, 1st Martha Wiggins, dau. of Benj., 2d, 1776, Catharine Bedell.
Isaac[4] b. 1755, m. 1791, Abigail Carman, he d. 1825.
Samuel[4] b. 1757, m. 1791, Sarah Searing, dau. of James, he d. 1824.
Alletta[4] m. Morris Simonsen.
Arrabella[4] b. 1763, m. John Marvin, she d. 1814.
Catharine[4] m. William Mott.
Mary[4] b. Sept. 12, 1745, m. Joseph Birdsall, she d. 1805.
Thomas[4] m. Amelia Clowes.

Clowes Family.

THOMAS[4] CLOWES and 1st wife Martha (Wiggins) had Sarah[5] and Benjamin.[5]

Children of 2d marriage:

Gerardus[5] b. 1777, m. Phebe Gildersleeve.

Samuel.[5]

John Gilbert[5] m. Hannah Burtis and had Thomas Henry.[6]

Mary Ann[5] b. 1786, m. Samuel Valentine, son of Jacob and Catharine.

COCK FAMILY.

JAMES¹ COCK and wife Sarah came from Setauket, L. I., to Oysterbay, about 1662, children:
Mary² b. 1655, m. 1693, John Bowne, had Ann and Ruth.
Thomas² b. 1658, m. Esther Williams, dau. of Robt.
Martha² b. 1661, d. 1770.
John² b. 1666, m. 1st ——————, 2d Dorothy Harcourt, dau. of Richard.
Hannah² b. 1669, m. James de la Plaine.
Sarah² b. 1672, m. Henry Franklin, son of Matthew.
James² b. 1674, m. 1698, Hannah, b. 1675, dau. of John Feke, she d. 1750, he d. 1728.
Henry² b. 1678, m. 1699, 1st Mary Feke, dau. of John, 2d Martha Pearsall, dau. of Nathaniel.
Martha² b. 1680, m.
JAMES² COCK and Hannah had:
Sarah³ b. 1700, unm.
Samuel³ b. 1702, m. Martha Alling.
Joshua³ b. 1704, d. 1778, unm.
Elisabeth³ b. 1706.
Josiah³ b. 1709, m. Rebecca Frost.
Martha³ m. Joseph Frost.
Mary³ m. Isaac Frost.
SAMUEL³ COCK and Martha (Alling) had:
Hannah⁴ b. 1731, m. Joseph Cole.
Samuel⁴ b. 1734, m. Jemima Powell, dau. of Wait and Mary, b. 1736.

Annie[4] b. 1736, m. James Titus.
Clark[4] b. 1738, Elisabeth Pearce. Will 1780.
Penelope[4] b. 1741, m. 1st a Loines, and had son Stephen Loines, 2d John Hawxhurst.
HENRY[2] COCK and Mary Feeks had:
Joseph[3] b. 1701, d. in P'a. 1733.
Benjamin[3] b. 1703, m. Ann Brinton of P'a.
John[3] b. 1705, m. Sarah Carpenter, b. 1712, dau. of Wm.
James[3] b. 1707.
Amy[3] b. 1709, m. Reese Jones of P'a.
Mary[3] b. 1711, m. Nathan Bane.
Henry[3] b. 1713, m. 1731, Mary Bowne, had dau. Hannah.
Twins { Sarah[3] b. 1715, m. 1741, Joseph Shotwell, son of John, of Elizabethtown, N. Jersey.
Elisabeth[3], m. William Townsend.
Children of JOHN[3] Cock and Sarah Carpenter:
Mary[4] b. 1730, m. Isaac Underhill, son of Amos.
William[4] b. 1732, m. 1st Dinah Hopkins, 2d Anne Feaks, 3d Clemence Feaks.
Henry[4] b. 1735, m. 1760, Elisabeth Robbins, dau. of Jeremiah.
Reese[4] b. 1738, m. 1761, Hannah Robbins, dau. of Jeremiah.
Elisabeth[4] b. 1740, m. 1765, Daniel Robbins, son of Jeremiah.
Anne.[4]
Elijah[4] b. 1745, m. 1773, Temperance Townsend.
Sarah[4] b. 1748, d. 1750.
Benjamin[4] b. 1754, m. 1779, Hannah Prior, b. 1756, she d. 1828, dau. of Thos., he d. 1835.
Amy[4] b. 1756, m. John Titus, dau. Amy, m. Benj. Seaman, son of Willet.

BENJAMIN[4] COCK and Hannah (Prior) had:
Abraham[5] b. 1780, m. Susan Wright.
Sarah[5] d. 1795.
Phebe[5] b. 1785, m. John Bird.
ABRAHAM[5] and Susan (Wright) had:
Alexander[6] d. an infant.
Elisabeth[6] m. Alfred C. Smith.
Benjamin[6] m. Martha Leggett.
Sarah[6] m. Manuel Fetter.
Jordan[6] m. Mary Willets, dau. of Seaman and Ann Willets.
William Henry[6] m. Mary J. Burrows.
Charles W.[6] m. Mary K. Holmes.

CORNELL FAMILY.

JOHN CORNELL, bro. of Richard (Cornkill) m. Mary Russell, and had:
Richard b. 1675, m. Hannah Thorne; Joshua, John, and Rebecca.
Caleb b. 1683, m. Phebe Hagner, she d. 1759.
Mary b. 1677, m. James Sands.
CALEB and Phebe had:
Mary b. 1714, m. Thomas Appleby, d. 1780.
Richardson m. and had Caleb, b. 1736, Elisabeth, m. John Sands; John, Susanna, Richard, William, Joshua, Margaret, m. John Willis.

CORNELIUS FAMILY.

1639. Adrian Cornelius, Capt. of the "Canary Bird," "respecting linen taken on board a prize."

1676. Capt. Cornelius, of Brooklyn, assessed for £128.—Dutch MSS.

1688. Aaron Cornelius, at Flushing, bought land of David Esmond.

John Cornelius, son of Adrian, m. Aug. 7, 1682, Mary Yates, dau. of Francis, all of Flushing.

There was a dau. Ann and probably a son Daniel, children of the 1st wife of Adrian. He married 2d Patience, their children were: Elias and Mary.

Adrian's will, proved 30th day of April, 1692, gave the homestead to son Elias; widow to live there till Elias was of age, during life, if she remained unmarried.

1698. John Cornelius and wife Mary lived at Flushing with children: John, Daniel, Samuel Joseph, Deborah, Mary, Phebe, Sarah and negro Zambo.

1713. Elias Cornelius and Sarah his wife, bought of Wm. Loines and Mary his wife, a place at West Neck, now known as the Minell place at Seaford. He died in 1718.

ELIAS[2] CORNELIUS (Adriaen[1]) m. Sarah? Harnett and had:

Elias[3] b. Nov, 2, 1703, m. Dec. 23, 1725, Elisabeth Rock Smith, dau. of Jonathan.

Mary Elisa[3] m. 1727, Nehemiah Dean, she d. 1750.

Cornelius Family.

Children of ELIAS[3] CORNELIUS and Elisabeth Rock Smith, dau. of Jonathan and Elisbeth, he d. June 25, 1743, she m. 2d 1745, Ezekiel Matthews:
Elias[4] b. May 12, 1729, he d. 1762.
Jane[4] b. Sept. 20, 1731, m. 1752, Johannes Covert.
Patience[4] b. 1734, lived single.
Jonathan[4] b. Mar. 26, 1736, m. 1757, Mary Baldwin, he d. 1820.
John[4] b. Dec. 22, 1739, m. 1766, Mary Powell, b. Dec. 30, 1739, he d. Apr. 10, 1814.
Moses[4] b. Jan. 4, 1743, m. Nancy Carman, he d. 1796.

JONATHAN[4] CORNELIUS (Elias[3] Elias[2] Adriaen[1]) and Mary (Baldwin) had:
Elias[5] b. 1757, became an M. D.
James[5] b. June 21, d. the 31st, 1759.
Nancy[5] b. 1760, William[5] d.
Elisabeth[5] b. 1763, Sarah[5] b. 1765, John[5] b. 1766, Mary[5] b. 1767, Phebe[5] b. 1770, Jane b. 1775, d. 1800.
Jonathan [5]b. 1778, m. Sarah, had dau. Ann, m. 1st a Powell, 2d 1801, George Weeks.
Daniel[5] b. 1780, M. D.

JOHN[4] CORNELIUS (Elias[3] Elias[2] Adriaen[1]) and Mary, dau. of Thos[3] Powell, had:
Mary[5] b. Jan. 31, 1767, m. May 6, 1789, Jesse Merritt, son of Nathaniel and Ann, she d. Sept. 11, 1840.

MOSES[4] CORNELIUS and Nancy Carman had:
Mary[5] m. Robert Powell, son of Solomon.
Samuel[5] m. Jemima Mott, sister of John the preacher.
John[5] b. 1773, m., d. 1829.
Henry[5] m. Jane Verity.
William,[5] Moses.[5]

Benjamin[5] m. Ruth Darby.
Elisabeth[5] m. Scudder Robbins.
SAMUEL[5] CORNELIUS (Moses[4] Elias[3] Elias[2] Adriaen[1]) and Jemima Mott had:
John,[6] Gideon,[6] Henry,[6] Carman,[6] Mott,[6] Jordan,[6] Samuel.[6]
Lott[6] m. a Valentine.
Hiram[6] m. a Smith.
BENJAMIN[5] CORNELIUS (Moses[4] Elias[3] Elias[2] Adriaen,[1] and Ruth Darby had:
John[6] m., Charles[6] m.
Carman[6] m. 1st Phebe Jane Combs, 2d Smith, widow Powell, he d, 1893.
Benjamin[6] d. 1894.
Children of JANE[4] CORNELIUS and Johannes[2] Covert, m. 1752.
William[2] b. 1753, m. Jane Stymits, son John[3] m. Loretta Lefferts, he d. 1841.
Jacob[2] b. 1758, was in Oysterbay in 1799, m. Catherine Powell, dau. of Joseph and Deborah.
John[2] m. 1781, Catharine Hoagland.
Elisabeth[2] m. Fulket Duryea.
Jane[2] m. Henry Lounsberry.
Moses[2] he d. 1787.
JOHN[3] COVERT and Loretta (Lefferts) had:
Jane[4] m. a Nichols, son of John, Elisabeth,[4] m. an Austen, Maria[4] m. a Purdy.
JACOB[2] COVERT and Catherine (Powell) had:
Joseph[3] m. had son Jacob.[4]
Deborah[3] m. a Bumpstead.
Another John Covert m. an unknown, 2d a Remsen, 3d Rebecca Striker.
JOHN and REBECCA (Striker) COVERT had:
William m. Helena Duryea and had Abraham, m. 1st a Mulineux, 2d Hannah Hicks.

Maria m. a Debevoise.
Hannah m. Jacob B.
MARY ELISA (Cornelius) and Nehemiah Dean, had Sarah, d. at 20 years of age.

Daniel Dean, b. 1731, d. 1753, Eunice, b. 1734, Phebe, b. 1738, Thomas, b. 1742, Kesia, b. 1745.

Nehemiah Dean was a weaver, at Oysterbay south, in 1764, and gave quit claims to Wm. Jones, for undivided lands of the estate of Elias Cornelius, deceased.

DEAN FAMILY.

Friends meetings were appointed in 1687, at Samuel Dean's, Jamaica, his dau. Sarah m. 1687, John Way, she d. 1707, Daniel Dean, m. 1699, out of meeting.

In 1703. A patent was granted to Christopher Dean and Madam Dean, persons of distinction, in Orange Co., N. Y.

Nehemiah Dean, m. 1727, Mary Elisa Cornelius. Children in the Cornelius list:

THOMAS DEAN m. Ann Verity and had:

Daniel m. Mary Haff (he d. about 1886), Elisabeth, John and Charles.

Children of DANIEL and Mary Dean:

Susan b. 1839, d.
Thomas b. 1841, m. Elisa Valentine.
Sarah b. 1844, m. John Jackson Seaman.
Stephen b. 1845, m. Elisabeth Smith, dau. of George.
Elbert b. 1847, m. Matilda Smith, dau. of Nathaniel.
Daniel H. b. 1855, d.
William b. 1864, m. Catharine Voorhees, dau. of Edward.

DERBY FAMILY.

Francis Derby, b. 1660, in R. Island; was at Southold, 1683, Samuel Derby from Salem, N. E., and wife Hannah Youngs, were at Southold, in 1700. They were Friends and probably the first of the name of Derby in the country; see Salem Records.

DOUGHTY FAMILY.

Francis Doughty, of Taunton, Mass., in 1639, removed to Long, Island in 1641, lived in Rhode Island awhile. "In 1649, Franciscus Douthy, an English clergyman here, came to N. E., at the time of the persecution in England. He betook himself under the protection of the Netherlands, in order that he may, according to Dutch Reformation, enjoy freedom of conscience, which he unexpectedly missed in New England.

In 1642. The Director granted and conveyed to him an absolute patent with manoral privileges. He added some families to his settlement, at Maspeth, L. I., in the course of a year, but the war breaking out, they were all driven off their lands, some were killed — and almost all they had was lost. They fled as all refugees did, to Manhattan, and Master Douthy was minister there. He was without means and his land was seized by the Director; Douthy appealed but the Director said there was no appeal, his decision must be final, and for his remarks, Doughty was sentenced to imprisonment 24 hours, and to pay 25 Guilders. The deed was for 6,666 acres of land, at Maspeth, from Gov. Keift. *Col. Rec.*

In 1685. The sons of Rev. Francis Doughty, viz : Francis, Charles, Elias and Jacob, of Flushing, petition for a grant of 250 acres each on L. I.

Doughty Family.

In 1680. Elias Doughty was to have 200 acres between Hempstead and Jamaica to settle his children on. Elias d. 1743.

In 1688. Elias Doughty gave deeds of gift to sons Francis, Charles, Elias, Jacob (Benjamin and William not of age).

"In 1648. Francis Doughty departed for the English Virginias;" he had previously conferred on his daughter Mary, on her marriage, in 1645, with Adrian VonDerDonck, his farm on Flushing bay, now owned by Abraham and John Rapelye.

CHARLES DOUGHTY m. Elisabeth Jackson, dau. of John and Elisabeth (Seaman), children:

Phebe m. 1734, Richard Cornell, son of Thomas, of Hempstead.

Mary m. 1747, Zebulun Dickinson, son of Joseph.

BENJAMIN m. 1737, Hannah Williams, dau. of Jeremiah and Philadelphia (Masters) and had children:

Charles b. 1741, m. 1771, Sarah Dusenberry b. 1738, dau. of Benjamin.[1]

Elisabeth.

William b. 1755, m. 1785, Mary, dau. of John and Elisabeth Williams.

Philadelphia m. Nicholas Townsend.

One m. 1787, John Hill, of Penn'a.

Hannah m. Charles Hull, went to Canada.

Benjamin.

Children of CHARLES DOUGHTY and Sarah Dusenberry.

Margaret b. 1772, Mary b. 1773, Benjamin b. 1775, Charles b. 1777, Sarah b. 1778.

WILLIAM and Mary, she b. 1757, Doughty had:

Benjamin b. 1785, Esther b. 1789, George Masters b. 1793.

DURYEA FAMILY.

JOOST¹ DURYEA emigrated from Manheim about 1675, wife Magdalena le Febre, he d. 1717, children.
    Antoinette² m. Lequier.
    Magdalena² m. Okie.
    Joost² m. he d. 1727.
    Abraham² m. he d. 1758.
    Charles² m. he d. 1758.
    Simon.
    Jacob, baptised 1686, m. Catrina Polhemus of Bushwick, he d. 1758.

JOOST² (Joost.¹) m. had sons Joost,³ Hendrick,³ Folkert.³

ABRAHAM² DURYEA (Joost.¹) m. had sons: Joost,³ Daniel,³ Johannes,³ Abraham.³

CHARLES² (Joost.¹) m. had sons:
Joost,³ Johannes,³ Charles,³ Tunis,³ Derrick,³ Abraham.³

JACOB² DURYEA, (Joost.¹) b. baptised 1686, m. Catrina Polhemus, of Bushwick, Long Island, children :
    Joost³ m. 1730, Willemptie Terhune.
    Daniel,³ Johannes,³ Abraham,³ Cornelius,³ Hendrick.³

JOOST³ DURYEA, (Jacob,² Joost¹.) m. 1730, Willemptie Terhune, children :
    Ruleff⁴ b. 1738.

Duryea Family. 201

John[4] b. 1739, m. Ann Pratt, dau. of Jonathan, she b. 1741, he d. 1781.
Jacob[4] b. 1750, Mann[4] b. 1752, Aaron[4] b. 1754.
JOHN[4] DURYEA (Joost,[3] Jacob,[2] Joost.[1]) m. Ann Pratt, children:
Ruleff[5] b. 1765, m. Waters.
Catharine[5] b. 1768.
Mary[5] b. 1771, m. Daniel Seaman.
Pratt[5] b. 1777.
RULEFF[5] DURYEA (John,[4] Joost,[3] Jacob,[2] Joost.[1]) m. Waters, children:
Elisabeth[6] m. James Smith.
Mary[6] Ann m. Ruleff Duryea.
Catharine[6] m. William Smith.
Jane[6] m. Andrew Powell.
John[6] m. Ketcham.
Elbert[6] m. Sally Ann Covert.
Henry[6] m. Margaret Nostrand, dau. of Peter.

At New Amsterdam, 1654, Albert, Albertse, Terhune and wife Geortje (Knit Ribbon Weaver). Their son Jan Albertse, m. 1683, July 1, Annetje Roelefse Schenck, he d. 1688.

Albert Terhune, son of Jan and Annetje, baptised at Flatlands in 1684, m. 1708, Aeltje Voorhees.

Willemtje Terhune, dau. of above, Albert and Aeltje Terhune, m. Joost[3] Duryea in 1730.

FEKE FAMILY.

Lieut. ROBERT FEKE of Watertown, N. E., and Wm. Palmer of Yarmouth, and Judith his wife, son and daughter of James Feke, late of London, Goldsmith, deceased, and Tobias Feke, aged 17, make Tobias Dixon, of London, their attorney in the settlement of the estate of James, 1638 to 41.

ROBERT[1] FEKE m. Elisabeth (Fones), widow of Henry Winthrop, son of John[1] and nephew of Gov. Winthrop. Their mother was a Winthrop.

Their children were:

Hannah[2] m. May 7, 1656, in Flushing, John Bowne, she d. 1677.

John[2] m. 1673, Elisabeth Prior, he d. 1724.

Tobias[2] b. at Watertown, came to L. I., in 1650, he d. 1668.

Elisabeth, who m. 1660, Capt. John Underhill, appears to have been the dau. of Elisabeth (Fones) and her 1st husband Henry Winthrop, to whom she was married about 1629; he was drowned on July 3, 1630, in attempting to swim a small river. The young widow came to Massachusetts bay, and subsequently, m. Robert Feaks. Elisabeth Underhill is generally supposed to have been his daughter, she having grown up with the Feaks children.

Children of JOHN[2] FEAKS and Elisabeth Prior, dau. of Matthew:

Feke Family.

Elisabeth³ b. 1674, m. 1710, Benjamin Field of Flushing.
Hannah³ b. 1675, m. 1698, James Cock.
Mary³ b. 1678, m. 1698, Henry Cock.
John³ b. 1679, d. 1683.
Robert³ b. 1683, m. Clemence Ludlam.
Sarah³ b. 1685.
Martha³ b. 1688, m. John Carpenter of O. Bay.
Abigail³ b. 1691, m. Josiah Coggshell.
Deborah³ b. 1695, m. 1716, Thomas Whitson, son of Thomas and Martha.
ROBERT³ FEAKS and Clemence (Ludlam) had:
Clemence⁴ m. Zebulun Wright.
Henry⁴ m. Elisabeth Prier.
Robert⁴ m. Eleanor Cousins.
John⁴ m. Abigail Wright.
Charles⁴ m. Catharine Tilley.
Deborah⁴ m. 1st James Cock, 2d Thomas Doughty.
Sarah⁴ b. 1729, James Cozens.
Elisabeth⁴ d.

1669. Robert Feaks d. wife named Sarah.

1670. James Feke gave release to Mary, widow of Tobias Feke, she having paid him all his claims the estate of Tobias, deceased.

FROST FAMILY.

WILLIAM FROST m. Rebecca (Wright) Leverich and had son:
  WRIGHT FROST m. Mary Underhill, dau. of 2d John and had:
  Joseph[3] m. Martha Cock, dau. of James and Hannah (Feak).
  William[3] m. 1st Hannah Prior, dau. of John and Elisabeth, 2d Jemima Coles, dau. of Benjamin.
JOSEPH[3] FROST and Martha had:
Anne[4] m. Benjamin Lewis.
Caleb[4] m. Sarah Halstead.
Jacob[4] m. Grace Scarlett.
Michael[4] single.
Elisabeth[4] m. Stephen Horton.
Wright[4] m. Sarah.
Hannah[4] m. 1774, Adolph Covert.
Sarah.[4]
WILLIAM[3] FROST and Hannah had,
  CHARLES[4] m. 1st Esther Cock, 2d Mary Rushmore. Their children were:
Isaac[5] m. 1807, Hannah Whitson, dau. of Amos.
Phebe[5] m. Samuel B. Titus.
  Sarah[5] m. Stephen Mott. son of James and Amy (Powell).
Jordan Frost, b. at O. Bay, L. I., Feb. 1754, m. 1781, Amy, dau. of Jacob and Amy (Hallock) Under-

hill, removed to Nine partners, Mo Me, thence in 1803, to Renselaerville, Mo Me. They had 5 children, he d. 1835, she d. 1799.

Israel Frost d. 1796, gave property to his brothers' children, viz: brother Nathaniel's children:

James, Israel and Mary.

Brother Townsend's children:

Elisabeth, Platt and Isaac; Ex., Uncle James Oakley, and brother Nathaniel, brother Platt, d. 1788, left property to his brothers.

Sister Elisabeth, widow of Thomas Merritt, she d. 1789. after receiving legacy from her brother, Platt Frost.

HALSTEAD FAMILY.

JONAS[1] HALSTEAD of Spattan Island, m. 1657, had sons, John, Joseph.
TIMOTHY[2] m. and had son Ezekiel.[3]
Thomas and perhaps others.
EZEKIEL[3] HALSTEAD m. 1730, at New Rochelle, had sons:
Ezekiel[4] m. 1758, Abigail Theall.
Joshua Halstead m. Mary, had dau. Phebe b. 1767, m. John Powell.

HAFF FAMILY.

George Haff was field Trumpeter, in Brazil, he married Twintie Strachman.

Son, Lawrence Haff, born in Brazil, m. 1676, Kniersie, dau. of Peter Mott and lived in Flushing.

Levi Vincent Haff, of Flushing, m. Esther De-Vaux Devoe.

1698. Lorus Haff and wife Cannerto, sons Jarwin, Peter, Johannes and Jacob; daus., Stinchie, Maria, Tuntie, Margaretta and Santa were living in Flushing, L. I.

Jacob Haff, m. had sons Joseph, Jacob and Lawrence m. and lived at Crum Elbow, Duchess Co.

Will 1753 says wife, Hannah, children: Ellis, Susanna, Isaac, Elisabeth and William.

1757. Will of Jacob Haff, jr., of Crum Elbow says, wife Margaret, sons Jacob, William and Lawrence, daus. Anne and Elisabeth.

1758. Will of Lawrence Haff, of Duchess Co., wife Sarah, sons Anthony, Peter, Lawrence and John, dau. Wynchie, Susanna and Mary.

1766. Wm. Huff's wife, of Cortland Manor.

1766. Leonard Huff, of Cortland Manor.

Jacob Haff, of Jerusalem South; now Seaford, m. Dean, children:

Stephen, William, Uriah, David, Fanny, Abigail, b. 1793, m. Samuel Verity, b. 1783, Dorothy, Mary and perhaps others.

Lawrence Haff, m. (now of Bellmore) and had two children, viz:

Lawrence and Elbert.

HAM FAMILY.

Rachel b. Aug. 9, 1749, m. Elisha Powell.
Frederic b. Jan. 20, 1751.
Catharine b. March 1753, m. Thomas Powell.
Mary b. Aug. 19, 1755, m. a Morrill.
Coenrad b. Sept. 29, 1757.
Margaret b. Feb. 7, 1760.
Casper b. Sept. 16, 1762.
Elisabeth b. March 10, 1764, m. a Coenly.
Abigail b. March 5, 1766, m. a Cooper.

HARNED FAMILY.

Edward^1 Harnett (or d) and family were at Salem, Mass., in 1640, and later suffered for harboring Quakers.

Edward^2 m. came to Huntington, L. I., with wife Elisabeth. (dau. of Jonathan and Eunice Porter), children probably :

Jonathan, who was in Huntington in 1672, and others ; supposed children of Jonathan were :

Jonathan in 1714, brother-in-law to Elias Cornelius, whose wife was Sarah ? Harned in 1700.

The Harned family increased and in 1816, Mary, wife of Jacob Harned requested to become a member of Jericho monthly meeting.

PORTER FAMILY.

JONATHAN^1 PORTER d. 1660, he and Eunice had:
Elisabeth^4 m. Edward Harned (or tt).
Eunice^2 m. James Chichester (name originally spelled Circencester) at Taunton in 1643, Salem, in 1650.
Mary^2 m. Stephen Jarvis.

HAWXHURST FAMILY.

Christopher[1] Hawxhurst, brother of Mary, widow of Robert Coles, came from Mass., to L. I.

Samson[2] Hawxhurst, m. Hannah Townsend, dau. of Mill John, children:

William,[3] Joseph,[3] m. had son, Wm.[4] who m. and had Ephraim[5] who m. Charity Titus.

Benjamin,[3] Samson,[3] m. Susanna, Daniel.[3]

Samson[3] and Susanna had:

William[4] m. Ann Pratt.

Samson[4] m. Amy.

Joseph,[4] Benjamin,[4] Daniel,[4] Amy,[4] Johanne[4] m. Daniel Birdsall.

SAMSON[4] HAWXHURST and Amy had:

John[5] m. Penelope (Cock) widow Loines.

Simeon[5] m. Lydia Rogers.

Henry[5] m. Phebe Oakley.

Jotham[5] m. Jane Seaman.

Will 1777, of Joseph Hawxhurst says wife Sarah, children: Hannah, Sarah, Elisabeth Merritt, Jacob, Jesse and William.

Will 1795, of Daniel Hawxhurst, New York City, says wife Hannah, children: John, Sarah, Almy, Mary, another Sarah.

HICKS FAMILY.

ROBERT HICKS the emigrant, m. 1st Elisabeth Morgan, dau. of John, children:
Elisabeth,² Thomas.²
John² m. 1st Herodias Long, 2d 1662, Rachel, widow Starr, he d. 1672.
Robert.¹
Stephen² m. 2d Margaret Winslow and had:
Samuel.²
Ephraim² m. 1649, Elisabeth Howland, dau. of John and Elisabeth, of the "Mayflower."
Lydia, Phebe.
Children of JOHN² and Hored (Long) Hicks:
Thomas³ b. 1640, m. 1st Mary (Butler, dau. of Richard, of Stradford) widow of John Washburne.
Hannah³ m. William Haviland.
Elisabeth³ m. Josias Starr.
Children of THOMAS³ and Mary Butler:
Thomas⁴ m. Deborah Valentine.
Jacob⁴ b. about 1669, m. 1690, Hannah Carpenter, he d. 1755.
Married 2d Mary Doughty and had:
Isaac,⁴ William,⁴ John,⁴ Charles,⁴ Benjamin,⁴ Charity,⁴ Mary,⁴ Elisabeth,⁴ Stephen,⁴ Phebe,⁴ m. Samuel Seaman, son of Capt. John.
JACOB⁴ Hicks (Thomas³ John² Robert¹) lived at Rockaway, m. Hannah Carpenter, had:
Samuel⁵ m. Martha Doughty.

Hicks Family. 213

Stephen,⁵ Thomas,⁵ m. 1730, Temperance Titus, dau. of Silas and Sarah Haight.
Joseph,⁵ Jacob.⁵
Benjamin⁵ b. about 1716, m. 1736, Phebe b. 1717, d. 1800, dau. of Silas Titus and Sarah, he d. 1744.
Elisabeth,⁵ John,⁵ m. 1st Martha Smith, 2d Phebe Powell.
Sarah,⁵ Hannah,⁵ m. David Titus, son of Silas and Sarah.

BENJAMIN⁵ HICKS and wife Phebe (Titus) had:
Silas⁶ b. 1737, m. 1762, Rachel, b. 1742, dau. of Samuel Seaman and Martha Valentine.
Benjamin⁶ b. 1739, m. 1765, 1st Elisabeth Mott, 2d 1774, Mary Mott, dau. of Jehu and Ruth (Powell).
Samuel⁶ b. 1741, m. 1st 1765, Phebe Seaman, 2d 1794, Amy (Shotwell, dau. of Joseph) widow of Charles Brooks.
Sarah⁶ b. 1744, m. 1764, Richard Albertson, she d. 1818.

BENJAMIN⁶ HICKS and 1st wife Elisabeth had son Mott⁷ Hicks, 2d had:
Elisabeth⁷ b. April 24, 1775, m. Cornell Willis.
Silas⁷ b. 1777, m. Sallie Titus, dau. of Silas.
Sarah⁷ b 1780, m. Henry Haydock.
Mary⁷ b. 1782, single.
Temperance⁷ b. 1784, m. 1812, Henry Mott.
Benjamin⁷ b. June 14, 1790, m. Mary Morrill.
Phebe⁷ b. 1793, m. Abraham Brookes, son of Charles and Amy.
Robert⁷ M. b. 1799, m. Rosanna Leggett.

Children of SAMUEL⁶ HICKS and (Phebe) Seaman:
Isaac⁷ b. 1767, m. Sarah Doughty, dau. of John and Abigail, he d. 1820.

Samuel[7] m.
Valentine[7] m. Abigail, dau. of Elias Hicks.
Phebe[7] m. John Clapp.
Elisabeth[7] b. 1771.
ISAAC[7] HICKS and Sarah Doughty had:
John[8] D. b. 1791, m. Sarah Rushmore, b. 1790, d. 1893, he d. Oct. 10, 1829.
Robert[8] m. Mary U. Mott.
Benjamin[8] m. Elisabeth Hicks, dau. of Whitehead.
Isaac,[8] Mary,[8] d.
Elisabeth[8] m. 1st Wm. Seaman, 2d Wm. T. Cock, son of Samuel.

JOHN[5] HICKS (Jacob[4] Thomas[3] John[2] Robert[1]) and Martha Smith had:
Samuel[6] m., Joseph[5] m., John[6] m.
Elias[6] b. 19, 3, 1748, m. Feb. 1, 1771, Jemima Seaman, dau. of Jonathan and Elisabeth, he d. Feb. 27, 1830.
Stephen[6] m. Mary Hewlett.

ELIAS[6] HICKS and Jemima had:
Martha[7] b. 1771, m. Royal Aldrich, son of Stephen and Mary, he d. 1839.
David[7] b. 1773, d. 1787.
Elias[7] b. 1774, d. 1789.
Elisabeth[7] b. 1777, d. 1779.
Phebe[7] b. 1779, m. Joshua Willets.
Abigail[7] b. 1782, m. Valentine Hicks.
Jonathan[7] b. 1784, d. 1802.
John[7] b. 1789, d. 1805.
Elisabeth[7] b. 1791, d. single 1871.
Sarah[7] b. 1793, m. Robert Seaman, son of David and Sarah, she d. 1835.

STEPHEN[6] HICKS baptised Sept. 9, 1750, m. Mary Hewlett, b. 1758, and had:
John,[7] Martha[7] m. James Poole.

Sarah[7] m. John Cornell.
Oliver[7] m., Phebe[7] m. William Imlay.
Mary[7] single, Stephen[7] m.
Abraham[7] m. Rachel Seaman, dau. of Gideon.
Whitehead[7] b. 1797, m. Mary Ann Merritt, dau. of Jesse and Mary.
Samuel.[7]

HAYDOCK FAMILY.

ROGER[1] HAYDOCK b. at Penketh, 3, of 1st month, 1643, m. 3, of 6th month 1682, Eleanor Lowe (his father d. 1670, mother d. 1684).
Children of ROGER and Eleanor:
Robert[2] b. at Penketh, 11, 1, 1687, m. 23, 6, 1709, Rebebca b. 1680, dau. of Daniel and Abigail Griffith, came to America in 1743, had 9 children; brought 6 with them: Eleanor,[3] Eden[3], Henry,[3] Rebecca,[3] Jane[3] and one more[3]; landed at Wilmington, spent the winter, established Eden in Phil'a., and moved to Flushing, L. I., in the Spring.
Eden[3] Haydock, of Philadelphia, son of Robert, of L. I., m. March 29, 1746, Elisabeth Forster, dau. of Reuben, of Philadelphia, Eden d. 1776, Elisabeth d. 1776.
HENRY[3] HAYDOCK of New York, son of Robert[2] of L. I., m. Catharine Rodman, dau. of Thomas, she d. 1760, between 29 and 30 years of age, he m. 2d Hannah Moode (or Mott) of New Jersey, dau. of Wm., she d. 1791, he d. 1798. He had previously m. in 1746, Mary Bowne, dau. of Robert and Margaret, she d. 1757.
Children of HENRY[3] HAYDOCK and Hannah (Mott):
William[4] b. 1764, d.

Haydock Family. 217

Mary[4] b. 1765, Rebecca and Hannah, twins, b. Dec. 24, 1766.
Henry[4] b. 1768, m. 1801, Sarah Hicks, dau. of Benjamin and Mary.
Elisabeth[4] Moode, b. 1770.
Eleanor[4] b. 1772.
Jane[4] b. 1774.
Robert[4] b. 1777, d. 1778.
HENRY[4] HAYDOCK and Sarah had:
Henry[5] b. Mar. 9, 1802, m. Martha Mott.
Hannah[5] b. Mar. 3, 1804.
Robert[5] H. b. Dec. 3, 1805.
Wm.[5] Wood b. March 13, 1808.
Mary[5] b. Sept. 29, 1809.
Elisabeth[5] b. April 24, 1812.
Jane[5] b. Jan. 29, 1816.
Sarah[5] b. July 18, 1820, m. John L. Griffin.
Richard[5] L. b. Mar. 28, 1823.
EDEN[3] HAYDOCK (Robt.[2] Roger[1]), of Phil'a, and Elisabeth Forster had:
Rebecca[4] b. 1748, m. Samuel Garigues.
Hannah[4] b. 1750, m. Hugh Hawell.
Robt.[4] 1754, m. Susanna Garigues.
Henry[4] b. 1758, m.
Elisabeth[4] b. 1765, d.
ROBERT[4] HAYDOCK and Susanna had:
Eden[5] b. 1779.
Samuel[5] b. 1780, m. Sarah Corlies and had:
Robert[6] m. Hannah Wharton of Philadelphia, dau. of Deborah (Rodman).

HOPKINS FAMILY.

William Hopkins (? came from England) wife Joanna, dau. of Thomas Arnold and Alice (Galley).
Thomas, (son) b. April 7, 1616, in England m. about 1648, Elisabeth, dau. of Wm. Arnold, of R. I., she was his cousin, he d. 1684, at Littleworth, Oysterbay, L. I., children:
William b. m., he d. July 8, 1723.
Thomas b. he d. April 1, 1718.
―――― b., m. Elisabeth, he d. in R. I. before his father left there; widow Elisabeth came to L. I., with her father-in-law, her son Ichabod, dau. Ann. and perhaps another dau. who m. Nathan Coles, widow subsequently m. Richard Kirby.
Ann dau. of ―――― and Elisabeth Hopkins, m. Thomas Kirby, son of Richard, had 6 children:
Icabod Hopkins was the progenitor of the Westchester and L. I. Hopkins family. He m. Sarah, dau. of Daniel and Maha, shal, lal, has, baz (Groton) Coles, children:
Thomas, of North Castle, Westchester Co., m. 1738, Margaret.
Daniel m. Amey Weeks, he d. 1763.
Elisabeth m. 1734, Benjamin Birdsall, of Rye.
Sarah b. 1719, m. 1736, Michael Mudge, she d. 1815.
Dinah m. Nehemiah Merritt.
Ann.

Hopkins Family.

Daniel and Amy had 12 children, viz:
William m. Rachel Coles.
Thomas m. Ann Mudge.
Martha m. Benjamin Downing.
Hannah m. John Trip.
Dinah m. Wm. Cock.
Amy m. George Downing.
Abigail m. 1734, Joseph Coles, a weaver.
Sarah m. Micah Mudge.
Temperance m. 1740, Derick Thorny Craft.
Elisabeth m. Caleb Coles.
Ann m. John Cromwell.
Mary m. David Tilley.
William and Rachel (Coles) Hopkins, children:
Daniel m. 1776, Susanna Ellison.
Phebe m. 1775, David Hopkins of Westchester.
Esther m. 1781, Samuel Carpenter.
Rachel m. Daniel Cromwell.
John m.
Amelia m. 1770, Aaron Robbins.
Daniel Hopkins and Susanna had:
Son Daniel m. 1st Phebe Gardner, dau. of Noah
  Gardner, m. 2d 1786, Sarah Wright.
Children of Daniel and Phebe:
Edwin b. m. 1st —— 2d Mary Hopper.
Sarah b., m. William Duke.
Milton b., m.
Edwin and 2d wife Mary have grandson Edwin Hopkins Seaman.

JACKSON FAMILY.

Richard Jackson had grant and deed of land in Southold from Earl Sterling as early as 1640, but sold it very soon to Goodyear, and he to John Ketchum. One Record says Richard remained in Massachusetts. He made a 2d marriage with the widow of Richard Brown, he died in 1672, aged 90 years.

ROBERT[1] JACKSON m. Agnes, dau. of Wm. and Jane Washburne. Their children were:

John[2] m. Elisabeth Seaman, dau. of Capt. John, he d. 1722.

Samuel[2] m. had children.

Sarah[2] m. Nathaniel Moore.

Martha[2] m. 1667, Nathaniel Coles, son of Robert.

Children of JOHN[2] and Elisabeth (Seaman) Jackson:

John[3] m. Elisabeth Hallet, dau. of Samuel.

Samuel[3] b. 1684, m. 1st Ruth Smith, 2d Abigail Seaman, dau. of Thomas.

James[3] m. 1730, Rebecca Hallett, dau. of Wm. and Sarah (Woolsey) she d. 1735.

Martha[3] m. Peter Titus, son of Edmond and Martha.

Elisabeth[3] m. Charles Doughty.

Hannah[3] m. Richard Seaman.

Mary[3] Jeremiah Scott.

Sarah[3] m. Joshua Barnes.

Children of John[3] Jackson and Elisabeth (Hallett):

John[4] m. Kesia Mott, dau. of Richbell Mott and Elis (Thorne).

Jackson Family.

Samuel[4] 1738, m. Mary Townsend, dau. of Richard and Ruth (Marvin).
Richard[4] m. Jane Seaman, dau. of Jacob.
Sarah[4] m. a Hallett.
Hannah[4] m. John Hewlett.
Phebe[4] m. Wm. Jones.
Mary[4] m. 1725, Samuel Titus, son of Samuel Titus and Elisabeth (Powell of Thomas.[1]

SAMUEL[3] JACKSON (John[2] Robert) m. 1st Ruth, 2d. Abigail and had Samuel,[4] Richard,[4] both d. unm. and intestate.

Ruth[4] b. 1709, m. Abel Smith.
Jemima.[4]
Thomas[4] m. 1748, Mary Willis, dau. of Samuel and Mary (Fry), he d. 1750. They had dau:
Mary[5] m. William Seaman.
Isaac[4] m. Mary Cornell, no children, he d. 1750.
Jerusha.[4]
Abigail[4] m. Jacob Mott, near Hempstead Harbor.

Children of JAMES[3] b. 1735, and Rebecca, Jackson, b. 1730, of Rocky Hill.

Mary[4] m. 1717, Jacob Willets.
Wm.[4] m. Prudence Smith.
Thomas[4] (the oldest) m. Mary Townsend.
Sarah[4] m. Samuel Clement.
Rebecca[4] m. Sylvanus Seaman.
John[4] m. Sarah Doty.
James[4] m. 1725, 1st Sarah Thorne b. 1702, 2d Mary Thorne.
Elisabeth[4] m. 1725, Nathan Field, son of Thomas.
Charity[4] m. John Dingee.
Hannah[4] m. John Hicks.
Joseph[4] m. Mary Rogers.
Richard[4] m. Mary Wright, dau. of Nathaniel Townsend.

Martha[4] m. Wm. Green.
Phebe[4] m. 1734, Edward Fitz Randolph, at Flushing meeting.
Robert[4] m. Sarah Hewlett.
Jemima[4] m. Henry Hicks.
Samuel[4] m. Sarah Carpenter.
Stephen[4] m. Mary Lewis.
Benjamin[4] m. Amy Paul, widow.
Two[4] d. young.

RICHARD[4] JACKSON (John[3] John[2] Robert[1]) m. Jane Seaman and had:
Richard[5] m. Rosetta Jackson, dau. of John.
Micah[5] m. ? Phebe Wright, dau. of Gilbert.
Jacob[5] m. Catharine Peters and had Jacob,[6] Jane,[6] and Phebe.[6]
Mary[5] m. John Tredwell.
Jane[5] m. 1771, Zebulun Seaman.

Children of RICHARD[5] JACKSON and Rosetta:
Micah[6] b. 1778, m. Elisabeth Jackson.
Jane[6] m. John Althouse.
Alma[6] m. Henry O. Seaman, he was a member of the Assembly from 1803 to 1808, a Justice of the Peace several years.

JOHN[4] JACKSON (John[3] John[2] Robert[1]) m. Kesia Mott and had:
Obadiah[5] m. Alma Seaman, dau. of Jacob, he d. 1779.
John[5] b. 1733, m. 1st Charity Smith Tredwell, 2d Margaret (Wright), widow of Noah Townsend.
Parmenus[5] m. Elisabeth Birdsall.
Martha[5] m. Thomas Seaman, son of Richard.
Elisabeth[5] m. Col. John Sands.
Jerusha[5] m. Morris Place.
Rosetta[5] m. Richard Jackson.
Abigail[5] m. Jacob Robbins.

Mary⁵ m. Benjamin Sands.
Ann⁵ m. John Hewlett
JOHN⁵ JACKSON and Charity Tredwell had :
Thomas⁶ Tredwell m. Catharine Britt.
John⁶ m. Sarah Udal, dau. of Joseph.
Tredwell.⁶
Samuel⁶ d. Intestate, left large estate.
Children of 2d wife Margaret (Wright):
Charity⁶ m. John Seaman.
Noah⁶ and Kesia,⁶ single.
Obadiah⁶ m. 1st Elisabeth Wright, 2d Rachel Underhill.
Mary⁶ m. Daniel Underhill, son of Adonijah.
THOMAS⁶ T. JACKSON and Catharine had :
Eliza⁷ m. William Wright.
Sarah⁷ m. Selah Carle.
Catharine⁷ m. Andrew Hageman.
John,⁷ Robert,⁷ Wm.⁷
OBADIAH⁶ JACKSON and Rachel (Underhill) had :
William,⁷ Elisabeth,⁷ John⁷ b. 12, 6, 1813.
PARMENAS⁵ JACKSON (John⁴ John³ John² Robert¹) Elisabeth (Birdsall) had:
Parmenas⁶ jr., m. Charity Coles.
Elisabeth⁶ m. Micah Jackson, son of Richard.
Rosanna⁶ m. Samuel Nichols.
John⁶ m. Margaret Cornell, dau. of Stephen.
Parmenas⁵ Jackson died of wounds received at his house, in Little Britain, near Jerusalem from a party of plunderers, Jan. 19, 1781 ; Revolutionary times.
OBADIAH⁵ JACKSON (John⁴ John³ John² Robert¹) and Alma Seaman had :
Elisabeth⁶ m. Thomas Jackson, son of Samuel.
Jacob⁶ Seaman b. 1763, m. Phoebe Coles, b. 1764, dau. of Benjamin, he d. 1828.

Jackson Family.

Major JACOB[6] SEAMAN JACKSON took oath of allegiance to U. S., in 1790, m. Phebe Coles and had:

Thomas[7] d.

Mary[7] b. 1784, m. Thomas Jones d. 1801, he m. 2d Ruth Jackson, dau. of Thomas and had Samuel.

Elisabeth[7] b. 1796, m. Thomas Jones, was his 3d wife and had Jacob S. I. Jones.

SAMUEL[4] JACKSON (John[3] John[2] Robert[1]) m. 1738, Mary Townsend and had:

Richard[5] m. 1st Phebe Kissam, 2d Elisabeth Brooks.

Townsend[5] m. Mary Seaman, dau. of Thomas.

Thomas[5] m. Elisabeth Jackson, dau. of Obadiah.

Ruth[5] and Elisabeth[5] both d.

Jemima[5] m. James Hewlett.

Letitia[5] m. Solomon Pool.

Mary[5] m John Pratt.

Martha m. Samuel Birdsall.

THOMAS[5] and Elisabeth Jackson had:

Obadiah[6] m. Sarah, dau. of John Boerum.

Jacob[6] m. Phebe Duryea.

Samuel[6] m. Martha Hewlett, dau. of Lewis.

Alma[6] d.

Ruth[6] m. Thomas Jones of West Neck.

OBADIAH[6] and Sarah had:

Timothy[7] m. Ethelinda Willis.

Thomas[7] m. Esther Willis.

Townsend[7] m. Margaret Nostrant.

Ruth[7] m. William Hicks.

Rebecca[7] m. Jacob Seaman Jackson Jones.

Sarah[7] m. Nehemiah Haydon, Margaret[7] m.

JACOB[6] JACKSON and Phebe Duryea had:

Townsend[7] m. Martha Willets.

Henry[7] m. Martha Eldred.

Jackson Family.

James[7] m. Julia.
Sidney[7] m. 1st Caroline Robbins, 2d Mary Jane Hubbs.
Mary[7] m. Townsend Willis.
Martha[7] m. 1st John Jackson, son of Richard, 2d Benjamin Albertson, widower.
Elisabeth[7] m. Benjamin Albertson, she d. early and he m. her sister Martha.
Emily[7] m. Isaac Thorne, son of Samuel and Maria.

THOMAS[4] JACKSON (Samuel[3] John[2] Robert[1]) and Mary Willets, dau. of Samuel and Mary (Fry) had:

Mary[5] b. 1749, m. 1763, William Seaman, son of Robert and Esther, (Tho's. d. 1750, and widow Mary, m. Thomas[4] Jackson, son of Thomas,[3] of James,[2] of John,[2] of Robert.[1])

THOMAS[4] JACKSON (James[3] John[2] Robert[1]) m. Mary Townsend and had:

Robert,[5] Amy.[5]
Thomas[5] m. Mary (Willis), widow of Thomas[4] Jackson, he d. 1750.
James,[5] Daniel,[5] Benjamin,[5] Rebecca.[5]
Samuel[5] m. 1773, Deborah Seaman, dau. of Solomon and Hannah.
Phebe[5] m. 1763, Isaac Seaman.

THOMAS[5] JACKSON and Mary (Willis) widow Jackson had:

David[6] m. Esther Whitson.
Charles[6] m.
Amy[6] m. Robert Hubbs.

DAVID[6] JACKSON and Esther (Whitson) had:
Jarvis[7] m. Mary Whitson.
Mary[7] m. 1803, Abraham Whitson.

JARVIS[7] JACKSON and Mary Whitson had:
William,[8] Nathaniel.[8]

Henry[8] m. Sarah Mott, dau. of John.

George[8] m. Elisabeth Underhill. dau. of Josiah I.

Charles,[8] Phebe.[8]

SAMUEL[5] JACKSON (Thomas[4] James[3] John[2] Robt.[1]) and Deborah had:

Solomon[6] m. Mary Brower, dau. of Jeremiah.

Thomas[6] m.

SOLOMON[6] and Mary had:

Jeremiah[7] m. Jerusha Powell, dau. of Rob't. he d. 1875.

Solomon[7] m. 1st Annie Titus, dau. of Ansel, 2d Esther Post.

Eliza[7] m. Stephen Dodge, she d. 1893.

Martha,[7] Amy.[7]

JEREMIAH BROWER a merchant in New York, died in N. Jersey, 1776, wife Elisabeth, eldest son Jeremiah,[2] Theophilus,[2] dau. Ianthe m. Peter Kipp: Wm., Henry, John, Elisabeth, Abraham. Mary born after her father's death, m. Solomon[6] Jackson. The eldest son Jeremiah was to have a birthright, and the residue, after each of the children had £250 apiece.

JONES FAMILY.

THOMAS¹ JONES came from Strabane, Ireland, to Rhode Island, thence to Long Island, m. Freelove Townsend, dau. of Thomas who gave them a large tract of land at Massapequa, where they settled and had:
    David² b. 1699, m. 1724, Anna Willet, she d. 1750, he d. 1775.
    Thomas² was drowned in crossing the ferry at Rye.
    William² b. 1708, m. Phebe Jackson, b. 1715, she d. 1800, he d. 1779.
    Freelove² m. Jacob Smith.
    Sarah² m. Gerardus Clowes.
    Margaret² m. Ezekiel Smith.
    Elisabeth² m. Jacob Mitchell.
First Thomas Jones, d. at Massapequa 1713, widow Freelove (Townsend), b. 1674, m. 2d Timothy Bagley.
    Children of DAVID² JONES and Anna Willet:
    David³ d. 1758.
    Thomas³ b. 1731, m. a Delaney, no children; he built the Mansion at Massapequa, he d. 1792.
    Anna³ m. John Gale.
    Arrabella³ b. 1734, m. 1757, Richard Floyd.
    Mary³ m. her cousin Thomas Jones, son of Wm. and Phebe.
In 1730. William² Jones bought a large quantity of land, of Timothly Bagley and settled at West Neck, where his grandson Thomas Jones afterward resided.
    Children of WILLIAM² and Phebe (Jackson):
    David³ m. Elisabeth Seaman.

Samuel³ m. Cornelia Herring.
William³ m. a Townsend.
Thomas³ m. his cousin Mary Jones, dau. of David.³
Gilbert³ m.
John³ m. Hannah, dau. of John Hewlett.
Walter³ m. 1st Esther Willis, d. 1801, aged 38, m. 2d Phebe Hewlett.
Richard,³ Hallett.³
Freelove³ m. Benjamin Birdsall.
Elisabeth³ m. Jacob Conklin.
Margaret³ m. Thomas Hewlett.
Phebe³ m. Benjamin Rowland.
Sarah³ m. John Willis.

THOMAS³ JONES (William² Thomas¹) and Mary had:
William,⁴ David,⁴ Thomas,⁴ Oliver⁴ and several daughters.

DAVID³ JONES and Elisabeth had:
William D.⁴ m. Almy Seaman, Thomas.⁴

By the will of the first Thomas Jones, the Massapequa property was to be entailed, to the male line of his eldest son, David.² In case there should be no male of that line left, then it was to go to the eldest son of David's² dau. Arabella,³ David⁴ Richard Floyd. The last of the male line died, and David⁴ Richard Floyd added Jones to his name and was allowed quiet possession of the property.

THOMAS JONES of Huntington, died 1669, his wife died leaving him four sons: Thomas, John and others. He married a 2d wife, Catharine, widow of Henry Scudder. Her father was Jeffrey Estes from Salem, Mass., he died 1657, being the first death in Huntington.

Thomas Jones and 2d wife Catharine had one daughter, Martha, who married Thomas Whitson, and was the progenitor of all the known Whitsons.

KIRBY FAMILY.

RICHARD KIRBY came from Mass., to L. I., settled at Littleworth, will Oct. 17, 1688, says wife Elisabeth, she was a widow Hopkins when he married her as his 2d wife. The mother of his son Thomas may have been Patience Gifford, as one of that name married a Richard Kirbie, and had daughter Temperance b. 1670, m. 1721, George Pearce b. 1662, son of Richard.

THOMAS[2] KIRBIE m. Ann Hopkins, dau. of widow Elisabeth, and had:
William[3] m. 1733, Sarah Willets, dau. of Richard of Islip.
Thomas[3] m.
Richard[3] d. 1749.
Daniel[3] m. Hannah Latting.
Mary[3] m. a Valentine.
Elisabeth[3] m. Benjamin Thorny Craft.

WILLIAM[3] KIRBY and Sarah (Willets) had:
Mary[4] b. 1738, d. 1781.♦
Willets[4] m. 1st 1764, Hannah Titus, dau. of Edmond, 2d 1787, (Mary Jackson), widow of Wm. Seaman.

Children of WILLETS[4] KIRBY and Hannah (Titus):
Jacob[5] b. 1765, m. 1790, Mary Seaman, dau. of William and (Mary Jackson).
Edmond[5] b. 1768, m. 1803, Sarah Loines, dau. of William and Sarah (Alsop).
Sarah[5] b. 1772, m. David Seaman, son of Wm. and Mary (Jackson).
Phebe[5] b. 1778, m. a Carpenter.

KETCHAM FAMILY.

EDWARD[1] KETCHAM of Ipswich, Mass., 1635, was a freeman 1637, land at Southold, L. I., in 1654.

John[2] Ketcham of Ipswich was a representative to the Government of Mass., he removed to Setauket, L. I. in 1648, went to Newtown in 1668, d. 1697, wife Bethia.

Children of JOHN[2] KETCHUM and Bethia:

John,[3] Samuel,[3] Edward[3] m. Mary, all at Huntington in 1672.

In 1665. John Ketcham and Thomas Weeks were Overseers at Huntington John Ketcham was a Grantee in the first Nichols patent of Huntington 1666.

Town made many grants of land from 1676 to 1687. Richard Harcourt had grandson Daniel Ketcham in 1696.

Lieutenant JOHN KETCHAM and wife Susan sold place in Southold Sept. 29, 1666 to Thomas Moore, Sr.

Children of JOHN[3] KETCHAM and wife Susan, b. in Huntington.

John[4] b. 1674, Thomas[4] b. 1676, Elisabeth[4] b. 1678, Philip[4] b. 1680, David b. 1683, Mary b. 1686.

SAMUEL[3] KETCHAM'S children were:

Samuel[4] b. 1672, Joseph[4] b. 1674, Mary[4] b. 1677, Nathaniel[4] b. 1679, Jonathan[4] b. 1682, Ephraim[4] b. 1685, Hester[4] b. 1687.

ISRAEL KETCHAM m. Esther Skidmore and had:

David, of Jericho, m. 1780, Jane Seaman b. 1746, dau. of Wm. and Martha.

Children of DAVID and Jane:

John m. Rebecca Sherman, dau. of Isaac and Margaret Fitzgerald.

David m. 1st Phebe Willets, dau. of Jacob, 2d Martha T. Hallock, dau. of James.

Martha unm. d. 1837.

Children of JOHN[2] and Rebecca (Sherman) Ketcham.

Phebe m. Thomas Hallowell.

William m. 1st Charry Jagger, m. 2d ———,went to Wisconsin.

Margaret S. m. William Jagger, she d. 1870.

Isaac S. m. 1st Mary, 2d Sarah Mann.

Martha S. m. David Hallock, son of Nicholas.

Jane d. a young woman, James d.

ISAAC SHERMAN b. Mar. 13, 1756, m. Apr. 20, 1791, Margaret b. Jan. 21, 1762, she d. 1799, he d. 1806. They had children, viz:

Rebecca b. Sept. 26, 1792, m. 1816, John Ketcham.

James b. 1794, m. Philadelphia Hallock, dau of James.

Anna b. 1797, m. Edward Hallock.

Margaret b. 1799, m. Joseph Townsend, she d. 1833.

KEESE FAMILY.

JOHN[1] KEESE of Flushing m. Mary Bowne and had:
Mary[2] b. 1721, William[2] b. 1723, Samuel[2] b. 1726.
John[2] b. 1729, m. 1750, Elisabeth Titus, b. 1729, dau. of Samuel and Mary (Jackson).
Eleanor[2] b. 1733.
JOHN[2] KEESE and wife Elisabeth, dau. of Samuel Titus, son of Samuel and Elisabeth (Powell) Titus, had children, viz:
Samuel.[3]
Stephen[3] m. a Haight, had son Samuel[4] and probably others.
William[3] m. Jemima (Baldwin), widow of Abraham Bunker.
Richard[3] m. Anna Hallock, had son Peter[4] and others.
John.[3]
Oliver[3] m. Paulina Lapham.
Sarah[3] m. a Thorn.
Mary[3] m. Peter Hallock.
Elisabeth[3] m. a Secor.
Phebe.[3]
SAMUEL[4] KEESE (Stephen[3] John[2] John[1]) m. 1st and had (m. 2d. Catharine Robinson) no children.
John[5] of Great Neck m. 1st ———, m. 2d Amy Barker, dau. of Caleb and Rachel.
WILLIAM[3] KEESE (John[2] John[1]) and Jemima had:
Julia[4] d.
Eliza Ann[4] m. William Shepherd.
Wm.,[4] Pamela,[4] Willets,[4] Jemima.[4]

LANGDON FAMILY.

Gilbert Opdyke to Alexander Briam, he to deliver Sept. 16, 1655, to Thomas^1 Langdon, three hollows over the run at East Meadow. In 1660, Thomas sold to Robert Williams Carpenter. Aaron Furman sold in 1662 (the property he bought of Adam Mott which was formerly the dwelling place of Christopher Foster), to Thomas^1 Langdon, Langdon died in 1666. Joseph^2 son of Thomas^1 Langdon had meadow in near Rockaway in 1675.

Children of JOSEPH^2 LANGDON and wife:

John,^{3} Samuel,^{3} Thomas,^{3} William,^{3} Hannah,^{3} Mary,^{3} Joseph.^{3}

Thomas^3 Langdon d. at Jerusalem in 1732–3, widow Mary, sons Joseph,^{4} Thomas^4, at Fishkill, Jonathan^4 on L. I., daus. Elisabeth^4 wife of Capt. John Birdsall, Deborah,^{4} Lewis.

LOINES FAMILY.

ROGER[1] LOINES was at Hempstead with wife Mary in 1647, was one of the first settlers of Jamaica in 1656, had sons:
    John[2] at Jamaica in 1660, at Hempstead in 1676, d. 1688.
    Nathaniel[2] m. 1679, Darmaris Baylis, had eldest son Nathaniel and others.[2]
    Thomas[2] m. Anna.
    Gabriel.[2]
    There is some evidence that John[2] Loines had son William[3] who m. Mary, dau. of George Baldwin and Mary Ellison, and had son William[4] who m. 1734, Ann Valentine, dau. of Obadiah.

WILLIAM[4] LOINES b. 1706 and Ann Valentine had:
    Mary[5] b. 2, 12, 1734, m. Dec. 7, 1754, Thomas Townsend.
    Stephen[5] b. 26, 9, 1737, m. 1759, Phebe b. 12, 12, 1735, d. 25, 3, 1815, dau. of Wm. Titus, he d. 1773.
    William[5] b. 25, 5, 1746, m. 1767, Sarah Alsop, dau. of Richard and Sarah.

Children of STEPHEN[5] and Phebe:
    John[6] b. 30, 8, 1760, m. 1779, Phebe b. 5, 9, 1755, d. 1843, dau. of Thos.[5] Seaman, he d. 1823.
    Phebe[6] m. 1791, Jacob Valentine, son of Charles.

Loines Family.

JOHN[6] LOINES and Phebe Seaman, dau. of Thomas and Hannah, had:
  Stephen[7] 20, 3, 1780, m. 1798, Phebe Weeks, m. 2d 1810, Sibbel (Powell).
  Simeon[7] b. 2, 9, 1783, m. Martha Willets, dau. of Richard.
  Hannah[7] b. 12, 4, 1786, Thomas b. 12, 2, 1789, d. 19, 11, 1792.
  Ann[7] b. 13, 3, 1797, m. John Searing.
STEPHEN[7] LOINES and Phebe (Weeks) had:
William[8] b. 1799, d. 1875.
Sarah[8] b. 1801.
2d wife Sibbel (Powell) had:
Mary[8] b. 1811, d. 1814, Jonas b. 1814, d.
John[8] b. 21, 2, 1818, m. 14, 6, 1843, Mary Bunker, dau. of Capt. Reuben.
Jonas P.[8] b. 27, 4, 1821, m. Martha Macy, no children, he d. 15, 12, 1873.
Robert[8] b. 17, 5, 1824, m. Caroline, no children.
JOHN LOINES (d. 5, 3, 1854) and Mary (Bunker) had:
Alice.[9] Stephen[9] m, Walter.[9]
WILLIAM[5] LOINES, son of Wm. and Ann Valentine, and Sarah (Alsop) had:
  James b. 1768, m. 1790, Phebe Wright, dau. of John.
  Richard b. 1769, m. a Hopkins, of Philadelphia, and had Richard and William.
  Anne b. 1773, m. 1792, Thomas Ross.
  Sarah b. 1781, m. 1803, Edmond Kirby, son of Willets and Hannah.
JAMES LOINES and Phebe had:
  William, Robert, Charles b. 1798, Nancy, b. 1801, Phebe b. 1804.
  ———[1] Loines m. Penelope Cox, dau. of Samuel, one child named Stephen[2] b. near Bethpage, L. I., in

1757, m. Jan. 28, 1778, Martha Underhill, she d. 1812, he d. 1845.

 Stephen² m. 2d 1814, Anne (dau. of Rowland Pearsall, widow) Allen, b. 1772, she d. 1840.

Anne Allen repented of marrying out of meeting in 1815.

Stephen spelled his name Lines, his great uncle Joshua Cox, in his will gave Stephen the silver watch that had been his brother Samuel's, Stephen's grandfather. The watch was with the Lines family in 1889. Penelope was soon a widow and m. 2d John Hawxhurst and had several children.

The children of STEPHEN² LINES and Martha (lived at Somers, was a Miller and Merchant) were:

Joshua² b. 1779.
Freelove b. 1781, m. William Bugbee.
John² b. 1794, m.
Samuel² b. 1787, m. Elisabeth Vanvareel.
Joseph² b. 1789.
James U.² b. 1792.
Jacob² b. 1795.
William² b. 1798.
Sally Ann² b. 1809.
2d wife had:
Martha² b. 1816, m. Stephen Horton, lived in Tioga Co., Richford P. O.

SAMUEL² and Elisabeth (Vanvareel) Lines had: Sally Ann³ b. 1809, Christianne³ b. 1810, Peter Williams³ b. 1813, Stephen³ b. 1815, Annie Allen³ b. 1817, Rowland Allen³ b. 1820, Henry Augustus³ b. 1829, Elvira³ b. 1833, and Mary.³

PETER WILLIAMS³ LINES m. Sarah Griffith, children:
William.⁴
Samuel⁴ m. Jane Crosby.

Stephen.[4]
Henry.[4]
Armanda.[4]

Dr. Ernest[5] Howard Lines (son of Samuel Lines and Jane Crosby) m. Elisabeth Lindsay James of New York.

Nathaniel Lynes (son of Roger) and Damaris (Baylis), eldest son Nathaniel m. Eunice Burroughs. He was a barber and lived in New York when they sold land at Jamaica in 1706.

1683. Ann Coles, widow of John being on the eve of a 2d m. with William Lynes, of Cow Neck gave half her land at Matinecock to her son Solomon Coles.

1689. Wm. Lyne bought land at Cow Neck of Elias and Sarah Doughty.

1691. Richard Osborne sold land to Wm. Lines of Cow Neck and wife Ann.

1713. William Lynes and Mary, his wife sold property at Jerusalem South, (or Oyster Bay, West Neck) to Elias Cornelius. Thomas Whitson lived many years on the place and sold it to Minell.

1745. William Loines bought land of Samuel Baldwin at Westbury.

1762. William Loines bought 60 acres at Westbury of Elisabeth and Richard Willis.

1776. Sarah Loines m. Samuel Gorham.

There were Loines' on New Haven Record, Ralph Loines m. Abiah Bassett.

1650. Henry Loines, son of John, of Badby, 2 miles from Daventry, 13 miles from Northampton had home in New Haven, he d. 1663, left widow, children:

John b. 1656, Joanna b. 1658, Samuel b. 1660, Hopestill b. 1661.

Ralph brother of Henry, m. children:
John b. 1655.
Joseph on list of proprietors in 1685, b. 1657.
Benjamin b. 1659.
Ralph b. 1772.
(On list of Births spelled Lines, on list of Proprietors Loines. Some of them were on the Isle of Wight. I cannot connect the families, but it seems possible that Roger, Henry and Ralph may have been brothers. The name is said to be French, De Loines. M. P. B.)

MERRITT FAMILY.

We find the arms of Merritt, of Wiltshire, England are Barry of Six, Gold on, Sable, a band of Ermine.

The earliest reliable record of this branch of the family is contained in the following receipts which were found amongst the papers of Nathaniel Merritt.

WESTCHESTER COUNTY, *March* 17, 1730.

Rec'd of John Merritt, the sum of 1 pound, 11 shillings, 7 pence half penny in full.

JAMES WOOD.

January 15, 1759.

Then received of Nathaniel Merritt, the sum of eighty-nine pounds, it being part of the taxes due from North Castle in the year 1758.

I say received by me,

WILLIAM WILLETT.

£ S D
113 16 10½
 89
―――――――
 24 19 10½

JOHN[1] MERRITT and wife ? Elisabeth or Mary had :

Nathaniel[2] b. 1725, m. Anne Fowler, dau. of Joseph and Hannah, he d. 7, 4, 1803.

Stephen[2] m. lived at White Plains.

Naomi[2] m. a White.

Mary² m. Alanson Lewis, she sent letter to her bro. N. from N. Brunswick.

Deborah² unm. d. 1820, some evidence of another dau. m. a *Lent*.

NATHANIEL² MERRITT and Ann Fowler had:

John³ b. 23, 3, 1758 at Cortland Manor, m. 1784, Phebe Weeks, dau. of Joseph, he d. 27, 10, 1833.

James³ m. 1788, Sarah, sister of Phebe, dau. of Joseph Weeks and Phebe (Underhill).

Jesse³ b. 20, 2, 1767, at Peekskill, m. 1789, Mary Cornelius, dau. of John, he d. 30, 3, 1843.

Anne³ m. John Ogden and had Jemima, Gilbert and Mary.

Jemima⁴ Ogden m. 1st JOHN¹ SMALL had son John⁵ d. m. 2d 1793, a Close.

Mary⁴ Ogden m. 1796, EBENEZER CHICHESTER had JOHN⁵ b. 1797, m. and had son Nathaniel⁶ m. lived at Amityville, L. I., Mary⁴ Ogden d. 1798.

Jesse³ Merritt and Mary d. 7, 11, 1840, (Cornelius) dau. of John and Mary (Powell) had:

Mary⁴ d. 1791.

Elisabeth⁴ b. 20, 10, 1793, m. 26, 3, 1817, Ardon Seaman, son of Zebulun, she d. 3, 2, 1875. he d. 2, 4, 1875.

John⁴ C. b. 2, 7, 1796, m. 1835, Phebe H. Albertson, he d. 26, 1, 1891.

Mary Ann⁴ b. 2, 1, 1799, m. 1st 1826, Whitehead Hicks m. 2d Robt, Seaman, she d. — 5, 1887.

John² son of Nathaniel¹ Merritt settled in New York.

In 1684. Was a Merchant, the firm name was Merritt & Webb, removed to New Brunswick in 6th month 1785, in partnership with his father at Gage Town. Returned in 1787, and in 1778, had farm at

Merritt Family. 241

Bethpage, L. I. His right of membership amongst Friends seems to have been acquired by his m. in 1784 with a Friend belonging to Amawalk Monthly Meeting, such being the rule of that day.

While at Bethpage, he was an active member of Westbury Monthly Meeting, was on the Committee when Jericho Monthly Meeting was set off from Westbury in 11th month 1789.

1792. John[2] Merritt and Phoebe his wife had certificates of removal from Westbury to Amawalk, M. M.

1793. Sold farm at B. to Moses Cornelius.

1798. Jericho Monthly Meeting sent certificate to New York, M. M. for Anne, dau. of John and Phebe Merritt.

1799. John in Flour Business in N. Y. 1802 the firm name was Merritt & Anderson.

The children of JOHN and Phebe (Weeks) Merritt.

Ann b. 1785, m. Nathan Comstock, she d. in Brooklyn 13, 9, 1860.

Phebe b. 1789, m. 1807, William F. Mott N. Y. she d. 1859.

Joseph b. 1791, 1794 Samuel d.

Deborah b. 1797, m. 1816, Richard Field, of Brooklyn, she d. 1875.

Louisa b. 1799, she d. 1818.

Nathaniel S. b. 1802, m. Mary King, he d. 1890.

John J. b. 1804, m. Hannah Brown, he d. 1871.

Sarah b. 1807, she d. 26, 4, 1827.

*James son of Nathaniel[1] Merritt, m. 1788, Sarah Weeks, sister of Phebe, lived in New York, They

---

*James became a member by request. The rule allowing one to come in by marrying had been abolished.

were daughters of Joseph Weeks and Phebe, nee Underhill, of Chappaqua, children :
Joseph, Nathaniel, Richard m. Maria Jones.
James m. Mary Finch.
Mary m. Richard Cromwell.
Phebe m. Nathaniel Hawxhurst.
Anne single.
Sarah m. John Cromwell.

Tradition says that Nathaniel Merritt of Peekskill, being a Tory, (or shall we say Loyal to his King) his neighbors set upon him to do him harm, and that he took his little Jesse into a small boat and rowed for New York. The rebels sent word ahead, so that when he reached N. Y. a mob on the dock seized him and some cried string him up, but the Mayor hearing the cry, went to the mob and telling them he would shut him (N. M.) up they desisted from their rash purpose. The Mayor then put him in the prison, and sent the son home to his mother in Peekskill. How N. M. got away is not told, but we next find him gathering a Company together as Militia men in the Kings service on Long Island, himself Captain, his son John a Corporal or ———. Soon tradition comes in again, and says, the wife got a pass for herself and her son Jesse and joined her husband on L. I.; finding her husband about to FIGHT against the Rebels, she said to him, "I can live in a cave, or on bread and water, or *even* starve if *need* be, but this *I cannot stand.* Tradition or no tradition, he passed his Company over to another Captain and opened a store at Raynortown, neither he nor his son ever went into the battlefield, but after the war was over they deemed it safer for them to join the exiles, and they all went to what was then called

Merritt Family. 243

Nova Scotia, now New Brunswick. Frederickton the capitol of N. B. was then called St. Ann, Tradition also says that Nathaniel Merritt's daughter Anne, wife of John Ogden, died on the way to N. S. and was buried at Sea.

Nathaniel Merritt was tax collector in North Castle, Westchester Co., in 1758, also engaged in the settlement of the Leases and Releases between Pierre VanCortland and Robert Gilbert Livingston.

The Lieut. Gov. and the Assembly appointed him to survey 4151 acres of land in 1760. He was constable of Cortland Manor from 1663 to 1666. In 1664 he surveyed a farm at Croton River in the tenure of Hicks Seaman, served as one of three arbitrators in a difference between J. McChain and Isaac Kronkhite, he was a merchant at Peekskill until 1776. In 1778 Loyalist in Long Island Capt. Nathaniel Merritt and his son John. In 1780 he had a store at Raynortown, L. I. Aug. 3, 1783, Captain Nathaniel Merritt's Company left New York in the ship Cyrus and arrived at St John's river the 11th day of Sept. They were supplied with rations about 3 monrhs.

In 1784 he was negotiating with Zephania[1] Kingsby for a store at Gage Town, N. Brunswick. N. B. was *then* separated from Nova Scotia, and Nathaniel Merritt's Company settled in that province. All his sons, and his son-in-law John Ogden were in company with him in the store at Gage Town in 1785, and there are store accounts at Waterborough, Queens Co. New Brunswick as late as April 15, 1788, and others at Amityville, Queens Co., L. I. as early as June 13, 1788.

N. Merritt was Notary Public, Registrar, Surveyor and farmer as well as merchant during the five years that he was in N. B. In 1788 Thomas Wetmore was registrar and N. M. passed the Book of Records over to him on the 23d of February, sd book contained record of the deeds &c. from No. 1 to No. 132, of Queens Co., N. B. N. M. sold his real estate in Waterborough to John Leonard for the consideration of £200. It consisted of two lots Nos. 12 and 14 of Coll Spry's grant on the St John river. May 1, 1789, N. and son Jesse Merritt were in partnership in two stores, one at Jerusalem in Obadiah Jackson's house, remained there till 1793, and Jesse's daughter Elisabeth, was born there, as may be proved by the store records. The other store was in Huntington Township. In the course of 1793 N. and Jesse Merritt bought 118 acres of land on Josiah's Neck, and in 1794, John and Sarah Hewlett, and Charles and Martha Hewlett of Oysterbay, sold to them Mill &c. at Oysterbay, West Neck for over £200, but they soon dissolved partnership and Nathaniel went to Brooklyn, and opened a store and public house in 1696, his wife died 23, 11, 1800. In 1802 he was boarding at Henry Whitsons, in Bethpage, town of Oysterbay, L. I., he built a small shop there. Last record in his book Jan. 15, 1803, says put £56, 14s, 6d, in Henry's desk. He (N. M.) died at his son Jesse's 17, 4, 1803, in Bethpage just across the street from Henry Whitson's. His will was dated Dec. 19, 1800.

Jesse Merritt, son of the above, born at Peekskill, 20, 2, 1769, was with his father on L. I. in 1781 when £3, 15s, 6d, was paid for his schooling. The home was then at Raynortown, (now 1888, Freeport) he (J. M.) next appears as one of the company on board the Cyrus, bound for St Johns river.

1785. Feb. 10, although 10 days less than 19 years old, he (J. M.) came into possession of lot No.

12, of Coll Spry's grant, which lot he afterward sold to his father. In Sept. 1785 he was in partnership with his father in the store in Waterborough Township, Queens Co. New Brunswick.

April 17, 1787.
This certifies whom it may concern, that Mr. Jesse Merritt, Deputy Surveyor, has attended my office for some time to qualify himself as a Deputy Surveyor, having before studied the theory of that business, and I do on a strict examination find him qualified in all respects to execute that duty.
GEO. SPROULE,
Surveyor General.

SURVEYOR GENERAL'S OFFICE, ST JOHN.
There is an Acc't of Records and papers delivered by Mr. Jesse Merritt (Deputy Clerk to James Cluert Esq.) clerk of Thomas Wetmore, Esq. the present clerk of Queens County, the eighth day of Oct. 1787.
1st the charter of Queens Co.
2d and 3d Deeds, &c., &c., &c.

Jesse Merritt requested and became a member of Jericho Monthly Meeting of Friends in 1788. He was married (by Friends ceremony the 6 of 5, 1789, at Bethpage) to Mary Cornelius, dau. of John and Mary (Powell). A warm friend of Elias Hicks he went with him as companion, on his very trying journey through the *then* far West in 1828. They traveled with their own conveyance over mountains and through wildernesses in Pennsylvania, Ohio and Indiana, taking six months for the trip. They held and attended many meetings, and his account of the opposition they met with is interesting, but sad. Besides his meeting business of which he did much, his store, farm and surveying business he was very useful in the neighborhood, being often called upon to write Wills, Deeds, &c. and to execute many kinds of offices necessary in the care of people's property.

His wife died 9, 11, 1840.

He died 30, 3, 1843.

In 1794. The partnership of Jesse Merritt with his father was dissolved, Jesse having become a strict Friend could not longer sell intoxicating liquor. An auction disposed of the goods, and he (J. M.) purchased the place of his father-in-law at Bethpage and thenceforth he and his family lived under the same roof with his father and mother-in-law, taking care of them in their old age, and making additions and improvements to the property until they died; he in 1814, and she in 1826.

Jesse and wife occupied the place during their lives, and transmitted it to their only son John C. Merritt, who has deeded it to his youngest son John C. Jr.

This property was purchased of the Indians by a Friend in 1695, as per deed which says he has had possession 7 years. A house was built in 1700, on the site occupied by the present one, and many friends have enjoyed the hospitality of the several occupants, none of whom gave friends a warmer welcome than Jesse Merritt.

Copy of Marriage Certificate.

WHEREAS: Jesse Merritt son of Nathaniel Merritt and Anne his wife at South Hempstead in Queens County and in the State of New York and

Mary Cornelius, daughter of John and Mary Cornelius of Oysterbay in the County and State aforesaid, having declared their intentions of marriage with each other before two several monthly meetings of the People called Quakers at Westbury, according to the good order used among them, and having consent of parents and nothing appearing to obstruct, was approved by said meeting.

Now these are to certify all whom it may concern, that for the full accomplishment of their said intentions this sixth day of fifth month one thousand seven hundred and eighty nine — They the said Jesse Merritt and Mary Cornelius appeared in a Public Meeting of said People and others at Bethpage, and the said Jesse Merritt, taking the said Mary Cornelius by the hand did in a solemn manner openly declare that he took her to be his wife promising by Divine assistance to be unto her a true and loving husband until death should separate them, And then in the said Assembly the said Mary Cornelius did in like manner declare that she took the said Jesse Merritt to be her husband promising by Divine assistance to be unto him a true and loving wife until death should separate them. And morever the said Jesse Merritt and Mary Cornelius, she according to the custom of marriage assuming the name of her husband, as a further confirmation thereof did then and there, to these presents set their hands.

JESSE MERRITT,
MARY MERRITT.

And we whose names are hereunto subscribed being present at the solemnization of said marriage and subscription have as witnesses thereto set our hands the day and year above written.

JOHN WHITSON,	MARY RUSHMORE,
DEBORAH WHITSON,	HANNAH WHITSON,
HENRY WHITSON, JR.	THOMAS WHITSON,
PHEBE WHITSON,	JOHN CORNELIUS,
MARY WHITSON,	MARY CORNELIUS,
ELISABETH PEARSALL,	MARTHA POWELL,
SARAH ALLEN,	PHILENA POWELL,
JOHN MERRITT,	ROWLAND PEARSALL,
JAMES MERRITT,	SAMUEL POWELL,
PHEBE MERRITT,	JAMES OAKLEY,
SARAH MERRITT,	ELISABETH OAKLEY,
ANNA PEARSALL,	THOMAS TITUS,
ISAAC POWELL,	DAVID WILLETS.

MARVIN FAMILY.

Robert[1] Marvin of Southampton, L. I. m. 1648 Mary, dau. of William Browne who d. 1650. Robert Marvin settled in Hempstead, in 1650 was Chosen Townsman, in 1650 held various offices in the Town and died about 1683.

Children of ROBERT[1] MARVIN and Mary (Browne):

John[2] m. Hannah Smith, dau. of John Smith nan and Anna (Gildersleeve).
Dau.[2] m. William Lee.
Children of John[2] Marvin and Hannah, he d. 1708.
Robert[3] jr. m. Phebe, he d. 1775.
Hannah[3] m. a Whitman.
Ruth[3] m. Richard[2] Townsend, son of Richard[1] and Elisabeth (Wicks).
Jemima.[3]
ROBERT[3] MARVIN and Phebe had:
Sarah[4] d. 1790, gave half her property to sister Hannah Rowland, ¼ to Phebe Mitchell and Winifred Tredwell.
Mary[4] m. John Rowland, d. 1776.
Hannah[4] m. 1740, Jonathan[2] Rowland.
Ruth[4] m. 1765, Samuel Rowland, she d. 1770.
John[4] b. 1722, m. 1755, Mary Smith, sister of Sylvanus and Timothy.
Robert[4] b. 1732.
Phebe[4] b 1736, m. Isaac Smith.
JOHN[4] MARVIN and Mary (Smith) had:
Jacob[5] b. and Baptised 1756, Sarah[5] b. 1757, John,[5] Phebe[5] b. 1763, Mary[5] b. 1771, Susanna.[5]

MOORE FAMILY.

Thomas[1] Moore b. in England before 1600, d. at Salem, Mass., 1636, wife Ann, dau Mary[2] m. Joseph Grafton of Salem.

Thomas[2] Moore, shipbuilder, at Salem in 1676, m. Martha Youngs b. 1613, dau. of Rev. Christopher Youngs (Vicar of Reyden, Suffolk Co. Eng. he d. 1640) and Margaret Elvin, dau. of Richard who d. in Boston 1647, "17 Feb. 1636–7, XX for Yong was received for inhabitant of Salem."

THOMAS[2] MOORE came to Southold, L. I. in 1650, wife Martha and 8 children followed in 1651, he d. June 27, 1691, 2d wife Catharine survived him, no children by her.

Baptized in Salem 1739, Martha[3] m. Capt. John Seaman, her father's Will says Symonds.

Hannah[3] m. a Symon, Elisabeth[3] m. a Grover.

Sarah[3] m. Samnel Glover, son of Charles.

Thomas[3] b. 1649, m. 1662 a Mott, of Mamaroneck.

Nathaniel[3] m. Sarah Vail, dau. of Jeremiah.

Benjamin[3] m., Jonathan.[3]

THOMAS[3] MOORE and wife had Thomas[4] b. 1663, Nathaniel,[4] Elisa[4] and Martha[4] m. John Peck.

MUDGE FAMILY.

Jervis[1] Mudge b. in England came to America in 1638, lived near Boston, m. 1649, Rebecca Elson and had children:
Micah[2] b. 1650.
MOSES b. 1652, m. Mary and had:
Jarvis[3] jr. single d. 1741. His heirs were his sisters Elizabeth, Mary and Jane.
William[3] m. Ann Coles, he d. 1713, Jane single.
Elisabeth[3] m. John Dusenberry.
Mary[3] b. 1701, m. 1723, Wait Powell.
WILLIAM[3] MUDGE and Ann Coles had:
Coles[4] b. 1711, m. Dorothy Coles.
MICHAEL[4] b. 1713, m. 1736, Sarah Hopkins, dau. of Ichabod and had:
Mary, Elisabeth[5] m. Peter Titus.
Sarah[5] b. April 17, 1746, m. Oct. 1, 1765, Daniel Merritt, of Quaker Hill, she d. 1833.
Daniel[5] m. Martha Coles.
Jacob Mudge and Hannah (Titus) had:
William m. Martha Willets, dau. of Richard.
Elisabeth m. John Titus Valentine.

MOTT FAMILY.

In 1646 Geo. Keift granted land at Green Point, L. I. to Adam Mott, married July 28, 1647, Adam Maet jm uyt Graefschaps Esseck
    en Jenne Hulet jd uyt Graefschap Buckingham
                from Dutch Church Records.

Adam and Jane settled in Hempstead in 1656, Jane d. and he m. 2d 1667, Elisabeth Richbell, dau. of John and Ann.

    Children of ADAM[1] MOTT and Jane:

Adam[2] b. and baptized 1649, in Dutch Church, N. Y. m. 1678 Mary Stillwell.

Jacobus[2] b. 1651, "(Rebecca Cornell one of the sponsors m. George Woolsey) m. 1607, Mary Richbell.

Grace[2] b. 1656, m. Jonathan Rock Smith.

Elisabeth[2] b. 1655, m. John Kissam.

Henry[2] b. 1657, m. Hannah, 3 children he d. 1681.

John[2] b. 1659, m. 1688, Sarah Seaman, dau. of Capt. John.

Joseph[2] 1661, m.

Gershom[2] b. 1653, m. a Bowne, dau. of John and Lydia had son Charles.

2d wife Elisabeth Richbell had:

Richbell[2] b. 1668, m. 1696, Oct. 14, Elisabeth had:

    Richbell b. 1768, m.(Adam[1]) and 2d wife Elisabeth Richbell.

Elisabeth Thorne.
Mary Ann[2] b. 1670.
Adam[2] b. 1672. m. 1731, Phebe Willets, dau. of Richard and Abigail (Powell) he d. 1738.
William[2] b. 1674, m. 1704, Hannah Ferris (dau. of John and Mary) d. 1759, he d. Jan. 20, 1740.
Charles b. 1676, m. he d. 1740.
ADAM[2] MOTT (Adam[1]) m. Mary, dau. of Nicholas and Ann Stillwell, children:
Adam[3] m. Elisabeth, dau. of Richbell and Elisabeth Mott.
Jane b. 1680, m. Richard Seaman, son of Capt. John.
Probably others.
JAMES[2] MOTT (Adam[1]) and Mary Richbell had: James[3] and Mary.[3] They lived at Mamaroneck.
JOHN[2] MOTT (Adam[1]) and Sarah (Seaman) had:
Henry[3] of Hempstead m. and had —— (he d. 1768.)
Henry,[4] Richard,[4] John,[4] Adam,[4] Abigail[4] m. a Foster, Sarah,[4] Elisabeth[4] m. a Hicks.
John jr.[3] m. Rebecca, he d. 1751.
James.[3]
Sarah,[3] Martha,[3] Jane.[3]
Patrick[3] b. 1707, m. Deborah, he d. 1774.
JOHN[3] Jr. MOTT (John[2] Adam[1]) and Rebecca had:
John[4] d. before 1751.
Samuel[4] m. had sons John,[5] Samuel,[5] Jehu[5] and Richard,[5] dau. Hannah.[5]
Micajah[4] m. Rachel.
Jehu[4] m. 1748 Ruth Powell, dau. of 3 Thomas and Abigail (Hallock) he d. 1781.
Sarah[4] m. a Hulse.
Martha[4] m. Daniel Carman.
Rebecca.[4]

Phebe⁴ m. Daniel Wright.

Jacob⁴ m. 1754, Kesia Seaman.

Samuel⁴ Mott, son of John³ jr. died 1781, Will says sons John, Samuel and Jehu. The children of my son Richard deceased, Amy and James and to such ch. or children as his wife is now like to have, &c.

My brother Jehu Mott and Gideon Seaman my Executors.

The will of Richard⁵ Mott of Hempstead says wife Phebe, daughter Amy, son James was small, brother Jehu, &c. Will made in 1775,

JAMES⁶ MOTT (Richard⁵ Samuel⁴ John³ jr. John² Adam¹) m. Amy Powell, dau. of Solomon and had:

Stephen⁷ m. Sarah Frost, dau. of Charles and Mary.
James⁷ m. Elisabeth Kirby.
Phebe⁷ single.
Amy⁷ single.
Jerusha⁷ m. a Cornell, no children.
Ann⁷ m.

STEPHEN⁷ MOTT and Elisabeth (Frost) had:
Mary F⁸ m. Daniel Wright.
Lydia P.⁸ m. William M. Valentine.

JAMES⁷ MOTT and Elisabeth (Kirby) had:
Cornell⁸ m. Hannah Albertson, dau. of Hicks and Elisabeth (Willis).
William⁸ m. Sarah Albertson, dau. of Hicks.
Others.

MICAJAH⁴ MOTT (John³ jr. John² Adam¹ and wife Rachel) of Hempstead made Will 1780, naming sons, Micajah,⁵ Israel,⁵ John,⁵ daughters Sarah Beets, Rebecca Mott and Rachel Mott, Executors my bro. Jehu Mott and my son-in-law Stephen Beets.

Mott Family.

MICAJAH[5] MOTT lived 2 miles west of Hempstead, m. children 6 daughters and:

Israel[6] m. 1797, Charity Haviland, son John[7] m. 1828, Gulielma Sutton dau. of Robert.

William.[6]

Oliver.[6]

JOHN[6] m. a Frost and had:

Sarah[7] m. Henry Jackson, son of Jervis, had sons John M. and others.

Hamilton[7] m. and had Oliver and Grace.

JEHU[4] MOTT (John[3] jr. John[2] Adam[1]) and Ruth (Powell) had:

John[5] m.

Mary[5] m. Benjamin Hicks.

Ruth[5] m. a Carman.

Rebecca[5] m. a Raynor.

Joseph[5] crazy, not 21 when his father died, he d. 1842.

John[5] called John of Hempstead, was to have £5.

JACOB[4] MOTT (John[3] jr. John[2] Adam[1]) and Kesia (Seaman) had:

Jacob[5] b. 1755.

Rachel[5] b. 1757.

Phebe[5] b. 1760.

Samuel[5] b. 1762.

Amy[5] b. 1765.

PATRICK[3] MOTT (John[2] Adam[1]) and Deborah had:

Sarah,[4] Rebecca,[4] William,[4] Richard,[4] Phebe b. 1754, and Gilbert.

In 1768. Elkanah[4] and Richard[4] Mott, grandsons of Henry[3] of Hempstead.

JOSEPH[2] MOTT (Adam[1]) m. and had, he d. 1733.

Joseph[3] m. Mary Mott, dau. of Richbell.

Samuel[3] m. 1728, Martha Smith.

Jacob³ m. 1735, Abigail Jackson.
Ann³ m. Samuel Cornell.
Jane³ m. Benjamin Seaman, she d. before her father.
JACOB³ MOTT and Abigail had :
Samuel⁴ m. Anna.
Ruth⁴ m. 1763, Jordan Lawrence.
Joseph.⁴
Jackson⁴ m. 1774, Glorianna Coles.
Jacob⁴ m. 1766, Deborah Lawrence and had Jacob L. b. 1784.
Miriam⁴ m. 1777, Benjamin Birdsall.
Richard⁴ m. 1770, 1st Martha Saxton, 2d Freelove Covert.
Isaac⁴ m. Anna Coles.
Elisabeth⁴ m. 1763, Samuel Smith.
Abigail⁴ m. Isaac Kirby.
Mary⁴ m. 1754, Aaron Duryea.
Jerusha.⁴

RICHBELL² MOTT (Adam¹) m. 1696, Elisabeth Thorne and had :
Elisabeth³ m. Adam Mott of Staten Island.
Mary³ m. Joseph Mott, of Cow Neck.
Anna³ m. Jonathan Townsend.
Jemima³ m. Stephen Wood.
Kesia³ m. John Jackson.
Deborah.³
Edmond³ m. Catharine Sands.
Richard³ b. 1710, m. 1740, Sarah Pearsall, had son James⁴ b. 1741.

JAMES⁴ MOTT b. 1741, m. 1765, Mary Underhill and had :
Richard⁵ b. 1766, m. 1787 Abigail Field.
Annie⁵ b. 1768, m. 1785, Adam Mott.
Robert⁵ b. 1771, m. Lydia P. Stansbury, dau. of Joseph.

Mott Family.

SAMUEL[5] b. 1773, m. Elisabeth Barnard and had :
Barnard[6] d. 1818.
Avis[6] b. 1797, m. James Everingham.
Andrew[6] b. 1799, unm.
Charles[6] b. 1801.
Martha[6] b. 1803, m. Henry Haydock.
Samuel[6] b. 1805, m. Ruth Saulsbury.
Elisabeth[6] b. 1807, m. a Brewster.
Matilda[6] b. 1809.

ADAM[2] MOTT b. 1672 (Adam[1]), m. 1731, Phebe Willets, he d. 1738, children :
Elisabeth[3] b. 1733, m. 1755, John Willis, son of Samuel and Mary (Fry).
Adam[3] b. 1734, m. 1755, 1st Sarah Willis, 2d Abigail Batty.
Stephen[3] b. 1737, m. Amy Willis, dau. of Samuel and Mary (Fry).

ADAM[3] MOTT and Sarah, dau. of Samuel Willis and Mary (Fry) had :
Elisabeth[4] b. 1756, she d. 1782.
Lydia[4] b. 1759, m. 1780, Solomon Underhill, she d. 1791.
Adam[4] b. 1762, m. 1785, Annie[5] Mott, dau. of James.
Samuel[4] b. 1773, m. 1796, Catharine Appleby.

ADAM[4] MOTT and Annie (Mott) had :
Mary[5] d. an infant.
James[5] b. 1788, m. 1811, Lucretia Coffin, he d. 1868.
Sarah[5] b. 1791, m. Silas Cornell, she d. 1879.
Mary[5] b. 1793, m. Robert Hicks, she d. 1862.
Abigail[5] b. 1795, m. Lindley Murray Moore, she d. 1846.
Thomas U.[5] b. 1798, d. 1801.

Richard[5] b. 1804, m. Elisabeth Smith, he d. 1888 he was Mayor of Toledo, Ohio in 1845.

STEPHEN[3] MOTT (Adam[2] Adam[1]) m. Amy Willis, dau. of Samuel and Mary (Fry), children:

Daniel[4] b. 1763, m. 1786, Amy Searing, dau. of John, he d. 1837.
Mary[4] b. 1768,
Phebe.[4]
Jane[4] b. 1771.
Abigail[4] b. 1773.
Stephen[4] b. 1779, d. 1781.
Henry[4] b. 1782, m. 1812, Temperance Hicks.

Children of DANIEL[4] and Amy Searing Mott:

Phebe[5] b. 1787.
Stephen[5] b. 1789.
Mary[5] b. 1791.
John[5] b. 1793.
Jane[5] b. 1796.
Joseph[5] b. 1798
Isaac[5] b. 1801.
Abigail[5] b. 1803.
Phebe[5] b. 1805.
Lydia.[5]

One, Richbell Mott, m. Mary Seaman, dau. of Richard[2] and had:

Richard, he d. 1779.
Seaman.
Sarah m. a Manlove.
Elisabeth m. a Seaman.

WILLIAM[2] MOTT (Adam[1]) and Hannah Ferris had:

Elisabeth[3] d. 1721.
Hannah[3] m. 1730, Phillip Pell and had Phillip, Hannah and Martha Pell.
Martha.[3]

Mott Family.

WILLIAM³ b. 1709, m. Elisabeth Valentine, he d. 1786. They had:
William⁵ b. 1742, m. 1789, Mary Willis.
Hannah⁴ b. 1744, d., James⁵ b. 1745.
Elisabeth⁴ b. 1747, m. David Underhill, son of Amos.
John⁴ b. 1749, d.
Samuel⁴ b. 1750, m. Sarah Franklin, he d. 1791.
Hannah⁴ b. 1753, John⁵ b. 1755.
Henry⁴ b. 1757, m. Jane Way, dau. of Samuel and Esther (Valentine).
Richard⁴ b. 1759, Joseph b. 1762, Benjamin b. 1765.
SAMUEL⁴ MOTT and Sarah Franklin had:
Wm. F.⁵ b, 1785, m. Phebe Merritt, dau. of John and Phebe, he d. 1867.
Walter⁵ b. 1786.
Samuel⁵ b. 1789.
Sarah⁵ b. 1791, m. a Wood.
WM. F.⁵ MOTT and Phebe had:
Mary⁶ m. Alfred Willis.
Ann⁶ m. Walter Franklin.
Wm. F.⁶ m.
HENRY⁴ MOTT (William³ William² Adam¹) and Jane (Way) had:
Way Mott.⁵
Dr. Valentine Mott.⁵
Elisabeth,⁵ Esther,⁵ Mary.⁵
CHARLES² MOTT (Adam¹) m. and had:
Gershom,³ Benjamin,³ John,³ Adam,³ Amos,³ grandsons Joseph⁴ Mott and Joseph Starkins,⁴ daus. Mary Ann³ m. a Carroll, Elisabeth² m. a Hunter.
In 1737. One Adam Mott m. Elisabeth Smith.
Adam Mott, of Staten Island, son of Adam² and Mary (Stillwell), had dau. Elisabeth, he was Clerk of Richmond County, Staten Island from 1728 to 1738.

Mott Family.

In 1774. Jacob Mott, of Portsmouth, R. Island was living on possessions that had been inherited by the same name for near a century and a half.

In 1794. Annie[5] Mott, dau. of James and Mary (Underhill) says we visited our cousin Jacob Mott, of Bedford, Rhode Island.

OAKLEY FAMILY.

John[1] Oakley came from England during the Dutch Rule, m. into a Dutch family and had numerous children, he was living in 1702.

Thomas[2] (supposed to be his son) b. 1688, m. Patience Cornell, perhaps the Thomas Oakley named in the divisions of land at Jamaica 1660 was the son of John[1] and father of Thomas b. 1688.

THOMAS OAKLEY and Patience Cornell had :
Thomas m. had son Timothy.
Phebe.
John.
Samuel m. Sally Wood and had Richard, Solomon, Timothy, Jacob and 4 daughters.
Andrew m. and had son Nathaniel.
Israel m. and had Anna m. Polly, Betsy, Nancy and Fanny.
Nathaniel.
Jesse b. 1748, m. Jerusha Peters and had 11 children.
Wilmot m. and had John, Phebe, William, Sarah and Daniel.
Anna Oakley, dau. of Israel m. a Ketcham, Betsy m. a Freeland and Nancy m. a Dissosway.

JESSE OAKLEY and Jerusha (Peters) 11 children :
Mary m. William Moore, George Peters m. Ruth Wilkinson.

Patience, Sarah m. Andrew Moore, Phebe m. Robert Wilkinson.

Thomas Jackson m. 1st Lydia Williams, 2d Matilda Cruger.

John Wilmot m. Harriet Badger, Martha m. Abraham Bokee.

Velina d., Jesse, Velina m. Gilbert Wilkinson.

The above is from *Martha Bokee Flint's* notes.

Thomas Oakley m. 1705, Mary Borroughs.

Nathaniel Oakley of Fosters Meadow, in 1630 m. a Foster.

Henry Oakley m. Hannah b. 1747, dau. of Giles and Letitia (Onderdonk) Seaman.

In 1789. James Oakley was Executor of the will of Elisabeth (Frost), widow of Thomas Merritt.

Martha Oakley b. 1706, m. John Powell.

Mary b. 1707, Sarah b. 1711, John b. 1713, Isaac b. 1715.

Elisabeth b. 1718, Rachel b. 1720.

POST FAMILY.

It is ordered at Southampton, L. I. in 1643, that Richard Post have two acres of unbroken ground adjoining his other two acres. In 1651 he was Constable at Southampton. Some of his children settled in Suffolk Co. and some came to Hempstead, Queens Co., he d. before 1700.

In 1729. Richard Post and Phebe deeded land in Hempstead to Thomas Carman, of the children of RICHARD POST and Phebe.

Richard m. 1st 1732, Mary Willis, dau. of Henry[3] and Phebe (Powell), 2d Elisabeth, dau. of William[3] Willis.

Joseph m. 1739, out of Friends meeting.

John m. 1740, Phebe Willis, dau. of John and Abigail.

Phebe m. 1744, Joshua Powell.

RICHARD POST and Mary (Willis) had, (she d. 1744).

Henry b. 8, 1, 1733, m. 1761, Mary Titus, dau. of Edmond of O. B.

Richard b. 17, 5, 1735, Mary b. 1737, had son Oliver.

Jotham b. 1740, m. 1763, Winnifred b. 1744, dau. of Benjamin Wright.

m. 2d Elisabeth Willis. dau. of William and Hannah (Powell), and had Stephen, Cotta, Sarah and several others.

JOHN POST and Phebe Willis had :
Phebe b. 1784, m. John Powell.
Abigail m. Henry Pearsall, son of Rowland.
Elisabeth m. Richard Valentine, son of Jacob.
Mary m. Gilbert Seaman.
Micah m. 1761, Elisabeth Powell, dau. of Thomas[3] and had :
Susannah m. Daniel Nostrand, Amy m. Caleb Saxton, Micah m. 1794.
Mary m. James Saxton, Phebe m. Gershon Saxton.
Elisha m. 1787, Sarah Seaman, dau. of John.
? Ruth Post m. Henry Powell, sister Hannah m. Stephen Losee.

Children of Henry Post and Mary (Titus),
Edmond b. 1762, m. 1788 Catharine Willets, Samuel b. 1765, m. 1793 Jane Titus, Daniel b. 1768, m. Rosetta Titus, Lydia b. 1772 d. 1772, Henry b. 1774, m. Mary Minturn, Sarah b. 1776, m. John Titus, Isaac b. 1779, James, b. 1785, m. 1811, Phebe Willis (of Samuel), he d. 1870.

Children of Edmond Post and Catharine :
Lydia m. Isaac Rushmore, Phebe m. Henry Willis, b. 1786, Edmond m. Mary Rushmore, Joseph m. Mary W. Robbins, Isaac m. 1st Hannah Kirby, m. 2d Amy Kirby, daus. of Jacob.

Daniel Post and Rosetta had :
Mary T. b. 1801, m. Elwood Valentine, William T. b. 1803, Edward b. 1808, m. Elisabeth Post, dau. of Joseph.

James Post and Phebe (Willis) had :
Elisabeth b. 1813, she d. 1858, Sarah b. 1815.
Charles b. 1818, m. 1844, Maria Amelia Townsend.
Rachel b. 1820, Mary b. 1823 m. Elias Lewis, she d. 1851.
Caroline b. 1826, m. 1847, Daniel Underhill.

Esther b. 1829, m. 1867, Solomon Jackson, his 2d wife.

Catharine b. 1833, m. 1883, Daniel Underhill, his 2d wife.

James Pine's Will 1689, sons James, Nathaniel, Jonathan, Samuel, Benjamin, John, cousin John Smith, loving neighbor John Smith Rock.

PIERCE FAMILY.

Richard Pierce of R. I. d. 1678, m. Susanna Wright.
GEORGE PIERCE b. 1662, m. 1st 1687, Alice Hart, dau. of Richard, and Hannah ———, he d. 1752. Their children:
Susanna b. 1688, James b. 1691, Samuel b. 1695, George b. 1699, Mary b. 1700, m. a Seaman.
2d m. 1721, Temperance (b. 1670) Kirby, dau. of Richard and Patience (Gifford) she d. 1761.
Samuel Pierce m. 20, May, 1738, Abigail Powell, dau. of Elisha and Rebecca.

PLATT FAMILY.

Richard Platt came from Hartfordshire, England to New Haven in 1638, he died there in 1684.
Children came to L. I., viz :
Isaac, he d. 1691, m. Elisabeth Wood, dau. of Jonas and had John, Elisabeth, Mary, Jonas, Joseph and Jacob.
Epenetus m. Phebe Wood, dau. of Jonas and had Mary, Epenetus, Hannah, Elisabeth, Jonas, Jeremiah, Ruth and Sarah.

PEARSALL FAMILY.

HENRY[1] PEARSALL one of the early settlers of Hempstead, d. 1667, wife Ann, sons-in-law Timothy Halstead, and John and Joseph, sons of Michael Williams. Sons:

Nathaniel[2] m. Martha Seaman, dau. of Capt. John, she d. 1712, he d. 1703.

Daniel[2] m.

George[2] m. had son Henry, and dau. Sarah m. 1721, John Titus jr. she d. 1753.

Thomas[2] m. Mary Seaman, youngest dau. of Capt. John.

Children of NATHANIEL[2] PEARSALL and Martha Seaman:

Nathaniel[3] b. 1676, d. 1679.

Thomas[3] b. 1679, m. 1708, Sarah Underhill, dau. of John and Mary.

Martha[3] b. 1681, m. Henry Cock, and had son Samuel.

Hannah[3] b. 1683, d. 1689.

Sarah[3] b. 1686, m. Thomas Townsend.

Elisabeth[3] b. 1688, Hannah[3] b. 1690, d. 1718, Phebe[3] b. 1693, d. 1702.

Samuel[3] b. 1695, d. 1720, Nathaniel[3] b. 1699, d. 1701.

Mary[3] b. 1703, m. 1726, Thomas Franklin, of Rye, son of Henry, of Flushing.

THOMAS[3] PEARSALL and Sarah (Underhill) had:
 Thomas[4] b. 1710, Nathaniel[4] b. 1712, m. 1735, Mary Latham, dau. of Joseph.
 Sarah[4] b. 1714, m. 1740, Richard Mott and had James, m. 2d 1747 Richard Alsop.
 Phebe[4] b. 1717, Martha[4] b. 1719, d. 1721.
 Hannah[4] b. 1721, m. Benjamin Hawxhurst, son of Samson and Hannah.
 Samuel[4] b. 1724.
 Mary[4] b. 1727, m. 1754, Obadiah Seaman.
THOMAS[4] PEARSALL (Thomas[3] Nathaniel[2] Henry[1]) m. and had (he was of Hempstead Harbor).
 Israel[5] b. 1733, Thomas[5] b. 1735, Nathaniel[5] b. 1737, Mary[5] b. 1742, Martha[5] b. 1743.
THOMAS[2] PEARSALL (Henry[1]) and Mary (Seaman) had:
 HENRY[3] b. 1690, m. 1717, Mary Titus, dau. of John and Sarah (Willis) and had, (he d. 1750).
 Rowland[4] m. 1748, Anna Powell, dau. of Wait and Mary (Mudge).
 Anna[4] b. 1722, m. 1740, Silas Willis, son of Henry and Phebe (Powell).
 Thomas[4] b. 1735, m. 1st 1754, Rachel b. 1720, d. 1759, dau. of John Powell and Margaret.
 John[4] m. Hannah.
ROWLAND[4] PEARSALL and Anna, of Bethpage had:
 Jane[5] b. 1749.
 Henry[5] b. 1751, m. 1785, Abigail, dau. of John Post.
 Mary[5] b. 1755, Phebe[5] b. 1757, m. 1791, John Thompson.
 William[5] b. 1759, m. Elisabeth Gaunt, b. 1767, dau. of Samuel.

Amy[5] b. 1761, Silas[5] b. 1764, was living at Bethpage in 1785.

Thomas[5] b. 1766, Rowland[5] m.

Wait[5] b. 1770, m. Hannah Brush. Anna b. 1772, m. 1st an Allen, 2d m. 1814, Stephen Lines, she d. 1840.

Children of WILLIAM[5] PEARSALL and Elisabeth Gaunt.

Samuel G.[6] b. 1787.

Amy[6] b. 1788, m.

Richard O.[6] b 1791. Jane[6] b. 1792, d. 1793.

Daniel G.[6] b. 1794. Mary[6] b. 1796.

Elisabeth P.[6] b. 1800, m. Edward Ballenger b. 1800, she d. 1888.

Martha[6] C. b. 1802.

William[6] b. 1804, m. Mary.

Edward B.[6] b. 1807. George T.[6] b. 1809.

Children of ELISABETH[6] P. (Pearsall) and Edward Ballenger:

William b. 1829, Mary Elisabeth b. 1831.

Jane Elisabeth b. 1834, m. Jacob Capron.

Edward b. 1836

WAIT[5] PEARSALL (Rowland[4] Henry[3] Thomas[2] Henry[1]) and Hannah Brush had:

Amy[6] m. John Seaman, son of Samuel and Kesia (Titus).

Rowland[6] m.

Anna[6] m. Samuel Seaman, son of Samuel and Kesia, Anna d.

Phebe[6] m. Samuel Seaman, his 2d wife.

Wait[5] Pearsall and Hannah requested, in 1797, to have their two little children, Amy and Rowland, joined in membership with Friends.

JOHN[4] PEARSALL m. 1771, Hannah, lived at Bethpage and had:

Hannah[5] m. 1793, Jacob Powell, son of Samuel.

John[5] m. 1793, Hannah Powell, dau. of Samuel.

THOMAS[4] PEARSALL (Henry[3] Thomas[2] Henry[1]) m. 1st Rachel Powell and had:
  Sarah[5] b. 1756, unm. m. 2d Ann Williams, dau. of Thomas and Mary, grandaughter of Thomas Powell.
  Samuel[5] b. 1764, m. Margaret Hicks, b. 1767, dau. of Gilbert, she d. 1833.
  Rachel[5] b. 1765, m. 1785, Samuel Willis, son of John and Elisabeth.
  Jacob[5] b. 1767.
  Edmond[5] b. 1768, m. 1794, Rachel Willets.
  Mary[5] b. 1770.
  Esther[5] b. 1772, m. Gilbert Lawrence.
  Amy[5] b. 1773, m. Henry Lawrence.
  Robert[5] b. 1776.

Thomas[4] Pearsall of Bethpage had Certificate of Removal to Flushing in 1786, for self, wife and 8 children.

Children of SAMUEL[5] and Margaret (Hicks) Pearsall.
  Mary H.[6] b. 1790, d. 1811.
  Ann[6] b. 1791, m. 1818, Seaman Willets, son of Daniel and Martha, she d. 1851.
  Gilbert H.[6] b. 1699, he d. 1879.
  Sarah[6] b. 1800.
  Samuel[6] b. 1802, d. 1805.
  Margaret H.[6] b. 1810.

In 1767, Mary Pearsall, widow of Nathaniel, and 4 daughters, Mary, Sarah, Hannah and Jane moved to New York and had certificate to Flushing Monthly Meeting.

In 1751, Mary Pearsall, widow of Henry had certificate to Little Egg Harbor, N. Jersey, signifying her clearness from Marriage engagements.

PRIOR FAMILY.

John and Daniel Prior, sons of John Prior, late of Watford, Hertford Co. England were at Scituate Massachusetts from 1638 to 41.

MATTHEW[1] PRIOR and Mary came from Setauket to Matinecock before 1670, she d. 1700. Their children were:

John[2] b. 1651, m. 1678, Elisabeth Bowne, he d. 1698.
Mary[2] b. 1652, m. 1668, John[2] Underhill.
Elisabeth[2] b. 1656, m. 1673, John Feaks.
Sarah[2] b. 1664, m. 1685, John Gould, son of Daniel and Wait of R. I.
Martha[2] b. 1672, m. 1693, Simeon Cooper.

Children of JOHN[2] PRIOR and Elisabeth:

John[3] b. 1679, d.
Hannah[3] b. 1681, m. William Frost.
Elisabeth[3] b. 1683, m. William Carpenter.
Mary[3] b. 1685, Sarah[3] b. 1687.
Matthew[3] b. 1690, m. Hannah Cock, dau. of John and Dorothy.
Samuel[3] b. 1692, m. 1728, Mary Powell, dau. of Thomas.[2]
Joseph[3] b. 1695.

MATTHEW[3] PRIOR (John[2] Matthew[1]) and Hannah (Cock) had:

Hannah[4] b. 1720.
Mary[4] b. 1723.

Prior Family. 273

Matthew⁴ b. 1729, m. Ann b. 1722 (Pearsall) widow of Silas Willis and had:
Henry⁵ b. 1755, no children.
James⁵ b. 1757, m. Theodosia Derby.
SAMUEL³ PRIOR (John² Matthew¹) and Mary (Powell) had:
Samuel⁴ b. 1729, d. 1732.
Joseph⁴ b. 1732, m. 1753, Phebe Titus, dau. of Edmond.
Thomas⁴ b. 1734, m. 1756, Martha Willets.
Mary⁴ b. 22, 3, 1738, m. 1765, John Searing, son of John.
JOSEPH⁴ PRIOR and Phebe Titus had:
Sarah⁵ b. 1753.
Edmond⁵ b. 1755, m. Phebe she d. 1791.
Thomas⁴ Prior and Martha (Willets) had:
THOMAS.⁴
Hannah⁶ b. 1757, m. Benjamin Cock.
Phebe⁶ b. 1759.
Elisabeth⁶ b. 1761, m. 1781, John Underhill of O. B.
Sarah⁶ b. 1765. Samuel⁶ b. 1770.

RICHBELL FAMILY.

John[1] Richbell of Southampton, England had two sons, John[2] and Robert. The later Richbells are from Robert; John came to America, had land in Delaware first, was in Oysterbay in 1663. In 1669, he became first Proprietor of Mamaroneck, one account says "8, 6, 1661, John Richbell of O. B. purchased Mamaroneck," he d. 1684, wife Anne d. 1700. They had no son. Her will says son-in-law John Emerson, dau. Ann Emerson, son-in-law Capt. James Mott, dau. Elisabeth, grand-daughters Ann Gedney, Mary Williams and Mary Mott, grandson James Mott, son of Capt. James Mott. Elisabeth[3] Richbell m. Adam Mott, Ann[3] Richbell m. John Emerson of Talbot Co., New Jersey, Mary[3] Richbell, m. Adam's son James[2] Mott.

ANN the wife of John[2] Richbell was a dau. of Margaret Parsons, other grandaughters of John and Ann were, Anna, Grace, Elisabeth and Jane.

ROBBINS FAMILY.

John Robbins of Huntington, in 1670 sold land there to Benj'm Jones. In 1680 he sold land at Matinecock reserving certain apple trees and a nursery of Apple and Peach trees. On the 25 of 5th month, 1747, there was laid out to John Robbins and Jeremiah Robbins, land which was formerly conveyed by Robert Williams unto John Robbins, and descended from the s^d John Robbins to his son Jeremiah Robbins, and from him by Will to his two sons above named.

John[1] Robbins m. had son:
Jeremiah[2] who m. and had sons:
John[3] m. 1731, Jane Seaman, dau. of Benjamin and Jane)Mott).
Jeremiah[3] m. Hannah Carr, dau. of Job and Hannah (Willets).
Children of John[3] and Jane (Seaman) Robbins:
Richard,[4] Benjamin,[4] Jacob,[4] ? Jeremiah.[4]
Phebe[4] m. an Ireland.
Martha[4] m. a Van Wyke.
Jane[4] m. a Willis.
Elisabeth[4] m. a Willis.
JEREMIAH[4] ROBBINS b. 1742, m. 1763, Hannah Cock, b. 1743, he d. 1802.
Mary[5] b. 1765, m. 1791, Jonathan Sweet.
Anne[5] b. 1768.
Daniel[5] b. 1772, m. Elisabeth Mitchell.

John[5] b. 1780, m. 1809, Sarah Carhart, dau. of Joshua and Phebe.
Jane[5] b. 1785.
DANIEL[5] ROBBINS and Elisabeth had:
Jeremiah[6] m.
Daniel[6] m. Matilda Frost.
Wm.[6] m.
Hannah[6] m. an Ely.
JOHN[5] ROBBINS and Sarah Carhart had:
John.[6]   Walter.[6]
Phebe Ann m. Thomas Seaman, son of Henry O. of Jerusalem.
JEREMIAH[3] ROBBINS (Jeremiah[2] John[1]) and Hannah (Carr) had:
Almy[4] b. 1733, Hannah[4] b. 1739, m. Rees Cock, son of John.
Sarah[4] b. 1742, m. John Titus, son of William.
Samuel[4] b. 1745, m. Elisabeth Cock, dau. of John.
Elisabeth[4] b. 1736, m. Henry Cock, son of John.
Isaac[4] b. 1748, m. Margaret Titus.
Stephen[4] b. 1750, m. Miriam Seaman, dau. of Samuel and Martha.
Phebe[4] b. 1752, m. Benijah Bedell.
Abigail[4] b. 1755, m. 1773, Samuel Titus.
Job[4] b. 1758, m. Mary Searing.
William[4] m.
STEPHEN[4] ROBBINS (Jeremiah[3] Jeremiah[2] John[1]) and Miriam (Seaman) had.
Mary[5] m. 1790, Robert Willets.
Willet[5] b. 1781, m. 1805, Esther Seaman, dau. of William.
Stephen[5] m.
Samuel[5] m.

Children of WILLET[5] ROBBINS and Esther (Seaman):
  Mary[6] b. 1806, m. Joseph Post.
  William[6] b. 1808, m. Elisabeth Willets, dau. of Obadiah and Elisabeth (Robbins).
  Elisabeth[6] b. 1810, d.
  Edward[6] b. 1813, m. Rachel Titus, dau. of Rowland.
  Matthew[6] F. b. 1815, m. Hannah Seaman, dau. of Robert and Sarah (Hicks).
  Willet S.[6] b. 1818, m. Dorinda Anderson.
  Stephen[6] b. 1821, m. Esther Carpenter.

ROWLAND FAMILY.

JONATHAN[1] ROWLAND in Hempstead, m. Martha Seaman, dau. of Benjamin and Martha (Titus) and had:

    Jonathan[2] b. 1704, m. 1740, Hannah Marvin, dau. of Robert and Phebe, he d. 1802.
    Samuel[2] m. 1745, Ruth Marvin, she d. 1770.
    Martha[2] ——— ? 2d m.
    John[2] m. Mary Marvin, she d. 1776.

JONATHAN[2] ROWLAND and Hannah (Marvin) had:

    Martha[3] b. 1741, m. 1761, Thomas Seaman, of Jerusalem, she d. 1824.
    Sarah[3] m. 1779, Israel Seaman of Jerusalem.
    David[3] m. 1784, Ida Sutphin of Flushing, had Jonathan b. 1785.
    Benjamin[3] m. Phebe Jones.
    Phebe[3] m. 1st Thorne, 2d Whitehead Cornell.
    Deborah.[3] Baptisms July 28, 1746. Martha and Sarah, daus. of Jonathan and Hannah Rowland.

Children of SAMUEL[2] ROWLAND and Ruth Marvin:

    Robert[3] b. 1747. Samuel[2] b. 1748.

Children of JOHN[2] ROWLAND and Mary (Marvin).

    Lorado[3] and Marvin.[3]

Mary (Marvin) Rowland in 1776. Wills property to son Marvin, provided he is a true and Loyal subject of King George III., and a true friend to good government.

RUSHMORE FAMILY.

THOMAS[1] RUSHMORE in Hempstead in 1659, with wife Martha in 1668, he d. about 1684. In 1703, Thomas[2] Rushmore and wife Sarah had:

THOMAS[3] m. Mary Hicks and had son:

ISAAC[4] m. Sarah Titus, she d. 1776. Their children were:

Phebe[5] b. 1758.
Mary[5] b. 1760, m. 1780, Charles Frost.
Stephen[5] b. 1763, m. 1787, Phebe Townsend.
Jane[5] b. 1768, m. 1790, Lewis Valentine.
Edmond[5] b. 1771, d. 1782.

Children of STEPHEN[5] RUSHMORE and Phebe (Townsend) of Westbury:

Isaac[6] b. 1788, m. Lydia Post.
Sarah[6] b. 10, 9, 1790, m. John D. Hicks, he d. 1829, she d. 15, 3, 1893.
Townsend[6] b. 1792, m. Amy Willis, dau. of Samuel and Rachel.
Mary[6] b. 1794, m. Edmond Post.
Jane[6] b. 1796, m. Valentine Willis.
Thomas[6] b. 1799, m. Jane Valentine.
Phebe[6] b. 1803, m. Isaac Gifford.
Ellen Tallman b. 10, 9, 1790, at Fishkill, m. John L. Bloomer, she d. 15, 3, 1893.

ISAAC[6] RUSHMORE and Lydia (Post) had:

Stephen[7] m. Matilda Powell, dau. of John.
Edmond.[7]

TOWNSEND[6] RUSHMORE and (Amy Willis) had:
Esther,[7] Maria,[7] Isaac[7] m., Phebe,[7] Samuel,[7] Mary[7] and William.[7]

THOMAS[6] RUSHMORE and Jane (Valentine) had:
Elisabeth,[7] Stephen.[7]

STEPHEN[7] RUSHMORE and Matilda (Powell) had:
Edward[8] m.
John Howard[8] m. Julia Barker, dau. of David and Julia.

A Will of Thomas Rushmore 1792, says wife Ruth, sons William and John, granddaughters, Abigail, Ruth and Elisabeth Valentine, brother Carman Rushmore.

ROGERS FAMILY.

JOHN[1] ROGERS, Martyr in 1655, son Noah[2] of Exeter had son John[3] of Dedham, had son Thomas[4] a passenger in the "May Flower" in 1620, had son Joseph, father of Jonathan, of Huntington, L. I. in 1659. In 1656, William Rogers, of Huntington supposed to be son of Isaiah a descendant of the Martyr, d. 1683. 1669 widow Ann Rogers, had children: Obadiah, John b. 1640, Noah, Samuel, Mary and Hannah.

RODMAN FAMILY.

JOHN[1] RODMAN and wife Ann, of Barbadoes had children, he d. 1686.

Thomas[2] b. Dec. 26, 1640, m. 2d in Barbadoes, Patience Malins a widow.

John[2] b. 1652, m. in Barbadoes, Mary, she d. 1747, aged 85 years, he d. 1731.

Ann.[2]

Catharine.[2]

Dr. THOMAS[2] RODMAN died at Newport, R. I. 1727, aged 87 years, his first wife was named Sarah, he m. 2d Patience, dau. of Peter Easton, widow Melius b. 1655. They came to R. I. in 1675, and had:

Thomas[3] b. 1683, m. 1706, Catharine Fry.

Ann[3] he m. 1691, Hannah Clark, dau. of Gov. Walter Clark, of Rhode Island and had: Hannah.[3]

Clarke[3] b. at Newport, March 10, 1669, m. Jan. 3, 1717, Ann Coggshell, dau. of Daniel, he d. Aug. 30, 1752.

John.[3]

Samuel[3] b. 1703, m. 1723, Mary Willett, dau. of Thomas.

Patience.[3]

William.[3]

Rodman Family. 283

Children of THOMAS[3] RODMAN and Catharine Fry:
Thomas[4] b. 1708.
Patience,[4] John,[4] Joseph,[4] Samuel,[4] Ann,[4] Robert,[4] William[4] Benjamin.[4]

CLARKE[3] RODMAN (Thomas[2] John[1]) wife Anne was dau. of Daniel Coggshall, who m. a dau. of Michael Wanton, a Physician and Minister of Portsmouth. They had 10 children amongst whom were:
Walter[4] b. 1719, m. 1739, a dau. of Abraham and Patience Howland.
Mary[4] b. 1722.
JOSEPH[4] b. Feb. 20, 1724, m. June 6, 1745, Mary Miller, dau. of Francis of Boston, and Mary his wife. They had 5 children.
Anna[5] b. March 18, 1746, m. Caleb Carpenter, she d. Sept. 10, 1834.
Mary[5] b. May 10, 1747, d. 1750.
Hannah[5] b. May 20, 1749, m. Oct. 29, 1767, William Mitchell, son of Richard and Mary, of Nantucket.
Clarke[5] b. April 10, 1750, m. Abigail Lawton, he d. Sept. 14, 1838.
Mary[5] b. 1752 d.

SAMUEL[3] RODMAN and Mary (Willett) had:
Thomas b. 1724, Hannah b. 1725, Charity b. 1728, Samuel b. 1730, William b. 1732, Elisabeth b. 1736, Ann ———.

Thomas[2] Rodman was the first Clerk of Rhode Island Yearly Meeting..

JOHN[2] RODMAN (John[1]) and wife Mary of Barbadoes had:
John[3] b. 1679, at Barbadoes.
Mary C.[3] b. 1681, d. 1682.

Samuel[3] b. at R. I. 1683.
William[3] b. 1687, d. 1704 at R. I.
Joseph[3] b. 1685, m. at R. I.
Ann[3] b. at Block Island, 1689, m. 1707, Walter Newbury.
Thomas[3] b. 1691 at Flushing, d.
Mary[3] b. 1693, at Flushing, m. 1714, John Willett.
Thomas[3] b. 1696 at Flushing, m. Elisabeth.
Hannah[3] b. 1700, in New York, m. 1716, Jonathan Dickinson of Phil'a.
Elisabeth[3] b. 1702, in Flushing, m. 1723, Thomas Masters, son of Thomas.

In 1699, Dr. John[2] Rodman lived in New York.

THOMAS[3] RODMAN b. 1696, and wife Elisabeth had:

Elisabeth[4] b. 1719, m. Benjamin Hicks.
Anne[4] b. 1721, m. 1746, Caleb Field, son of Thomas and Hannah.
Hannah[3] b. 1723. John[4] b. 1726. Mary[4] b. 1729.
Catharine[4] b. 1731, m. Henry Haydock of N. Y. she d. 1760.
Caroline[4] b. 1734, m. 1762, James Bowne, son of Samuel and Sarah.
Penelope[4] b 1737. Thomas[4] b. 1739.
William Rodman, son of Joseph, d. 1712. Ann dau. of Joseph, d. 1713. Samuel Rodman, son of Joseph, m. 1737, Mary Hicks, dau. of Wm.

Hannah, dau. of Thomas, and Mary Rodman, of Newport, R. I. m. 1793, Samuel R. Fisher of, Philadelphia.

SANDS FAMILY.

Capt. JAMES[1] SANDS born in England in 1622, died in America 1695. He came from Reading, Berkshire, England. He followed Ann Hutchinson in her exile on the banks of the Hudson, N. Y., and returned to Rhode Island in 1664. He m. Sarah Walker, dau, of John and Catharine, she d. 1709. Their children were :

John[2] J. b. 1650, m. Sybil Ray, b. 1665, d. 1733, dau. of Simeon and Mary (Thomas) he d. 1712.

Sarah[2] m. 1671, Nathaniel Niles, son of John and Jane, he b. 1642, d. 1723, she d. 1726.

Mercy[2] m. 1683, Joshua Raymond, b. 1644, son of Joshua and Elisabeth (Smith), she d. 1704.

Capt. James[2] b. 1662, m. 1694, Sarah Cornell, b. 1679, dau. of John and Mary (Russell).

Samuel[2] b. 1666, m. 1699, Dorothy Ray, dau. of Simeon and Mary (Thomas), he d. 1730.

Edward[2] b. 1672, m. 1693, Mary Williams, dau. of John and Ann (Alcott), he d. 1708, she d. 1708.

Children of JOHN J.[2] SANDS and Sibyl :

John[3] b. 1684, m. Catharine Guthrie, he d. 1763.

Nathaniel[3] b. 1687, m. an O'Neil.

Edward[3] b. 1691, m. Mary Cornell, dau. of Richard of Cowneck.

George[3] b. 1694, d. 1704.

Mary[3] b. 1697, m. Joseph Silleck.

Catharine[3] b. 1700, m. Edmond Mott.

Dorothy[3] b. 1703, m. John Bowne.
Abigail[3] b. 1708, m. 1728, John Thomas.
JOHN[3] SANDS (John J.[2] James[1]) and Catharine Guthrie had:
John[4] b. 1708, m. 1st 1734, Elisabeth Sands, 2d 1736, Elisabeth Cornell, dau. of Caleb.
Robert[4] b. 1710.
Edward[4] m. 1732, Hannah Tredwell.
George[4] m. 1757, Jemima Smith, dau. of Abel and Ruth.
Annie[4] b. 1723, m. 1st Christopher Dean, had son, 2d 1745 David Brooks.
Nathaniel[4] b. 1724, m. Mercy Sands.
Joshua[4] b. 1725, m. 1748, Mary Smith.
Simon[4] b. 1727, m. 1757, Catharine Tredwell, 2d 1765, Sarah Sands.
Gideon[4] b. 1729, m. Mary Sands.
Mary[4] b. 1732, m. 1757, Samuel Gifford.
Benjamin[4] b. 1735, m. 1758, Mary Jackson.
JOHN[4] SANDS and 1st w. Elisabeth Sands had:
John[5] b. 1735, m. 1757, Elisabeth Jackson.
2d wife Elisabeth Cornell had:
Cornell[5] m. 1767, Elisabeth Hull.
Robert[5] m. 1759, Phebe Carman.
Comfort[5] m. 1769, Sarah Dodge.
Stephen[5] m. 1772, Mary Bronson.
Richardson[5] m. 1777, Lucretia Logan.
Joshua[5] m. 1780, Ann J. Cott.
JAMES[2] SANDS (James[1]) and Sarah Cornell had:
Othniel[3] b. 1699, m. Susannah Laing.
James[3] b. 1702, m. 1st 1731, Hannah Haviland, 2d Rebecca Bagley.
Abijah[3] m. 1730, Hannah Waring.
John[3] b. 1716, m. Catharine Greene.
Mary[3] m. Joseph Sutton.

Zerviah[3] m. Aaron Smith.
Jerusha[3] m. John Carman.
Bathsheba[3] m. Thomas Everett.
Sarah[3] b. 1728, m. John Aspinwall.
SAMUEL[2] SANDS (James[1]) and Dorothy Ray had:
Sybil[3] m. Jonathan Rogers.
Mary[3] m. Richard Stillwell.
Anna[3] m. a Kenman.
Sarah[3] m. 1713, Nathan Silleck.
Mary[3] m. —— John Reid.
Samuel[3] m. Mary Pell, dau. of Thomas; his mother, dau. of an Indian Chief.
Children of SAMUEL[3] SANDS and Mary Pell:
Samuel[4] b. 1723, m. Mercy Gedney.
Pell[4] m. 1753, Sarah Ackerly, had Samuel[5] m. 1777, Esther Seaman.
Thomas[4] m. Mary Ketcham.
Mercy[4] m. Nathaniel Sands, had David b. 1745, m. Clement Hallock, b. 1746.
Mary[4] m. Jonathan Belknap.
Sarah[4] m. Thomas Powell, son of Solomon.
Phebe[4] m. Armont Cannon.
SAMUEL[5] SANDS and Esther Seaman had:
Obadiah m. Susan Bussing.
Rachel m. Samuel Ketcham.
Martha m. Wm. Edmondson.
Henry m.
Edmond, Samuel, Nathaniel, William.
James[2] Sands and Sarah Cornell settled at Sands Point, L. I.

SCUDDER FAMILY.

Dr. Henry Scudder presided at a committee of clergyman appointed by the King, at Westminister Abbey, England, 1643.

THOMAS^1 SCUDDER, sr. (supposed to be his son) came from Groton, England with wife Elisabeth, in 1636. Settled at Salem, Mass., died there in 1657, children :

Elisabeth,^{2} Thomas,^{2} Henry^2 and John^2 came from Salem to Southold, L. I. in 1651. In 1656, all sold out to John Baylis, and removed to Huntington, L. I. Later some of the families went to Jamaica, L. I. to reside.

HENRY^2 SCUDDER m. Catharine Este, dau. of Jeffrey, he d. 1661, children :

Jonathan^3 m. 1680, Sarah Brown. Moses.^{3} David^3 m. Mary.

Mary,^{3} Rebecca.^{3}

JOHN^2 went to Maspeth, 1660, m. Joanna Betts, their son, Samuel^3 m. Phebe Titus about 1680.

In 1710. Henry Scudder m. Mary Willets, dau. of Richard* and Abigail (Powell). They were cousins. He d. 1715, and she m. Thomas Williams.

SEARING FAMILY.

SIMEON[1] SEARING shared in the first division of land, in Hempstead, in 1647. In 1674, Simeon Searing and others petitioned to have a minister, he sold land in Oysterbay to Christopher Hawxhurst, in 1655.

John[2] son of Simeon Searing paid taxes in 1685, his Will dated 1713, names wife and children, John,[3] James,[3] Simeon,[3] Jonathan.[3]

JAMES[3] SEARING (John[2] James[1]) m. Temperance (Williams) dau. of John and widow of David Seaman, and had children, (he d. 1746).

James.[4]
Daniel.[4]
Sarah[4] m. Jacob Fowler.
Mary[4] m. Daniel Williams.

JOHN SEARING b. 1734, m. Martha Smith, she b. 1737, and had:

Samuel b. Aug. 5, 1756, m. Phebe Seaman, dau. of Zebulun and Phebe.
Sarah b. Apr. 4. 1758.   Daniel b. June 28, 1759.
James, b. July 31, 1761.
Ruth b. March 28, 1763.   Susannah b. Feb. 7, 1765.   Mary b. June 26, 1767.
John b. Sept. 8, 1769.   Jemima b. Oct. 28, 1771.
Martha b. Sept. 14, 1774.
Jane b. July 30, 1776.   Rebecca b. July 30, 1779.

JAMES SEARING b. 1761, m. 1786, Mary Fowler, b. 1767, and had:
Cynthia b. 1788, James Smith b. 1791. John Parker b. 1794. Daniel b. 1797.
Harriet b. 1799. Silas b. 1802. Samuel S. b. 1804. George F. b. 1806.
Agnes A. b. 1808. Silas C. b. 1813.

JOHN SEARING m. Mary Prior, b. 1738, dau. of Samuel and Mary (Powell), children:
Mary b. 1764. John b. 1766. Amy b. 1768.
Phebe b. 1773, m. 1795, Thomas Willis, dau. of Fry and Anna.

SAMUEL SEARING, son of John and Martha (Smith) had:
John b. 1796, m. Annie Loines.
Rebecca m. Townsend Hawxhurst.
Leonard m. Rebecca Albertson.
Richard m. Mary. Esther and Zebulun did not marry.

DANIEL SEARING d. about 1763, sons John, Coe, Moses, James and Daniel, daus. Jemima and Sarah.

Will of John Searing, the elder in 1795, says wife Mary, and gives to Amos Searing, son of Michael. To children of John Marvin, Deceased, to wit, John Marvin, Susanna Smith and Sarah Willis. To two daus. of Jecamiah Marvin, to Jane Smith, widow of Timothy and her five children, viz: Deborah, Mary, Rebecca, Jane and John. To children of Sylvanus Smith, Deceased, Joseph, John, Timothy and Sylvanus, and to Elisabeth Hicks's children.

Abigail Embree's Will 1792, gives to sister Mary Searing, Dr. James Searing and his wife Sarah, and also to his six children. To Wm. Nichols, son

Samuel. To sister Hannah Hewlett's children and to Abigail Nostrant.

Will of Samuel Searing, wife Lavinia (Toffy) money to support my mother; granddaughter Phebe to be decently brought up. Remainder of estate to Elisabeth Hicks's children.

JOHN STRICKLAND'S FAMILY was from County Westmoreland, England.

He was an original settler of Charlestown in 1629–30. Made Freeman of Massachusetts in 1631. Became a member of the church at Watertown, afterwards was at Weathersfield and Fairfield, Conn. His son Thwaite settled at Weathersfield.

Son Samuel came to L. I. Of his daughters one, Elisabeth m. Capt. John Seaman.

Joanna m. Jonas Wood from Halifax.

In 1644. The Charter of Hempstead was granted unto John Strickland, Robert Fordham, John Ogden, John Carman, John Lawrence and James Wood.

In 1647. John Strickland shared in the first division of land. In 1650, Mr. Strickland of Hempstead, by his deputy, Jonas Wood, his son-in-law, drew a three hundred pound lot in Southampton.

In 1653. Mr. Strickland, Mr. Washburne and Mr. Gildersleeve were appointed by the authorities at Fort Amsterdam to administer the law and justice in the village of Hempstead to the best of their knowledge and information in accordance with their privileges and the laws of New Netherland.

1663. Strickland was of Jamaica, he d. 1672, a widower. He was in Dedham, Mass., in 1631. The children of his son THWAITE and wife Elisabeth, born in Dedham were Elisabeth b. 1647, John b. 1648, Joseph b. 1654, Jonathan b. 1657.

Edmond Strickland was on L. I. in 1656.

Jonathan Strickland had land in Hempstead Swamp, L. I., in 1669, had wife on L. I. in 1691.

Will of Nicholas Stilwell, of Staten Island, 1671, his wife's name was Ann. They had children:

Elias, wife Rebecca, youngest son Jeremiah, others.

Nicholas, wife Mary, daus. Mary m. Adam² Mott, and others.

Nicholas² Will 1750, wife Mary, sons Nicholas and Thomas, daus. Catharine, Mary, Susanna, Ann, Francis and Sarah.

Died 1765. Samuel Stillwell, a merchant of New York.

William Stillwell m. Mary Powell, he b. 1757, d. 1797.

ROCK SMITH FAMILY.

JOHN[1] ROCK SMITH in Stamford, Conn. in 1640, at Hempstead, L. I. in 1644, says that at Stamford he was called Rock John for distinction. There were several John Smiths in that settlement. He was a Judge. He was born about 1615, he d. 1706, and the Hempstead records show his long life to have been spent in an active, enterprising manner, surrounded by neighbors and friends who were ever ready to transact business with him, and hold him in good esteem.

The name of his wife does not appear in any of the deeds or exchanges of land or in his will. The names of his sons are of frequent occurrence, sometimes disposing of property jointly with their father.

Children of JOHN[1] ROCK SMITH:

John[2] m., died before 1690. Children, Richard, Timothy, Mary and Sarah.

Joseph[2] m. had son Joseph.

Jonathan[2] m. Grace Mott, dau. of Adam[1] and Jane (Hewlett), he d. about 1724.

Mary[2] m. Samuel Denton.

Martha[2] m. Francis Chappel, she d. before her father.

One dau.[2] m. a Rushmore and had Ann and Mary.

Hannah[2] m. John Tredwell.

JONATHAN[2] ROCK SMITH (John[1]) in 1698, a Lieutenant in the King's service, had commission signed and sealed by Richard Earl, of Belmont, Commission is still in the possession of one of his descendants who bears the name of Rock Smith, and lives on the farm that he owned and occupied at Merrick, L. I. The old house has been moved back from the road and is kept as an heir loom.

Children of JONATHAN[2] and Grace (Mott) Rock Smith:

Thomas[3] m. had dau. Grace, he d. previous to 1724.
Jonathan jr.[3] m. Elisabeth, he d. 1746.
Mary,[3] Jane,[3] Grace.[3]
Gersham m.

JONATHAN[3] jr. and Elisabeth had:
Jonathan[4]
John[4] m. Rachel.
Henry Cornell.[4]
Philena.[4]
Elisabeth[4] b. 1708, m. 1725, Elias Cornelius, m. 2d Ezekiel Matthews.
Jane[4] m. Benjamin Haviland.
Hannah[4] m. Timothy Beadle.

JOHN[4] ROCK SMITH (Jonathan[3] Jonathan[2] John[1]) m. Rachel and had:
Joseph[5] m. Elisabeth Gildersleeve.
Son-in-law, Benjamin Smith, daus. Phebe,[5] Ann[5] and Elisabeth.[5]

JOSEPH[5] and Elisabeth (Gildersleeve) Rock Smith had the homestead, and son WILLIAM, who m. Amy Smith, dau. of George and had:
Elijah m. Delia Fish. dau. of William.

GERSHAM[3] ROCK SMITH (Jonathan[2] John[1]) d. about 1732, had wife Mary, and children:
Gersham,[4] Thomas,[4] Uriah,[4] Israel,[4] Mary,[4] Martha[4], Sarah,[4] Jane[4] and Elisabeth.[4]

Children of Gersham[4] Rock Smith and wife:
Adam[5] m. Elisabeth Raynor and had Raynor[6] Rock Smith, m. 1st ――, 2d Elisabeth.
Richard,[6] Thomas,[6] Gersham,[6] Catharine,[6] m. a Seabury.

RAYNOR[6] R. SMITH (Adam[5] Gersham[4] Gersham[3] Jonathan[2] John[1]) and Elisabeth[2] Moxon had:
dau, m. 1st Charles Powell, 2d m. Carman Cornelius.

ZOPHAR SMITH b. March 23, 1749, m. 1779, Glorianna Carman, b. May 10, 1756, he d. July 25, 1814, children:
Benjamin b. 1780, m. ――, he d. 1820.
Ruth b. 1781.
James b. 1782, m. Elisabeth Duryea, he d. 1848.
Hannah b. 1784. Mary b. 1786. Silas b. 1787.
William b. 1789, m. 1817, Catherine Duryea.
Clarissa b. 1791. Fanny b. 1792, d. 1795.
Samuel b. 1794.
Carman b. 1801.

JAMES SMITH and Elisabeth (Duryea) had:
Gelston m. Esther Seaman, dau. of John and Mary (Whitson).
Hewlett m. Nancy Post, dau. of Oliver and Mary (Birdsall).
Maria m. 1st Braddock Seaman, 2d m. John B. Post.

WILLIAM SMITH of Huntington. d. before 1684, his sons were:
Thomas, Joseph, Nehemiah and Wait.
Benjamin Smith formerly of Huntington, L. I., with wife Sarah, lived at Milford, New Haven, in 1684.

JONATHAN SMITH (had sister Abbie Carpenter of Snarlington) m. 1st and had Sylvanus, m. Jane Ireland, dau. of Thomas; lived at Bethpage. Sylvanus had half sisters.
Phebe Dorland, m. Wait Wells.
Amy Dorland, m. a Wilson.

Sir John Underhill m. Mary Moseley.

UNDERHILL FAMILY.

Capt. JOHN UNDERHILL born in Warwickshire, England about 1596, came with John Winthrop and his 900 emigrants to Boston in 1630—his wife Helena was a member of the "Old South Church" in 1633. She was the mother of John² baptised 1642. She died at Southold, L. I. 1658. John² married Elisabeth, dau. of Henry Winthrop, and wife Elisabeth. After his fighting the Indians successfully in N. E., the Dutch Government invited him to come to New Amsterdam in 1649, and help them. He came then; and again in 1653, the Mass. Government allowed him, and Capt. Edward Hull to come and fight the Indians on L. I. He bought (1657) a place in Southold and brought his family in 1658, but losing his wife soon, he sold his home in 1659, to Thomas¹ Moore,—came west, and receiving a grant of land in Oysterbay, settled again, at a place which he named Kenilworth, joined the Society of Friends, raised a family, and died at his home, 21, 7, 1672.

Capt. John Underhill was one of the 8 men to assist the Governor of New Netherlands in 1648-9.

1639. Petronella Underhill, wife of Ulrich Leopold had money, lived west end of L. I.

1642. John Underhill, at Flatlands, bought land of Andries Hudd.

Underhill Family.

1674. Humphrey Underhill, west end of L. I. refused to pay for the support of the clergy.

1646. Deborah, dau. of Capt. John Underhill was at Flatlands,

1697. Jemima Underhill m. Benjamin Wyncoop.

1695. Sarah Underhill m. Joseph Budd.

1654. John Underhill was at Southold, L. I.

Elisabeth, dau. of Capt. John and Helena Underhill b. 1636.

Capt. JOHN¹ UNDERHILL and 2d wife Elisabeth Winthrop had:

Deborah² b. 1659–60, m. Henry Townsend.

Nathaniel² b. 1663, m. 1685, Mary Ferris, dau. of John and Mary.

Hannah² b. 1666, m. Thomas Alsop, son of Richard, she d. 1751.

Elisabeth² b. 1669, m. Isaac Smith.

David² b. 1672, m. Hannah.

JOHN² UNDERHILL (John¹) m. 1668, Mary Prior, b. 1651, she d. 1698, was dau. of Matthew and Mary Prior. John² b. 1631, d. 1693, had:

John³ b. 1670, m. 1st Elisabeth Willets, dau. of Thomas and Dinah, 2d Susannah Birdsall.

Daniel³ b. 1672, d   Samuel b. 1674, died early.

Mary³ b. 1677, m. Wright Frost, son of William.

Abraham³ b. 1679, m. Sarah Townsend, dau. of Thomas.

Deborah³ b. 1682, m.

Samuel³ b. 1685, m. 1700, Hannah Willets, dau. of Thomas and Dinah.

Sarah³ b. 1687, m. 1708, Thomas Pearsall.

Jacob³ b. 1689, m. Mary Wright, dau. of John and Mary (Townsend).

Hannah³ b. 1690, m. 1716, Thomas Bowne, son of Samuel.

JOHN³ UNDERHILL (John² John¹) and Elisabeth Willets had:
Daniel⁴ b. 1700, m. Abigail Cruger.
Amos⁴ b., m. 1729, Elisabeth b. 1710. dau. of Benj'n. and Jane (Mott) Seaman:
Isaac⁴ d. 1723.
Deborah⁴ m. Joseph Prior.
Mary.⁴
Thomas⁴ m. Sarah Powell, dau. of John of Bethpage.

AMOS⁴ UNDERHILL and Elisabeth Seaman had:
Isaac⁵ b. 1732, m. Mary Cock, b. 1730, dau. of John and Sarah.
Annie⁵ b. m. Townsend Drick.
David⁵ b. 1743, m. 1773, Elisabeth b. 1747, dau. of William Mott of Hempstead.
Solomon⁵ b. 1749, m. 1780, Lydia Mott, dau. of Adam and Sarah, he d. 1827.
Edmond⁵ b. 1754, m. Frances Carpenter.
Amos⁵ m. Mary Woodhull.
Benjamin⁵ m. Letitia Townsend.
Deborah⁵ m. Richard Townsend.
Hannah⁵ m. Willett Bowne, son of William.

DAVID⁵ UNDERHILL and Elisabeth (Mott) had:
William⁶ b. 1774. Elisabeth b. 1778. Miriam b. 1786.

SOLOMON⁵ UNDERHILL and Lydia (Mott) had:
Isaac⁶ b. 1781. Sarah⁶ b. 1783. Elisabeth⁶ b. 1786, d. 1801. Samuel⁶ b. 1788, Henry⁶ b. 1790.

ABRAHAM³ (John² John¹) and Sarah (Townsend) Underhill had:
Thomas⁴ a mariner, m. Freelove Alling.
Sarah⁴ m. James Dickinson, William m.

BENJAMIN[5] UNDERHILL and Letitia (Townsend) had:

Elisabeth[6] m. John B. Coles, and Townsend[6] m. Almy, dau. of Dr. James Townsend.

SAMUEL[3] UNDERHILL (John[2] Capt. John[1]) m. Hannah Willets and had:

Anne[4] b. 1702.

Dinah[4] b. 1705, m. 1737, John Bowne.

Samuel[4] b. 1708, m. 1737, Ann, dau. of Joseph and Mary Carpenter of O. B.

Abraham[4] b. 1715, m. 1754, Dinah, dau. of Isaac and Clement Willets.

Children of SAMUEL[4] UNDERHILL and Ann Carpenter:

Joseph[5] b. 1738.

Samuel[5] b. 1740, m. 1770, Ann b. 1768, dau. of Richard and Hannah Willets, of Islip.

Robert[5] b. 1742.

Mary[5] b. 1745, m. 1765, James Mott. son of Richard and Sarah,

Andrew[5] b. 1746, m. 1774, Deborah Willets, son of Richard and Hannah.

James[5] b. 1751, d. 1752. Hannah b. 1727, d. 1760.

Thomas[5] b. 1755.

Children of SAMUEL[5] (b. 1740) UNDERHILL and Anna (Willets) b. 1748).

Richard[6] b. 1772, m.

Hannah[6] b. 1775. Robert[6] b. 1778. Mary b. 1780. Joseph[6] b. 1783.

Anna[6] b. 1785, m. 1810, William Willis, son of Edmond and Abigail.

ANDREW[5] UNDERHILL (Samuel[4] Samuel[3] John[2] John[1]) and Deborah (Willets had:

Samuel[6] b. 1774, m. 1796, Elisabeth W. dau. of Phineas and Mary Buckley.

Ann[6] b. 1780, m. 1808, Asa Moore, son of Thomas and Elisabeth, of Va.

Elisabeth[6] b. 1783, m. 1708, Abraham Bradbury, son of Abraham and Phebe Norley.

James[6] b. 1787.

ABRAHAM[4] UNDERHILL (Samuel[3] John[2] Capt. John[1]), and Dinah (Willets) had:

Israel[5] m. Mary, dau. of John and Phebe (Seaman) Wright.

Children of ISRAEL[5] and Mary (Wright) Underhill:

Samuel[6] b. 1778, m. 1809, Hannah Titus and had Jordan Underhill, m. Hannah Willets.

Sarah[6] b 1781, m. Andries Seaman, son of Jordan.

Charles[6] b. 1783.

Phebe[6] b. 1787, m. 1st Daniel Underhill, 2d Jacob Crooker.

Isaac[6] b. 1789, m. 1809, Rachel Seaman, dau. of Jordan, he d. 1832.

Mary[6] b. 1791, m. Saul Alley.

Hannah[6] b. 1793, m. Stephen Titus.

Willet[6] b. 1786, m. 1st a Prior, 2d m. Susan Hopkins.

Elisabeth[6] b. 1798.

Rebecca[6] b. 1701, m. a Cox.

ISAAC[6] UNDERHILL and Rachel Seaman had:
Abraham.[7]   Wm. S.[7] m. Elisabeth Wigham.

WILLET[6] UNDERHILL and —— Prior had:

Elisabeth[7] m. Absalom J. Barrett   Susan m. George Townsend, son of Jacob P.

2d wife Susan Hopkins had:

Isaac[7] m. a Voorhees, and had several children,

THOMAS[4] UNDERHILL (John[3] John[2] John[1]) and Sarah (Powell) had:

Adonijah[5] m. Phebe, dau. of Daniel Willets and Phebe (Powell.

Jacob[5] m. Catharine Willets.
Elisabeth[5] m. John Powell, son of John and Martha.
John[5] m. a Prior.
Freelove[5] m. Penn Frost.
ADONIJAH[5] UNDERHILL and Phebe had:
Daniel[6] m. 1st 1793, Mary Jackson, dau. of John, 2d Phebe Underhill, dau. of Israel.
Rachel[6] m. Obadiah Jackson.
DANIEL[6] UNDERHILL and Mary (Jackson) had:
Samuel[7] J. b. 1797, m. 1824, Mary Willets, dau. of Samuel and Hannah.
Adonijah[7] m. Phebe Hicks, dau. of Valentine, no children.
Amy[7] m. Isaac Willets, son of Samuel and Hannah.
2d wife Phebe Underhill had:
Jackson[7] m.
Mary[7] m. Samuel A. Barrett.
Elisabeth[7] m.
Children of SAMUEL[7] J. UNDERHILL and Mary:
Daniel[8] b. 1826, m. 1st Caroline, 2d Catharine Post, daus. of James and Phebe.
Phebe[8] b. 1830, m. Elias Hicks Seaman, son of Robert and Sarah (Hicks).
JACOB[5] UNDERHILL (Thomas[4] John[3] John[2] John[1]) and Catharine Willets had:
James[6] m. 1788, Mary, dau. of John Titus and Sarah.
Mary[6] m. Thomas Leggett.
Richard[6] m. 1784, Pamela Townsend, dau. of Tho's. and Mary (Loines).
RICHARD[6] UNDERHILL and Pamela had:
Thomas[7] m. Sarah Whitson, dau. of Henry.
Wm.[7] m. Elisabeth Kissam. Jacob[7] single.

Adonijah[7] m. Sarah Underhill, dau. of Israel, and had dau. Sophia.
Mary[7] single. Catharine[7] single.
Phebe[7] m. William Willets.
James[7] m. Margaret Rogers.
Samuel[7] m. Hannah W. Seaman, dau. of Elijah.
Sarah T.[7] b, 1803, m. Richard S. Powell, son of Benjamin.
Alfred[7] m. 1st Jane Underhill, 2d Hannah Sutton, 3d Rebecca Burling, 4th Hannah Seaman.
Rebecca[7] m. Henry M. Carpenter.

ALFRED[7] and Jane Underhill had:
Phebe[8] m. Ezekiel Miller. Caroline[8] m. Joshua Washburne.

NATHANIEL[2] UNDERHILL (Capt. John[1]) and Mary Ferris had:
Nathaniel[3] b. 1690, m. Mary Honeywell, dau. of Israel — son Israel m. Mary Lispenard.
Thomas[3] m. Phebe Davenport,
Abraham[3] m. Hannah Cromwell.
Benjamin[3] and perhaps others. John, Mary and Wm.

Children of THOMAS[3] UNDERHILL and Phebe Davenport:
Isaac[4] b. 1732, m. Mary b. 1730.
Phebe[4] b. 1734, m. Joseph Weeks.
Thomas[4] b. 1738, m. Sarah Weeks.
Benjamin[4] m. 1st Amy Weeks. 2d Elisabeth Dean.
Samuel[4] m. Phebe Dodge.
William[4] m. Mary Sutton.
Nathaniel[4] m. Phebe Weeks.
James[4] m. Prudence Rogers.
Caleb[4] m. Hannah Carpenter.
Charity[4] m. 1st Joseph Thorn, 2d John Church, 3d Jesse Weeks.

Mary⁴ m. Joshua Hutchins.
Sarah⁴ m. Robert Dodge.
Abel.⁴

ABRAHAM² UNDERHILL (Nathaniel John¹) and Hannah (Cromwell) had:

Abraham³ m. 1746, 1st Phebe Hallock, 2d Kesia Farrington.
Mary³ m. a Horton.
Isaac³ m. 1756, Sarah Field.
Jacob³ m. 1747, Amy Hallock.
Hannah³ m.
Martha³ m. Jabez Lockwood.

ABRAHAM³ UNDERHILL and Phebe Hallock had:

Abraham⁴ m. Phebe Pugsley.
John⁴ m. a Fowler.
Isaac⁴ m. Fanny Pugsley and had Tabitha m, John Powell,
Phebe⁴ m. Foster Hallock.
Clementine⁴ m, Henry Whitson,
Children of 2d marriage:
Hannah⁴ m. James Birdsall.
Sarah⁴ m. Samuel Sutton.
Daniel⁴ m. 1786, Sarah Cox, dau. of Reese and Hannah.
Martha⁴ m. Walter Haight.
Israel⁴ m. Zervia Haight.
Amos⁴ m. Amelia Baxter.
Amy⁴ m., Isaac Pierce, son of James and Martha.
Joseph⁴ single. Rebecca.⁴ Ann.⁴
Solomon⁴ m. Phebe Conklin.

ABRAHAM⁵ UNDERHILL (Abraham⁴ Abraham³ Nathaniel² John¹) and Phebe Pugsley had:

William.⁶
James⁶ m. 1st Lydia Carpenter, 2d

Underhill Family. 305

Phebe[6] m. James Carpenter.
Hannah[6] m. Josiah I. Underhill.
JAMES[6] UNDERHILL and Lydia Carpenter had:
Abraham[7] m. Eliza Ostrander.
Phebe[7] m. Job Carpenter, she d. and Job m. her sister.
Bailey[7] m. Mary Griffin.
Maria[7] m. Job Carpenter.
Jane[7] m. Thomas Carpenter.
Wm.[7]
Daniel[7] m. Mary Carpenter.
Elias H.[7] b. 1826, m. Elisabeth Underhill, dau. of David.
of 2d m. Cyrus m. Sarah Ann Kipp.
DANIEL[5] UNDERHILL (Abraham[4] Abraham[3] Nathaniel[2] John[1]) and Sarah (Cox) had:
Adonijah[6] m. a Sutton.
Stephen[6] m. 1712, Phebe Cornell. dau. of Ben'j. and Alice, of Scarsdale.
Andrew[6] m. Sarah Upton.
Levi.[6]
David[6] m. Sarah Pierce.
Abraham[6] m. Elisabeth Buckley.
Israel.[6] Ephraim.[6]
Esther[6] b. 1800, m. 1824, Robert Haviland.
Hannah[6] m. 1st John Griffin, had John L. 2d, Solomon Haviland.
Deborah[6] m. Stephen Archer.
ISRAEL[6] UNDERHILL (Abraham[4] Abraham[3] Nathaniel[2] John[1]) and Zervia (Haight) had:
Sarah[6] m. Adonijah Underhill and had Sophia,[8] m. Henry T. Willets.
Phebe[6] m. Thomas Carpenter.
Charlotte[6] m. Charles Carpenter.

39

SOLOMON[5] UNDERHILL (Abraham[4] Abraham[3] Nathaniel[2] John[1]) and Phebe (Conklin) had:
Caroline[6] m. Aaron Quimby.
Jane[7] m. Alfred Underhill.
Isaac[6] m. Jane Underhill, dau. of Adonijah.
Townsend[6] m. Emily Smith.
David[6] m. Emeline Brady.
Elias[6] m. Jane Carpenter.
John[6] m. Sarah Young.

ISAAC[4] UNDERHILL (Abraham[3] Nathaniel[2] Capt. John[1]) m. Sarah Field and had:
CALEB[5] Underhill m. Elisabeth Quimby and had:
Josiah I.[6] m. Hannah Underhill, dau. of Abraham.[5]
Aaron[6] m.
Richard Mott[6] m. Hannah Griffin.
Alexander[6] m. 1st Phebe, 2d Caroline Albertson, daus. of Silas.[3]
William[6] m. Phebe Griffin.
Willett[6] m. Phebe Smith.
Charles.[6]
Phebe[6] m. Stephen Wood.

Children of JOSIAH I.[6] UNDERHILL and Hannah:
Euphemia[7] m. 1st John Haskins, 2d a Beardsley.
Phebe T.[7] m. John Yellott.
Susan[7] m. Rev. Joshua Butts.
Elisabeth[7] m. George Jackson, son of Jarvis.
Mary[7] m. Daniel Smith.
Ann[7] m.
Clarkson[7] m.
Aaron.[7] Howard.[7] Jane[7] m.

JACOB[4] UNDERHILL (Abraham[3] Nathaniel[2] John[1]) m. 1747, Amy Hallock and had:
Amy[5] m. 1781, Jordan Frost, b. 1754, d. 1835, she d. 1799, moved to Rensselaerville, in 1803.

James[5] m. 20, 4, 1785, Phebe Cock, dau. of Reese and Hannah (Robbins).

JACOB[5] m. Ann Conkling, dau. of David, and had: David[6] m. Hannah Hatfield and had Elisabeth m. Elias H. Underhill.

? Joseph Underhill m.   his sister Martha, m, 1778, Stephen Loines, she d. 1845.

VALENTINE FAMILY.

The WILL of RICHARD[2] VALENTINE dated 1725, says wife Sarah, eldest son Richard,[3] youngest son Jonathan,[3] other son David,[3] daughters Sarah[3] Smith, Phebe[3] Downing, Anne[3] Carle and Hannah[3] Pine.

The Will of Richard[4] Valentine, of Hempstead Harbor, son of Richard, now living in 1763, says "wife Phebe and small children, son Richard to have a double share of property, daus. Abigail, Sarah, Mary, Phebe and Martha, brother in-law Benj'n. Robbins."

The Will of Richard[3] Valentine, of Hempstead Harbor, 1768, says "sister Ann Pearsall, son Joseph, daughter-in-law Phebe Valentine, deceased son Richard's children, grandson George Weeks to have his own, and the share of his brother Richard, deceased, grandson Richard Kirk — and granddaughters Jemima Baker and Abigail Weeks."

Sarah Valentine, dau. of Richard and Phebe, was living in Bethpage, in 1836.

RICHARD[1] VALENTINE, one of the first settlers of Hempstead, took his share in the first division of land in 1647.

In 1657. R. V. had land at Merrick in company with Richard Cornell.

In 1659. Richard Vallingtyne was one of the five chosen Townsmen of the town of Hempstead. The other four were Francis Wicks, Robert Marvin, Adam Mott and Richard Brutnall.

In 1676. R. V. was Overseer, and in 1679, he was Constable.

In 1684. The widow was named in the Tax List, — also four sons, viz :

Obadiah[2] m. Martha.　　Will made 1743.

William.[2]

Ephraim.[2]

Richard[2] jr. 1676, had grant of land, Richard,[3] son of Richard had brother-in-law Thomas Clement, in 1700. Timothy Halstead gave to his son-in-law, Richard Valentine, Will in 1686. Deborah Valentine, dau. of Rich'd., probably R.[3] m. 1736, Samuel Weeks had dau. Abigail Weeks, who m. 1770, Rich'd. Titus, her father gave her some Valentine Manuscript, still preserved by their descendants.

Deborah Valentine m. 1674, Wm. Foster, d. 1687.

Jacob Valentine of North Hempstead, m. 1800, Sarah Carman.

Valentine Family.

Samuel Valentine, m. 1805, Mary Ann Clowes.
David Valentine m. 1810, Mary Langdon.
Charles Valentine m. 1813, Phebe Bedell.
Obadiah Valentine m. 1815, Martha Willets.
Will of Ephraim Valentine made 1729, proved 1737, says wife Rachel, dau. Phebe, sons William, Ichabod, Richard and Ephraim.

OBADIAH[2] (Richard[1] Valentine[1] d. 1684) m. Martha, she d. 1743, children:

    William[3] d. 1744, gave his property to his brothers and sisters.
    Obadiah[3] b. 1690, m. 1716, Martha Willets, he d. 1769.
    Jacob[3] m.
    Thomas.[3]
    Henry[3] m. Mary Kirby, dau. of Thomas and Ann (Hopkins),
    Ruth[3] m. a Dean.
    Phebe[3] m. Sept. 10, 1726, Peter Demilt.
    Sarah.[3]
    Ann[3] b. 1715, m. 1734, William Lynes (Loines or Loynes) name spelled all these ways in her father's Will.

OBADIAH[3] VALENTINE (Obadiah[2] Richard[1]) m. Martha Willets, dau. of Richard[2] and Abigail (Powell), children:

    Martha[4] b. 1717, m. 1736, Samuel Seaman, son of Nathaniel.
    Mary[4] b. 1719.
    Phebe[4] b. 1721, m. 1743, Zebulun Seaman, son of David and Temperance (Williams).
    Elisabeth[4] b. 1724, m. 1747, John Williams, son of Thomas and Mary (Willets).

Valentine Family.

Esther[4] b. 1733, m. Samuel Way, had children:
Valentine Way b. 1756. Jane Way b. 1761, m. Henry Mott and had Dr. Valentine Mott, of New York.
Sarah Way m. 1781, a Franklin.
? JACOB[3] VALENTINE ? (Obadiah[2] Richard[1]) m. and had:
William[4] b. 1741, m. 1764, Phebe Smith.
Richard[4] m. 1st   2d Elisabeth Post, dau. of John.
WILLIAM[4] and Phebe Smith had:
Mary[5] b. 1765, Caleb[5] b. 1767, Ann[5] b. 1769, Phebe[5] b. 1772, Smith[5] b. 1774, Charles[5] b. 1776, David[5] b. 1779.
William[5] b. 1781, m. Phebe Myers, d. 1863.
WILLIAM[5] and Phebe Myers had:
Wm. M.[6] b. 1809, m. Almy Seaman, dau. of Henry O., had James Edgar, she d. and he m. 2d Lydia P. Mott, dau. of Stephen.
RICHARD[4] VALENTINE (Jacob[3] Obadiah[2] Richard[1]) and 2d wife Elisabeth (Post) had:
Martha.[5]   JACOB[5] m. Hannah Wood and had:
Ann[6] m. Daniel Lewis.
Ruth[6] m. Daniel Searing.
John[6] m. Maria Vandewater.
William[6] m. Marian Bedell, had son.
Jacob[7] m. Martha Powell, b. 1727, dau. of John and Elisabeth Cox).
Obadiah[3] Valentine m. 1716, Martha Willets.

Present as witnesses.

OBADIAH VALENTINE,	NATHANIEL SEAMAN,
MARY VALENTINE,	RICHARD SEAMAN,
THOMAS VALENTINE,	TAMAR SEAMAN,
REBECCA WHITSON,	THOMAS SEAMAN,

Phebe Willets,
Elisabeth Titus,
Silas Titus,
Thomas Underhill,
Peter Titus,
Sarah Pearsall,
Thomas Powell, Sr.
Thomas Powell, Jr.
John Powell,
Wait Powell,
Thomas Townsend,
Jacob Seaman,
Benjamin Seaman,
Samuel Powell,
Mary Powell,
Mary Powell, Jr.
Rachel Powell,
Thomas Powell,³
Jacob Townsend,
Abigail Willets,
Jacob Willets,
Elisabeth Willets,
Henry Willets,
(perhaps Willis).

DAVID³ VALENTINE b. 1689, (Richard² Richard¹) m. 1716, Charity Coles, b. 1695, dau. of Nathan and Rachel (Hopkins) Coles and had.

Charity⁴ b. 1717.
Jacob⁴ b. 1718, m. 1740, Mary Coles.
Mary⁴ b. 1721.
Sarah⁴ b. 1725.

Children of JACOB⁴ VALENTINE and Mary Coles:

Mary.⁵
Charles⁵ b. 1742, m. Mary Frost.
David⁵ b. 1745, m. Hannah Townsend, dau. of George.
Susanna⁵ m. Thomas Udall.

CHARLES⁵ VALENTINE (Jacob⁴ David³ Richard² Richard¹) and Mary Frost had:

Jacob⁶ b. 1763, m. 1791, Phebe Loines, dau. of Stephen and Phebe (Titus).
Lewis⁶ b. 1765, m. 1st 1790. Jane Rushmore, 2d Jane (Titus), widow of Samuel Post, he d. 1821.
Sarah⁶ b. 1767.

Letitia⁶ b. 1769, m. William Willets, son of Joseph and Hannah.
Elisabeth⁶ b. 1770, Theodosia⁶ b. 1776, Frost⁶ b. 1778, Isaac⁶ b. 1780, David⁶ b. 1783.
Daniel⁶ b. 1785.

DAVID⁵ VALENTINE (Jacob⁴ David³ Richard² Richard¹) and Hannah Townsend had:
Susannah,⁶ Sarah.⁶
George⁶ m. Mary Frost.
Elwood⁶ m. Mary Post, had Caroline,⁷ Emily,⁷ Susan.⁷
Charles⁶ m. Catharine Adee and had David⁷ and Charles.⁷
Townsend⁶ d. 1807. Mary d. 1799.

LEWIS⁶ VALENTINE (Charles⁵ Jacob⁴ David³ Rich'd² Richard¹) and Jane Rushmore had:
Jacob⁷ m. Martha, dau. of Samuel Titus and Abigail (Robbins.)
Stephen⁷ m. Ann Titus, dau. of Samuel Titus and Abigail, of 2d m. with Jane (Titus), widow Post.
Townsend,⁷ John T.,⁷ Jane,⁷ George.⁷

JACOB⁷ VALENTINE and Martha had:
Charles⁸ m. Kesia Coles.
Mary⁸ m. William Willets, son of Isaac and Amy.
Lewis⁸ m. Anna C. Thorne.
Jane R.⁸ died.

STEPHEN⁷ VALENTINE and Ann (Titus) had:
Martha⁸ m. Henry Griffin.
Sarah⁸ m. Charles Griffin.
Samuel T.⁸

VAN BERGEN FAMILY.

ADRIAEN VAN BERGEN 1599, Dutch Rec. say that he was exporter and part owner of the turf boat that ran down the river to Breda, and by capturing the city, assisted in freeing Holland from the Spanish yoke.

Agatha Van Bergen, dau. of Adriaen m. —— Van Der Donck, and was the mother of Adriaen Van Der Donck who came to New Netherlands in 1641, with W. Van Twiller, as sheriff of Rensalaer Wycke.

In 1645. Gov. Kieft in order to make presents to the Indians, was obliged to borrow money of A. Van Der Donck, Sheriff of Rensalaer Wycke.

The Prince Stadtholder of Holland, taking a Royal English wife, the dau. of Charles I. set the Dutch boys an example which many were willing to follow. "One of the most noted was Adriaen Van Der Donck; Dr. of both Laws."

"Married, Oct. 23. 1645, in the Reformed Dutch Church, at New Amsterdam: Adriaen Van Der Donck, j. m., Van Breda en Maria Douthy, j. d., of Van Hempstead." She was a dau. of Rev. Francis Doughty.

In 1648. Doughty departed for the English Virginias," he had previously conferred on his daughter Marie on her marriage in 1645, his farm on Flushing bay, now owned by Abraham and John J. Rapelye. Doct. Van Der Donck familliarly called the Yonker (or young Lord), obtained a patent for the farm in 1648. In 1649, Adriaen Van Der Donck, President of the Board of nine men, was called President of the Commonwealth of New Netherlands. He with two others was accredited to the "Mighty Sovereigns" and sent in 1650 to carry a Remonstrance written by himself on behalf of the People.

In 1652, April 26, while in Holland, "Adriaen Van Der Donck, of Breda, Patroon of the Colonie Nipperham, by him called Colendonck (Yonkers) was empowered to dispose of his Colonie and property by Will. His Will gave the Colonie to his wife. He returned in 1653. His wife, mother, brother, sister, &c., preceded him about a year.

"In 1655. Patent to Cornelius Van Der Donck land on the north side of Manhattan Island. The boundaries of New Netherlands extended to Cape Henlopen, 4 leagues south of Cape Cornelius, Lat. 38 degrees.

Adriaen Van Der Donck died 1655,—his widow removed to Pawtuxent, Maryland with her father— later m. 2d Rev. Hugh O'Neile.

Deleware papers say "in 1666, Van Der Donex, widow will enter again into possession of Nipperham. She claims also land in Maspeth, L. I." N. *Van Amstel.*

In 1664. The English purchased of the Indians all the land between West Chester and the North River, including the land which old Van Der Donck, his children and partners divided into Boweries and plantations, but which were deserted in the time of the massacre in 1655.

A Survey was made of 640 acres being a mile square upon the main patent belonging to (Yonkers) Van Der Donck, at Yonkers.

Three of the name supposed to be sons of Adriaen and Marie were on Long Island about 1672. They were Adriaen, Andrew Adriance and Hendrick Onderdonck, last named Baptized in N. Y. in 1665, Apr. 29,— m. Mary Foster, lived at Fosters Meadow, L. I., he d. 1732. Had only a daughter, Letitia who m. 1735, Giles Seaman, son of Richard. Their grandson Henry Onderdonck Seaman was in the Assembly several years.

Letitia was baptised in the Dutch Church at Jamaica, Dec. 22, 1722. She afterwards became a member of the Society of Friends at Jericho.

VAN DER DONCK FAMILY.

ANDREW² ADRIANCE (Adriaen¹) m. in Flatbush, Nov. 11, 1683, Maria Van Der Vliet and had:
Adrian³ b. 1684 m. Sarah Snedeker.
Andrew³ b. 1686, m. Jan. 2, 1742, Gertrude Lott.
ADRIAN³ and Sarah Snedeker had:
Andries,⁴ Gerrett,⁴ Abraham,⁴ Adrian,⁴ Isaac,⁴ Jacob,⁴ Elsie,⁴ Hendrick,⁴ Maria,⁴ John,⁴ Sarah.⁴ Most of these removed to Rockland Co., or New Jersey, descendants are numerous.
ANDREW³ ONDERDONCK (Andrew² Adrian¹) and Gertrude had:
Maria⁴ m. Jacobus Montfort.
Catharine⁴ m. Daniel Hegaman.
Andries⁴ b. 1711, m. Sarah Remsen, removed to Tappan.
Gertrude⁴ m. Jacobus Hegaman.
Anatie⁴ blind.
Dorothy⁴ m. Adrian Hegaman.
Sarah⁴ m. Thomas Dodge.
Hendrick⁴ b. 1725, m. Phebe Tredwell.
Adrian⁴ b. 1727, m. Maria Hegaman.
Peter⁴ b. 1730, m. Elisabeth Schenck.
HENDRICK⁴ ONDERDONCK (Andrew³ Andrew² Adriaen¹) and Phebe (Tredwell) had:
Benjamin,⁵ Gertrude,⁵ Phebe,⁵ Andrew.⁵
Sarah⁵ m. David Richard, Floyd Jones.
Henry,⁵ Maria,⁵ John,⁵ Phebe.⁵

ADRIAEN[4] ONDERDONCK (Andrew[3] Andrew[2] Adrian[1]) and Maria (Hegaman) had:

Gertrude[5] m. Peter Lyster.
George[5] b. 1752, m. 1796, Sarah Rapalye.
Sarah[5] m. Thomas Thorne.
Maria[5] m. Abraham Hoagland.
Joseph[5] b. 1766, m. 1789, Dorothy Montfort.
Lott,[5] Phebe,[5] Catharine,[5] Susannah,[5] Andrew.[5]

GEORGE[5] ONDERDONCK b. 1762, and Sarah Rapalye had:

Catharine,[6] Jacob,[6] Elisabeth.[6]
Maria H.[6] m. Henry Onderdonck, jr.

JOSEPH[5] ONDERDONCK and Dorothy Montfort had:

Maria,[6] Catharine,[6] Adrian,[6] George,[6] Andrew,[6] Elisabeth,[6] Andrew[6] Lott·
Henry[6] jr., b. 1804. m. 1828, Maria Hegaman Onderdonck, Horatio Gates,[6] James M.[6]

Henry[6] jr. and Maria[6] had Elisabeth,[7] Adriaen[7] b. 1831, m. 1856, Mary W. Pearsall.

WHITSON FAMILY.

HENRY[1] WHITSON was resident of Hempstead, L. I. in 1647, his wife was a Foster. They removed to Huntington about 1653, where he died in 1669, leaving a widow and minor son, Thomas, who afterwards m. Martha, dau. of Thomas Jones and Catharine (Estes), dau. of Jeffrey, he d. 1657, the first death in Huntington. Thomas Whitson purchased 1-3 of the Bethpage Purchase in 1700, died there in 1742, aged 90 years.

Children of THOMAS[2] and Martha Whitson:

Thomas[3] b. 1689, m. 1716, Deborah Feeks, b. 1695, he d.

Martha[3] b. 1691.

Ruth[3] b. 1694.

John[3] b. 1697, m. 1722, Esther Seaman.

Rebecca[3] b. 1699, m. 1719, Amos Willets, son of Thomas and Dinah.

David[3] b. 1701, m. Clement Powell, dau. of John and Margaret.

Henry[3] b. 1705, m. 1739, Hannah Powell, dau. of Thomas,[2] he d. 1790.

Hannah[3] b. 1707, she d. 1789.

THOMAS[3] WHITSON (Thomas[2] Henry[1]) and Deborah (Feeks) had:

John[4] b. 1718, m. 1744, Deborah Powell, b. 1715, dau. of Thomas,[2] he d. 1804.

Thomas[4] m. went to N. Jersey or Penn'a.

Whitson Family. 319

Children of JOHN[4] and Deborah (Powell) Whitson:
Mary[5] b. 1745, m. 1767, Jonathan Titus, b. 1743.
Deborah[5] b. 1747, m. James Rushmore, b. 1745, she d. 1796.
Elisabeth[5] b. 1749.
Amos[5] b. 1751, m. 1772, Amy Willets, dau. of Joseph.
Children of AMOS[5] and Amy (Willets) Whitson.
Thomas[6] b. 1773, m. 1797, Hannah Willets, dau. of Amos of Jericho (of Herricks).
Robert[6] m. 1809, Annie Whitson, dau. of Isaac.
Rebecca[6] b. 1780, m. 1804, Enos Alley.
Joseph[6] b. 1782, m. 1804,—— Smith, dau. of Jacob.
Hannah[6] b. 1784, m. 1807, Isaac Frost, son of Charles.
Deborah[6] m. 1818, David Willets, son of Jonah.
Children of Deborah[6] Whitson and James Rushmore:
Jacob b. 1767, m. Esther Dingee, he d. 1824.
John b. 1770, d. 1775.
Mary b. 1772, d. 1796.
Deborah b. 1778, d. 1857.
Annie b. 1781, m. Elkanah Wood and had son Dr. James R. Wood, of N. Y.
MARY RUSHMORE dau. of Jacob and Esther (Dingee) Rushmore, m. ALFRED CROSSMAN and their children were named Alonzo, Jacob, Cornelia m. Edward Willets, Frank m. Emily, Alice m. Dr. Marsh of N. Y. Huntington, West Neck.

JOHN[3] WHITSON (Thomas[2] Henry[1]) m. 1722, Esther Seaman, dau. of Nathaniel,[1] children:
John[4] m. 1747, Martha Whitman, in church at Huntington.

Nathaniel[4] m. 1749, Mary Powell, dau. of Wait.

Children of JOHN[4] and Martha (Whitman) WHITSON.

John[5] m. Mary, dau. of Daniel Powell.
Richard[5] m. Abigail, dau. of Joseph Powell.
Isaac[5] m. Rachel, dau. of Joseph Powell.
Silas[5] m. 1772, Sarah, dau. of Wait Powell.
Ruth[5] b. 1761, m. 1781, Willets Powell, son of Richard.
Phebe[5] m. Richard Powell, son of Richard.
Rachel[5] m. Benjamin Mott, she d. 1835.
Martha[5] m. a Collier.

Children of NATHANIEL[4] and Mary (Powell) Whitson:

Esther[5] b. 1755, m. 1778, David Jackson, son of Thomas and Mary (Willets), of Jericho.
James[5] b. 1750.
Sarah[5] b. 1757, m. a Jackson.

JOHN[5] WHITSON (John[4] John[3] Thomas[2] Henry[1]) and Mary (Powell) had:

Eliphalet[6] m. Annie Powell.
Ruth b.— m. John Powell.

ISAAC[5] WHITSON (John[4] John[3] Thomas[2] Henry[1]) and Rachel had:

Jane[6] m. Solomon Oakley.
Ann[6] m. 1809, Amos Whitson.
Rebecca[6] m. a Mitchell.
Hannah[6] m. a Mitchell.
Rachel[6] m. Abraham Weeks, son of Isaac.
Henry[6] m a Carle and had son Isaac.[7]

SILAS[5] WHITSON and Sarah, dau. of Wait Powell and Mary had:

Mary[6] b. 1773, m. John Seaman, son of Samuel.

ELIPHALET[6] Whitson and Annie Powell had:

James[7] m. Damaris Powell.

Whitson Family. 321

Jarvis[7] m. Abigail Plummer.
Daughter[7] m. a Lawrence.
DAVID[3] WHITSON (Thomas[2] Henry[1]) and Clement Hallock had:
Ruth[4] b. 1732.
Mary[4] b. 1736.
Amy[4] b. 1739, perhaps Ancestress of Edward Magill.
Solomon[4] b. 1741, m. 1766, Phebe Willis, dau. of Silas.
Children of 2d m., family removed from Bethpage to Buckingham, Penn'a., about 1761. Edward Magill of Swathmore College is a descendant of David[3] Whitson.
David[4] b. 1743.
Clement[4] b. 1751.
HENRY[3] WHITSON (Thomas[2] Henry[1]) m. 1739, Hannah Powell, dau. of Thomas[2]. They always lived on the old Whitson Homestead, at Bethpage, they had children:
Mary[4] b. 1740, m. a Jackson.
Hannah[4] b. 1742, m. a Cary.
Henry[4] b. 1745, m. 1772, Clementine Underhill, dau. of Abraham and Phebe (Hallock).
Thomas[4] b. 1747.
Kesia[4] b. 1753, m. 1777, Isaac Coles, she d. 1789.
Children of HENRY[4] WHITSON and Clemma.
Mary[5] m. Jarvis Jackson, son of David and Esther.
Abraham[5] m. 1803, Mary Jackson, dau. of David and Esther.
Thomas[5] m. 1804, Ann Willets, dau. of Jacob.
Hannah[5] m. Charles Willets, son of John and ? Anna Jones or ? Sarah.
Phebe[5] m. 1825, John Cromwell, she d. 1860.
Henry[5] b. 1786, m. 1811, Sarah Collier.

Kesia⁵ b. 1788, m. 1813, Silas Albertson.
Sarah⁵ m. 1819, Thomas Underhill.
Children of ABRAHAM⁵ WHITSON and Mary (Jackson):
Esther⁶ m Edward S. Willets.
Amy⁶ m. Edward S. Willets.
Samuel⁶ m. Phebe Jackson, dau. of George and Elisabeth.
Charles.⁶
Children of THOMAS⁵ WHITSON and Ann (Willets):
Hannah⁶ m. Joseph Townsend.
Martha⁶ m. Edmond Willets.
Daniel⁶ m.
Jacob⁶ b. 1813, died.
Ann⁶ b. 1814, m. William Willets, she d. 1833.
Jacob H.⁶ b. 1818, m.
Thomas⁶ b. 1821, m. Mary Willets, dau. of Isaac and Amy.
Phebe⁶ b. 1824, m. James Wright, son of John D.

THOMAS³ WHITSON (Thomas² Henry¹) m. 2d in 1747,— by a Priest, makes acknowledgment, is retained a member of the Monthly Meeting and says that he and his son, Thomas, being about to remove into the Jersies, desire certificates to Bethlehem, M. M., that for the son to express clearness of marriage engagements. Thomas³ sold his homestead in Bethpage, in 1739, to his son John.

Westbury Monthly Meeting issued certificates in 1761, to Buckingham, M. M., for David Whitson, one son and three daughters.

WEEKS FAMILY.

Francis Weeks was at Dorchester, Massachusetts, in 1636. When John Smith (Miller) was banished with Roger Williams, he asked to be allowed to take a boy named Francis Weeks with him, to Providence. The boy went and was allowed to join the 14 settlers, and signed the agreement, some time later, when he became of age. In 1657, he was on Long Island with his wife Elisabeth (Luther) and some children.

FRANCIS WEEKS b. 1616, m. Elisabeth Luther, he d. 1687, children:

George m. Mary.
Joseph m. st 1 Hannah Ruddick, dau. of Henry and Mabel, 2d Hannah Crooker, 1698, he d. 1754.
John m.
Samuel m. Elisabeth Ruddick, dau. of Henry and Mabel.
Thomas m. Isabella Harcourt, dau. of Richard.
James m. had son Edward.
Daniel m. Mary Alling, he d. 1697.
Elisabeth m. Nicholas Simpkins.
Ann m. Joseph Carpenter.

JOSEPH[2] WEEKS (Francis[1]) and Hannah Ruddick had:

Henry[3] m. Susanna Alling.
John[3] m. Mercy Forman.
Joseph[3] m.

Samuel[3] m. Hannah Ruscoe.
Amy[3] m. Daniel Hopkins.
Sarah[3] m. Tristram Dodge.
Abigail[3] m. Amos Weeks.
JOSEPH[2] WEEKS m. 2d Hannah Crooker and had:
Charles[3] m. Anna Longhick.
Micah[3] m. 1741, Sarah Weeks.
Mary[3] m. Charles Ludlam.
HENRY[3] WEEKS (Joseph[2] Francis[1]) and Susanna Alling had:
  Freelove[4] m. 1737, Richard Powell, b. 1704, d. 1774, she d. after 1744.
  Robert[4] m. 1728, Jerusha Lewis, dau. of Jonathan. he d. 1741.
Freelove, wife of Richard Powell died about 1745, and he m. 2d 1748.
Jerusha (Lewis) widow of her bro. Robert Weeks.
SAMUEL[3] WEEKS (Joseph[2] Francis[1]) and Hannah (Ruscoe) had:
  Joseph[4] b. 1725, m. 1st Phebe Underhill, 2d Sarah Peas, he lived at Northcastle, d. 1795.
  Samuel,[4] Thomas[4] and Benjamin,[4] of Queens Co., L. I.
  John,[4] of Westchester and Jesse, of L. I.
Children of JOSEPH[4] WEEKS and Phebe, of Westchester Co.
  Jesse[5] b. 1752, m. 16, 12, 1773, Sarah, dau. of Joseph Carpenter.
  Thomas[5] b. 1754, Samuel[5] b. 1756, Richard[5] b. 1758, Joseph[5] b. 1761.
  Joshua[5] b. 1763, m. Hannah.
  Phebe[5] b. 1765, m. 1784, John Merritt, son of Nathaniel.

Weeks Family.

Sarah[5] b. 1767, m. James Merritt, son of Nathaniel, at Amawalk.
Abel[5] b. 1769, Amy[5] b. 1772.
Dorothy[5] b. 1776, m. Zopha Jones.
SARAH (CARPENTER) widow of Jesse[5] Weeks, m. 1784, Robert Dodge.
In 1794, Joseph Weeks and wife, Sarah, visit her son, Peas, in Nantucket.
THOMAS WEEKS m. Sarah Townsend, b. 1685.
Thomas Weeks' Will 1761, says sons, George and Gilbert, grandson Richard, son of son Thomas.
RICHARD WEEKS b. 1746, m. Martha Rushmore, b. 1750, dau. of Jeremiah and Elisabeth, he d. 1829, children were:
Hannah b. 1772.
Phebe b. 1775, m. 1798, Stephen Loines, she d. 1808.
Elisabeth b. 1776, m. Jacob Crooker, she d. 1828.
Sarah b. 1779, m. Rowland Titus.
Rachel b. 1781, Freelove b. 1783, d. 1805, R. d. 1820.
Anne b. 1785. m. Phineas Carman, she d. 1802.
Richard b. 1787, m. Samantha Mead.
Silas b. 1789, m.——, his son Isaac has the Bible.
James b. 1791.
Samuel b. 1793, m. Sarah Downing, he d. 1827.
Martha b. 1795, m. at 50, Jacob Willis, she d. 1889.
Mary, m. John B. Thorne, he b. 1795, d. 1828, she d. 1879.

WHITMAN FAMILY.

From London to New England in the "Freelove" Gibbs Master 1635.
Zacharia Whitman, aged 40.
Wife Sarah Whitman, aged 25.
Zacharia, jr., aged 2 1-2.
Joseph Whitman. sr., was at Huntington, L. I. from 1661 to 1686.
Joseph Whitman m. Sarah Cecum, their sons were: Nathaniel, Nathan, Samuel and Zebulun.
ZEBULUN WHITMAN m. Sibel Lewis, b. 1685, at Huntington. She was a daughter of Jonathan Lewis and Jemima Whitehead, dau. of Daniel Whitehead, of Oysterbay. They had dau:
    Martha Whitman m. 1733, Isaac Powell, son of Thomas.[2]
I think the Martha Whitman, who in 1749, m. John Whitson was a niece of Martha (Whitman) Powell, but do not find the note to that effect.

WILLIAMS FAMILY.

Thomas[1] WILLIAMS FAMILY of Hempstead, he m. 1st and had sons Richard,[2] Thomas[2] and William[2] died, m. 2d and had:

John[2] b. 1718, m. 1747, Elisabeth Valentine, his cousin.
Esther[2] b. 1720, m. 1743, Robert Seaman, son of John.
Elisabeth[2] b. 1724, m. 1754, George Hewlett, she d. 1794.
Samuel[2] b. 1726, not able to maintain himself.
Phebe[2] b. 1728, m. 1755, Richard Doty, son of Isaac.
Jacob[2] b. 1731, m., lived at Rockaway.
Ann[2] b. 1733, m. Thomas Pearsall, of Bethpage, moved to Flushing.

Thomas[1] Williams d. May 12, 1736, William, son of Thomas,[1] d. Sept. 13, 1737. Mary (Willets) Williams, widow of Thomas, d. Feb. 25, 1749-50.

JOHN[2] WILLIAMS (Thomas[1]) and Elisabeth (Valentine) had:

Mary[3] m. 1785, William Doughty, son of Benjamin.
Martha[3] m. 1767, Jacob Willets, son of Richard and Ruth, of Jericho.
VALENTINE[3] m. Elisabeth and had Jane[4] m. George Hewlett.
Samuel[4] m a Hagner and John[4] m. a Cheeseman.

Richard[2] Williams (Thomas[1]) m. 1st Elisabeth Hicks, she d. 1750, he m. 2d 1768, Mary. Children of Richard[2] and Elisabeth:

Richard,[3] Thomas,[3] Jacob,[3] Mary,[3] Elisabeth.[3]

Children of 2d marriage:

William,[3] Easter,[3] Austen,[3] Phebe,[3] Pelatiah,[3] Charity.[3]

In 1640. Mary Williams, widow of Thomas[1] lived north side of the plains; a memorial of her by Clement Willets says, "she was a worthy woman and justly deserves our grateful remembrance, to me she was like a mother — and not to me only, but to many of her poor neighbors also, who felt the benefit of her bountiful hand. She was very careful not to let her left hand know what her right hand did."

The original deed from the Indians to Robert Williams for the Plains in Oysterbay, was executed on the 20 of May, 1648.

Robert appears to have resided a part of the time in Hempstead, was living there in 1659. The Indian Deed for Oysterbay was executed in 1653 to Robert Williams and others, he was one of the patentees of Dosori's, O. B. in 1668. Some accounts say that he was born in Wales, and was a brother of Richard Williams, of Huntington, and a near relative of Roger Williams, of R. I., all of which may be true; I have not seen any of it verified, suffice it he was our Ancestor, and disposed of 1-3 of his property in Jericho to his wife's sister, Mary (Washburne), widow of Richard Willets; in 1667 — thus paving the way for many pleasant Ancestral homes in that vicinity.

ROBERT[1] WILLIAMS m. Sarah, dau. of Wm. and Jane Washburne, he d. about 1680, she d. 1693. Their children were :

Phebe m. John Townsend, son of Richard and his 2d wife Elisabeth Wicks.

John m. Leah, dau. of Richard Townsend and his 1st wife Deliverance Cole.

Hope m.

Sarah m. John Champion.

Patience m. a Barnes.

Williams Family.

Mary m. 1st a Jessup, 2d m. John Cole.
Hester m. Thomas Cock.
JOHN and Leah Williams had two daughters, co-heirs of their father's property.
 Temperance m. 1st David Seaman, 2d m. James
  Searing.
 Hannah m. John Seaman, brother of David, they were sons of Jonathan.
HOPE WILLIAMS had dau. Sarah, m. 1723, Joseph Clements.
 Jeremiah Williams born near Boston, came to L.
  I., m. 1708, Philadelphia Masters, dau. of George
  and Mary (Willis) Masters.
Flushing minutes say he had certificate of clearness from other marriage engagements from both Rhode Island and Philadelphia meetings.
 Children of JEREMIAH and Mary (Masters) Williams:
 Joseph, d., Hannah b. 1711, m. 1737, Benjamin
  Doughty, son of Charles m. 2d Mary (Newbury),
  widow Howland, of R. I., and had:
 Ann b. 1719, Walter b. 1720, m. Benjamin b. 1722,
  m. Mary b. 1724, Jeremiah b. 1726, Lydia b. 1729.
He may have descended from Roger Williams.
 James Williams d. 1621, wife Alice d. 1634, in Wales, her will names sons, Sidraeke, Roger, Robert and Whightman, dau. Katharine, wife of John Davies, kinsfolks:
Roger Bryan and Alice Harris:
ROGER WILLIAMS born in Wales, in 1599, came to Boston in 1630, in the "Lyon" with wife Mary.
 Children of ROGER and Mary Williams:
 Mary b. 1633, at Plymouth, Massachusetts.

Freeborn b. 1635, at Salem, m. 1st Thomas Hart, of Newport, 2d Gov. Walter Clark.

Mercy b. 1640, m. 1st Resolved Waterman, children, 2d Samuel Winson, children, 3d John Rhodes, children.

Providence b. 1638, died unmarried in 1686.

Daniel b. 1642.

Joseph b. 1643, m. 1669, Lydia Olney.

There are Jeremiahs in the next generations.

In the "Primrose" for Virginia in 1635.

Richard Williams aged 28.

Robert Williams aged 21.

WRIGHT FAMILY.

Nicholas Wright b. 1609, wife Ann, he d. 1682.
Peter Wright[1] and wife Alice, she m. 2d Richard Crabb, she d. 1685.
Anthony Wright died 1680, gave property to sister-in-law, Alice Crabb, and his brothers' children:
NICHOLAS[1] WRIGHT and wife Ann had:
Caleb[2] b. 1645, m. Elisabeth.
John[2] m. Mary Townsend, dau. of Henry.
Sarah[2] m. Josias Latting.
Edmond[2] m. Sarah Wright, dau. of Peter and Alice.
Mercy[2] m. Robert Coles.
Rebecca[2] m. 1st Eleazer Leverich, divorced, she m. 2d 1672, William Frost.
Deborah[2] m. Nathaniel Coles.
CALEB[2] and Elisabeth had:
William[3] b. 1680, m. Elisabeth Rhodes, he d. 1759.
Elisabeth[3] m. Joseph Cole.
Penelope[3] m. David Reynolds, of Conn.
JOHN[2] WRIGHT and Mary (Townsend) had:
Rose[3] m. 1691, 1st Nathaniel Coles, jr., he d 1705, 2d m. John Townsend, he d. 1709, 3d Samuel Birdsall.
Eliphal[3] m. 1st Henry[3] Townsend, he d. 1709, 2d Daniel Wright.
Mary[3] m. 1st Jacob Underhill, 2d Richard Latting.

EDMOND[2] and Sarah Wright, dau. of Peter and Alice, had:
Nicholas,[3] Caleb.[3]
Edmond[3] m. Sarah Townsend, dau. of Mill John.
Daniel,[3] Eliphal Wright, Jacob.[3]
WILLIAM[3] WRIGHT (Caleb[2] Nicholas[1]) and Elisabeth had:
- John[4] b. 1701, m. 1736, Zervia Wright, dau. of Edmond.
- Caleb[4] m. Freelove Coles, dau. of Wright Coles, son of Nathaniel Coles and Rose (Wright).
- Mary[4] m. Joseph Cooper.
- Sarah[4] m. 1738, John Townsend, son of John and Esther.

EDMOND[3] WRIGHT and Sarah Townsend had:
- Nicholas[4]
- Daniel.[4]
- Jotham[4] b. 1708, m. Tabitha Sammis, he d. 1777.
- Thomas[4] m. Sarah Cooper.
- Edmond.[4] Jacob.[4]
- Zervia[4] m. 1736, John Wright, son of Wm. and Elisabeth.

PETER¹ WRIGHT FAMILY.

PETER¹ WRIGHT and Alice had:
Hannah² b. 1651. The Devotee, d. 1675.
Peter² b. 1651.
Gideon² m. Elisabeth Townsend.
Job² m. Rachel Townsend.
Adam² m. Mary Dennis.
Sarah² m. Edmond Wright.
Elisabeth² m. 1693, James Townsend, son of John.
Mary² m. 1663, Samuel Andrews moved to N. Jersey in 1683.
Lydia² m. 1684, Isaac Homer.
ADAM² WRIGHT and Mary (Dennis) had:
Dennis³ m. Susanna.   Adam.³   George.³
Joseph³ m. Temperance (Seaman), widow of Arthur Kirk.
Peter³ b. 1698.
JOSEPH³ WRIGHT and wife had:
Adam⁴ m. Elisabeth.
John⁴ b. 1729, m. 1753, Phebe (b. 1733) Seaman, dau. of Thomas, of Wheatly.
Mary.⁴
Joseph.⁴
Charles.⁴
Job.⁴
JOHN⁴ WRIGHT (Joseph³ Adam² Peter¹) and Phebe (Seaman) had:
Charles⁵ b. 1754, d. 1824.

Obadiah⁵ b. 1756, m. 1777, Jane Sayre, he d. 1794.
Mary⁵ b. 1757, m. Israel Underhill, she d. 1834.
Isaac⁵ b. 1760, m. 1784, Sarah Titus, dau. of William.
Jordan⁵ b. 1762, m. 1786, Elisabeth Titus, dau. of Richard and Elisabeth.
Sarah⁵ b. 1764. m. 1786, Noah Gardner, son of Seth and Sarah.
Phebe⁵ b. 1771, m. 1804, James Loines.
Lydia⁵ b. 1776, d. 1778.

Children of JORDAN⁵ and 1st w. Elisabeth Titus Wright.²

Jane⁶ b. 1788, m. John White.
Susan⁶ b. 1789. m. Abraham Cock, son of Benjamin.
Charles⁶ b. 1791, d. 1794.
Eliza⁶ b. 1793, d. 1795.
Margery⁶ b. 1795, m. John Franklin, son of Anthony.

JORDAN⁵ WRIGHT m. 2d Rebecca Dunbar, dau. of Daniel and Naomi.

Children of 2d marriage.

John D.⁶ m. 1st Mary Bird, dau. of James, had James⁷ m. Phebe Whitson and John⁷ Howard.
Mary b., m. Henry Guliger.
Catharine b., m. David L. Rogers.
Charles b.
Harriet b., m. John K. Townsend.

ZEBULUN⁴ WRIGHT (Gideon³ Gideon² Peter¹) m. Clemence Feaks, dau. of Robt. and Clemence.

Ann⁵ m. Henry Townsend.
Elisabeth.⁵
Margaret⁵ m. 1st Noah Townsend, 2d Daniel Thorn, 3d John Jackson.
Martha⁵ m. 1765, Joseph Latting.
Daniel⁵ m. Sarah.

Lydia Wright (Peter and Alice) m. Isaac Horner and had:

Isaac Horner m. 1718, Eleanor Bowne, dau. of Samuel.

Deliverance b. 1685, m. Thomas Stokes, of N. Jersey.

MARY WRIGHT, dau. of Peter and Alice, m. Samuel Andrews, son of Edward and had:

Mordecai b. 1664, m. 1691, a French woman, Peter died.

Peter b. 1671. Hester b. 1673. Hannah b. 1675, d. 1686.

Edward b. 1678, m. 1694, Sarah Ong, dau. of Jacob and Sarah.

Jacob b. 1680, d. 1686.

Mary b. 1683.

GARDINER FAMILY.

When Lyon Gardiner came from Saybrooke Fort, to L. I., in 1638, he was the first settler within the present bounds of Easthampton, and his settlement of Gardiner's Island in 1639 was the first English *settlement* in what is since the State of New York, being one year anterior to the settlements, at Southold and Southampton.

Lyon Gardiner wrote in his Bible:
"In the year 1635, July 10, came I, Lion Gardiner, and my wife, Mary, from Worden, a town in Holland, where my wife was born, being the daughter of one, Derike Willemson, Deurant, her mothers name was Hackin, and her aunt, sister of her mother, was the wife of Wouter Leonardson, old burgomaster. We came from Worden, to London, and from there to New England, and dwelt at Saybrooke Fort, 4 years, it is at the mouth of the Connecticut river, of which I was Commander; and there was born to me a son named David, 1636, the 29th of April, the first born in that place, and in 1638, a daughter was born to me, called Mary, the 30th, of August; and then I went to an Island of mine own, which I bought of the Indians, called by them Mannehonake, by us, the Isle of Wight, and there was born another daughter, named Elisabeth, the 14th of September, 1641, she being the first child of English parents, that was born there."

In 1653, he removed to East Hampton, he died there in 1663, wife died 1665.

Children of LYON[1] GARDNER and wife Mary:

David[2] b. 1636, m. Mary Leringmore, he d. 1689.

Mary[2] b. 1638, m. Jeremiah Conklin, of East Hampton, she d. 1726.

Elisabeth[2] b. 1641, m. Arthur Howell, of Southampton, she d. 1664.

DAVID[2] and Mary had:

John,[3] David,[3] Lyon[3] and Elisabeth.[3]

In the Spring of 1640, a company of dissatisfied and restless men, who had been in Wethersfield, Conn. about 6 years, having sought in vain to end contentions there; looked about for a place to remove with their minister, Rev. Mr. Denton. He had been a minister, in Halifax, England.

New Haven people bought Rippowams or Stamford of the Indians, and offered it to the Wethersfield people on certain conditions.

Twenty-nine men agreed while at Wethersfield, to begin the settlement, others came in later. These people are spoken of as part of Capt. Mason's 500, who came to New Hampshire, in 1631–3.

In 1636, there were Articles of agreement between the Governor of Manhattan, and the Indians on Nassau Island, relating to, and extending over that part which was afterwards settled under the name of Hempstead.

In 1643, John Carman and Robert Fordham made the first purchase of the Indians, for themselves and others. In 1644, Gov. Kieft issued a patent, Bearing Date the 16th day of November, 1644.

Thomas[1] Gildersleeve, father of Richard[2] came to L. I., in 1664. They both sent in their allegiance to Connecticut Colony.

Richard² was one of the number who came from Stamford, to Hempstead, in 1644. Some of the others were, Rev. Richard Denton, Jonas Wood, Hal, Capt. John Underhill, Robert Jackson, John Karman, John Ogden, Matthew Mitchell, Robert Fordham, Robert Coe, Andrew Ward, William and Thurston Raynor, Thomas Armitage, William Mead, Symon Searing and Thomas Weeks.

Richard² (b. 1601), Gildersleeve's wife, named Experience. Their dau. Anna, m. John Smith, nan.

In 1652, Richard² Gildersleeve was a magistrate

In 1656 he and John Seaman were appointed. They were Magistrates many times.

1674, Richard Gildersleeve (sr. and jr.), in behalf of others petition the governor.

When Gov. Dongan issued a patent for the town of Hempstead, in 1722, John Jackson (son of Robert and Agnes) was the only surviving patentee of the first patent under Gov. William Kieft, in 1644.

The other patentees in 1722 were, John Seaman, son of Capt. John, Symon Searing, James Pine, sr., Richard Gildersleeve, sen., and Nathaniel Pearsall.

Robert Jackson's Will dated 1683, says wife Agnes, she was a dau. of William and Jane Washburn.

Their children were:

John m. Elisabeth Seaman, dau. of Capt. John.

Samuel m., had children.

Sarah m. Nathaniel Moore.

Martha m. son of Nathaniel Coles.

In 1650, the Society of Friends began to keep Records of births, marriages and deaths, of members of the Society in England.

The earliest Record in Friends Meeting House in, 20th street, New York — relates to a case in law. Mary, dau of William Ashwell and Ann (Ridge) dau.

Gardiner Family.

of Thomas, had property left her by her father at his death.

Her legitimacy was disputed because the marriage of her father and mother had been performed by Friends Ceremony, in England.

After much litigation she was allowed to have her rights.

The second entry in the Book of Records was in 1663, viz: the marriage of Samuel Andrews, son of Edward Andrews, of Barbadoes, and Mary Wright, daughter of Peter and Ann Wright.

Samuel and Mary Andrews removed to New Jersey, in 1683.

Third entry, 1665, Samuel Spicer m. Casher Hilton.

Fourth entry, John Underhill m. 1668, Mary Prior.

Fifth entry, John Wilson m. 1670, Mary Coats.

John Feaks, m. 1673, Elisabeth Pryor.

John Hilton, m. 1674, Deborah Darby.

John Pryor m. 1678, Elisabeth Bowne.

Pryor was of Killingworth and Bowne of Flushing (we now have the first notice of) a committee of inquiry in relation to their clearance from other marriage engagements, and the committee consisted of Ann Hobbs, Elisabeth Adams, Mary Willets and Mary Andrews.

George Masters, of N. Y., m. 1678, Mary Willis.

John Horner m. 1682-3, Lydia Wright.

Thomas Loyd, of Phil'a., m. 1684, Patience Story, of Flushing.

Richard Willets m. 1686, Abigail Bowne.

John DeLavalle m. 1686, Hannah Loyd dau. of Thomas.

In 1685, a certificate of clearness in relation to other marriage engagements was sent from Rhode

Island, for John Gould, son of Daniel and Wait Gould. He married Sarah Prior, dau. of Matthew and Mary Prior, of Matinecock.

Henry Clifton m. 1686, Rebecca Adams, both of Flushing.

William Willis m. 1687, Mary Titus.

Simon Cooper, son of Mary, m. 1693, Martha Pryor, dau. of Mary.

Joseph Thorne m. 1695, Martha Bowne, dau. of John.

Daniel Kirkpatrick m. 1696, Dinah Yates.

Isaac Gibbs, son of Richard and Sarah, m. 1696, Hannah Dickinson.

Martyn Jervis, of Penn'a., m. Mary Champion, of O. B.

James Cock, son of Sarah, m. 1698, Hannah Feaks, dau. of John.

Henry Cock, son of Sarah, m. 1698, Mary Feaks, dau. of John.

Richard Osborn m. 1698, Jane Coats.

Richard Ridgeway m. 1701, Mary Willets, dau. of Hope.

William Haig, m. 1702, Mary Masters, dau. of George.

Samuel Tatem m. 1701, Mary Southwick, late of R. I.

Joseph Willets, son of Hope, m. 1702, Deborah Seaman, dau. of Solomon.

Silas Haight m. 1704, Patience Titus.

Silas Titus, of Westbury, m. 1704, Sarah Haight, of Flushing.

John Powell m. 1704, ye 9th day, of 11 month, called January, Margaret Hallock.

Thomas Willets, m. 1706, Catharine Hallock.

Thomas Potts, of Penn'a., m. 1712. Judith Smith.

William Glading m. 1707, Mary Fry, dau. of William.
Walter Newbury, of Boston, son of Walter, of R. I., m. 1707, Ann Rodman.
John Shotwell, son of John, of Staten Island, m. 1709, Mary Thorne.
Samuel Bowne m. 1709, Hannah Smith.
Thomas Pearsall, son of Nathaniel, m. 1708, Sarah Underhill.
Benjamin Field, of Flushing, m. 1710, Elisabeth Feaks.
David Heustis, of Westchester, m. 1711, Mary Haight, of Flushing.
Abraham Shotwell son of John, of S. I., m. 1711, Elisabeth Cowperthwait.
Thomas Farrington m. 1715, Elisabeth Way, dau. of John.

In 1713, Friends began to require those who wished to perform their marriage in the meeting to get consent of parents.

John Fry, son of John and Mary, m. 1711, Mary Urquhart, dau. of John, now of East Jersey.
John Haight, of Flushing, m. 1715,   Titus of, Newtown.
Matthew Farrington, jr., m. 1716, Hannah Hedges.
Thomas Whitson, m. 1716, Deborah Feaks.

POWELLS.

Powells of Stonage Park, County Radnor, descended through Walter Powell, living in Queen Elisabeth's time, from Rhys Aap, King of South Wales.

Coat of Arms, 6 Lions heads — Lions Rampant Or gold mullet and gold border.

Powells (Boughton Moncheusy, Co. Kent, Ednop Newtown), descended from Ethelystan, Glodrydd, Prince of Ferlys, of this family was Richard Powell, of Ednor, author of the Pentarchia, a short History of the Royal Tribes of Wales and their descendants, written in 1623. Sir Nathaniel Powell, of Ewherst, and H. was son of Meredith Powell, and grandson of John Ap Howell of Ednop.

In 1623, living in Virginia on the eastern shore, Thomas Powell and wife Gody.

In 1626, patent granted to Capt. Nathaniel Powell and nine others, Land on the northerly side of the James river.

His share was 600 acres.

In 1626, patent granted to Capt. William Powell and others in the territory of Tappahanna over, against James Ciltie. His share was 750 acres.

In 1635, July 24. From London to Virginia in the ship "Assurance," Samuel Powell, aged 19 years, and Elisabeth Powell, aged 17 years.

In 1635, a warrant from the Earl of Carlilse, sent Thomas Powell, to Barbadoes or Virginia.

In 1635, In the Brig "Matthews," from London to Virginia, Thomas Powell, aged 21 years, and in June, in the "Thomas," James Powell, aged 12 years.

NEW HAVEN THOMAS POWELL.

From 1638 to 1681, there was a Thomas Powell living in New Haven with wife named Priscilla. They were members of the first Church there, and we find by the Church Records, and his Will dated 1681, that they had five children, viz: (he d. 1681.)

Hannah b. 1641, baptised 1643. m. 1661, Thomas Tuttle. she d. 1710.

Priscilla b. 1642, baptised 1644, m. 1666, John Thompson.

Mary b. 1645, m. 1669, Ephraim Sandford, of Milford.

Martha b. 1651, died early.

Esther b. 1653, died early.

No connexion has been traced between these New Haven Powells and our first Thomas Powell, of Long Island, and the subject would not have been alluded to, if Thompson's History of L. I. had not suggested that he, of Newhaven, was identical with the L. I. Thomas Powell,—and we should not have gone to N. H. to search for a possible father of our Thomas.

M. P. B.

Some Powell marriages by license from Gov. of New York.

1761. Elisabeth m. John Etherington.
1761. Edmond m. Mary Rowland.
1759. James, a mariner, m. Ann Bruce.
1764. James m. Eleanor McKenney.

1768. Eleanor m. Pierce Donoven.
1769. Thomas Washburton m Elisabeth McEwen.
1778. Ruth m. Robert Petit.
1779. Elisabeth m. Benjamin Carman.
1781. James, a Refugee, m. Elisabeth Smith, of Hempstead.
1804. James m. Martha Townsend.
1819. Cornelius Powell, of Westbury, son of Reuben and Ann, m. Rachel Healy, dau. of Christopher and Alice.

Born 1765, Jane, dau. of James and Elaniah Powell.

Thomas. son of John Allen Dyer, of Norwich was admitted to Cambridge in 1624.

Roger Alling, Deacon of Church at New Haven, he d. 1674. His wife was Mary Nash, she d. 1683.

Peter Cæsar Alburtus was at Flatlands in 1641; his daughter Francena Alburtus, born 1654, m. John Allen.

Samuel Allen was at Hempstead, bought land of Joseph Young, in 1664.

John Allen, Freeholder in 1666, at Newtown, L. I. Capt. John Allen or Alline.

Nathaniel Alline on Record, in 1671.

William Allen, a Quaker at Newtown in 1676.

John Allen at Foster's Meadow 1681, 1684, at Maspeth Hills, sold his land at Foster's Meadow to Henry Maybe, land was laid out to John Ellison.

Thomas Allen ? of 1698.

Samuel Allen, Proprietor of New Hampshire, purchased the right of Mason in 1697.

Henry Allen bought land of Abel Smith, in 1711, once Thomas Champion's.

Sarah Allen m. 1723, John Seaman.

New Haven Thomas Powell.

David Allen m. 1724, Mary Birdsall.

Henry Allen m. 1731, Phebe Williams — in 1733, they sold the place on Mad Nan's Neck, to Mary Allen, widow of Henry, father of the present Henry.

Mary Allen b. 1701, dau. of Henry and Mary Allen, of Great Neck, m. 1728, Reumourn Townsend.

John James was Town Clerk of Hempstead, several years, being chosen first, in 1657. His Will dated 1660, makes it appear that he had no near relatives in this country, and no family of his own.

COPY OF WILL.

I, John James, of Cardiffe, in the County of Glamorgan, in principality of Wales — being at present sick in body, but blessed be God, of good & perfect memory; do by these presents for ye well ordering of ye blessings of God bestowed upon me, for my relief; I bless his name for it & for his merciful providence over me all ye days of my life.

Imprimis, My Will is y^t my debts shall be paid in ye oats & other grain in my lodging of each a part, y^t is to say one hundred & seven Gilders, eighteen Stivers unto Mr. Samuel Dryssius minister of ye church of Christ at Manhattans. Item unto Mrs. Bridges twenty-one pound of butter Dutch weight, there is sufficient on my book to pay it.

Item I give and bequeath unto John Smith Rock junior my feather bed & bowlster and two blankets one red & another blue, to be given at the death of his parents or on his day of marriage, or when he shall keep house with his parents consent.

Item I give unto Hanna Smith my Byble, and if her brother die without issue my bed and appointments.

Item, I give & bequeath unto Joan Brudnell six pounds sterling to be paid in oats & other grain a month after my decease, I doubt not but there will be so much overplus, when my debts are paid. It is to buy her part of a house.

Item, I give unto Thomas Jeacock's children 3 1-4 of trading cloth, that is on my bed to cloathe them. Item I give and bequeath unto Richard Hicks one sheet for a winding sheet — To Josias fforman one sheet, — to goodwife Champion one sheet, and ye other to make a winding sheet for myself. Item I bequeath to William Scaddin one English ell of Holland; — and to John Smith Rock ye remainder for his children. I bequeath unto John Beadle my Dublet & black cloth breaches & 40^s his father owes me to keep him to school. Item I give unto Mr. Hicks the use of my books of Arithmetick   Item I give unto Mr. Gildersleeve my chair and ffree of all accounts between us. Item I give my table and bench & cupboard to John Smith Rock & doe appoint him to be executor of this my last will & testament & Wm Scaddin to assist him. Item I give & bequeath my white blanket to goodwife Simmons, living near ye wall on Mr. Dryssius land at Manhattans. She is a washer woman pray send it safe to her. Item I desire my executor to see me decently buried, & to have so much wine or drams as may in moderation be drank. Iff I have been too large in giving I leave to their discretion. If there be any thing over to give unto pious uses — half to help repair ye meeting house ye other half to ye church at Flatbush, and thus in conclusion I commend my poor soul into ye Merciful hands of God, hoping to enjoy ye kingdom of Heaven forever more.

DATED at Hempstead ye 13 day off *March* 1660.

SMITH FAMILY.

AMOS SMITH m. and had:
George m. 1802, Amy Mott, b. Jan. 11, 1784, dau. of Samuel.
Sarah m. 1st George Williams, m. 2d Thomas Seaman.
Mary m. Edmond Smith.
Stephen.
Jacob.
GEORGE SMITH and Amy (dau. of Samuel Mott, b. 1742, and Amy Raynor, b. 1750), had children, viz:
Oliver b. 1803, Amy M. b. 1804, m. William Rock Smith, Willet b. 1806, Carman b. 1807, Benjamin b. 1809, George b. 1810, Samuel b. 1812, Elisabeth b. 1815, Phebe b. 1817, Melicent b. 1819, Phebe b. 1822, L. Maria b. 1824, S. Ann b. 1826.
Edmond Smith, Whitehead, Smith, James Smith (brothers).
EDMOND m. Deborah and had:
Edmond m. Mary Smith, dau. of Amos.
Sarah m. Richard Seaman, son of Giles, she d. 1833, he d. 1834.

INDEX.

Albertson, 166–9.
Albertus, 344.
Allen, 344–5.
Almy, 117.
Althouse, 149, 150, 180.
Andrews, 170, 335, 339.
Baldwin, 68, 69, 80, 182, 193, 234.
Bedell, 33, 172–6.
Betts, 183,
Birdsall, 177–83.
Bowne 184–6.
Brower, 182, 226.
Bunker, 61, 162, 235.
Carman 164–6.
Carpenter, 37, 53, 76, 83, 99, 167, 189, 203, 212, 305.
Carr, 89.
Chichester, 46, 54, 210, 240.
Clapp, 97, 98, 101, 214.
Clements, 128, 141, 185.
Clowes, 186–8.
Cock, 188–90.
Coles, 179, 204, 251, 256.
Cornelius, 192–5.

Cornell, 191, 256, 257, 261, 278.
Covert, 194.
Crossman, 319.
Dean, 195–6.
Derby, 32, 197.
Doughty, 198–9.
Duryea, 200–1.
Feke, 202–3.
Ferris, 58, 157, 253, 258, 298.
Frost, 204–5.
Fry, 129, 132, 341.
Gardiner, 336.
Gildersleeve, 337.
Gould, 340.
Haff, 207.
Hallock, 96–102.
Halstead, 40, 41, 206.
Ham, 31, 208.
Harned, 209.
Harnett, 54, 192.
Hawxhurst, 58, 118, 121, 160, 189, 211, 269.
Haydock, 216–7.
Hewlett, 124, 125, 129, 130, 134.

Hicks, 212–5.
Hinton, 64, 69, 154.
Hopkins, 218–9.
Horner, 335.
Hughes, 85, 86, 87.
Hull, 100.
Jackson, 179, 220–6, 338.
Jones, 227–8.
Keese, 232.
Ketcham, 230–1.
Kirby, 229.
Langdon, 233.
Lines, 236.
Loines, 234–8.
Ludlam, 203.
Mann, 100.
Marvin, 249, 290.
Merritt, 239–48.
Moore, 250.
Mott, 252–60.
Mudge, 30, 36, 251.
Oakley, 261–2.
Onderdonck. 316–7.
Parrish, 123.
Pearsall, 268–71.
Phillips, 30.
Pierce. 266.
Pine, 128, 158, 160, 265.
Platt, 267.
Plummer, 61.
Porter, 210.
Post, 263–5.
Powell, 29–71, 342.
Prior, 272–3.
Richbell, 274.

Robbins, 275–7.
Rodman, 282-4.
Rogers, 281.
Rowland, 278.
Rushmore, 279–80, 319.
Sands, 285–7.
Scudder, 288.
Seaman, 134–63.
Searing, 289–91.
Sherman, 99, 100, 123, 125, 231.
Smith, 293–6, 347.
Stillwell, 292.
Strickland, 291.
Terhune, 201.
Thorne, 99, 105, 122, 184. 191, 221, 256.
Titus, 103–16.
Townsend, 118–25.
Underhill, 297–307.
Valentine, 307–12.
Van Bergen, 313.
Van Der Donck, 313–7.
Washburne, 73, 220.
Way, 310.
Weeks, 30, 323–5, 303.
Whitman, 326.
Whitson, 318–22.
Willets, 72–95.
Williams, 326–30.
Willis, 126–33.
Wood, 32, 122, 125, 256, 261, 267, 319.
Wright, 331-4.
Zane, 127, 133.

www.ingramcontent.com/pod-product-compliance
Lightning Source LLC
Chambersburg PA
CBHW070012010526
44117CB00011B/1522